Directions in Applied Sociology

Presidential Addresses of the Society for Applied Sociology 1985-1995

Directions in Applied Sociology

*Presidential Addresses of the
Society for Applied Sociology
1985-1995*

Edited by

**Stephen F. Steele
Joyce Miller Iutcovich**

A publication of
Society for Applied Sociology

Directions in Applied Sociology
Presidential Addresses of the Society for Applied Sociology 1985-1995

SOCIETY FOR APPLIED SOCIOLOGY
Administrative Office
101 College Parkway
Arnold, MD 21012

Copyright © 1997 Society for Applied Sociology

Publisher: Society for Applied Sociology
Composition: L. Antoine Dennison
Proofreading and Editing: Teri Kepner and Cynthia LoPresto

LIBRARY OF CONGRESS CATALOG CARD NUMBER: 97-66102

ISBN: 0-9656883-0-5/338pp./1997/$15.00 [paper]

Printed in the United States of America

We dedicate this book...

To Alexander Boros, the founder of the Society for Applied Sociology, whose dedication and vision of sociology as a *workable myth* made this volume possible.

To our families: Cindy, Scott, and Matt Steele, and Mark, Mara, and Nadia Iutcovich--two families who understand the value of practice and who have been supportive of our efforts to advance applied sociology.

To the contributors who know and understand the intrinsic value of sociology and advancing its applied side.

Preface

This book marks both an end as well as a beginning. While it would be woefully inaccurate to suggest that applied sociology started in the last two decades, we suggest that its reemergence has occurred over this period. The works included herein are valuable indicators of the path on which sociology, in general, and applied sociology, specifically, find themselves. In a sense, they are data, they monitor the recent rebirth of a part of the discipline that has lain dormant for many decades.

Contributions from the presidents of the Society for Applied Sociology, each a significant player in this rebirth of applied sociology, are reprinted in this volume. They give insight into the development of applied sociology, the challenges it faces, its relationship to the discipline of sociology, and a vision for its future. Furthermore, this volume provides an understanding of the context in which these recent developments in applied sociology have occurred. Not only does it detail the history of Society for Applied Sociology (SAS), but it also examines its development and growth in relation to other applied and clinical initiatives--both nationally and internationally.

There are four major sections in this volume: *Applied Sociology's Past and Future; Applying Sociology: What We Do and How We Do It; Social Change and Intervention in Applied Sociology; and A Vision for Applied Sociology.* In addition to the articles in each of these sections, the appendices contain a number of important historical documents from the archives of the Society for Applied Sociology.

When we examine these articles, we find two central themes: an emerging identity for applied sociology and directions for applied sociology's future. We will briefly summarize each theme.

APPLIED SOCIOLOGY'S IDENTITY

After reading these articles, there is little doubt that we can answer reasonably well the question: "What is applied sociology?" In this sense, we have reached the "end" of the discussion. Five factors are part of this definition. As applied sociologists:

We know that sociology contains valuable knowledge, methods, and skills. We recognize the usefulness of our discipline. Sociology provides a different lens to analyze and understand human social life. The application of sociology provides the acid test for theories already developed through basic research and it is, paradoxically, both an end and a beginning. The application of sociology is an end because it is often, in and of itself, adequate to solve real-world problems, stop a social leak, rewire a social system, monitor a social structure. It is a beginning because the successes or failures in the use of sociology provide a reality test for basic knowledge, helping basic researchers to further refine their theories.

We use what we know. We are practical and pragmatic. We place high value on the ability to use our knowledge and skills to understand and solve problems. For us, *the theory is not the problem*, theory is *one of the tools for solving the problem.* If the theory does not work, it becomes a problem.

We are real-world problem centered. We are interested in problems that people have in living their collective lives. We seek to enhance the quality of life in a community, not test a theory of community. For example, we want to solve a problem of teen suicide in a local high school, not develop a theory of suicide. Moreover, we are willing to search other sources of knowledge, often outside sociology, to find the solution to problems.

We are intervention oriented. We will intervene and take action to solve problems through informed, rigorous application of our sociological imagination. Practicing sociologists are willing to "get their hands dirty," often working in less than ideal settings, with far from perfect environments for testing their ability and skills.

We are change oriented. Whether monitoring change or directly impacting it, we recognize that social change is a key element in human social behavior. As such, it is central to the work of applied sociologists.

When taken together, these five components of an applied sociologist's identity are sufficient to distinguish us from other sociologists. Enough said about who we are; let's see where this identity takes us.

DIRECTIONS FOR APPLIED SOCIOLOGY'S FUTURE

If this work marks the end of an identity crisis, it also underscores the beginning of a future for applied sociology. All of the presidential addresses of the Society for Applied Sociology directly or indirectly offer a vision and a sense of direction for the future. Unlike the identity issue, reaching a consensus on the future direction of applied sociology is not as easy. On one hand, there appears to be some level of consensus among certain presidents in the articulation of their visions. On the other hand, alternate paths for applied sociology are depicted by some of the other presidents.

Visions of a Future Where There Is A Consensus

Applied sociology will enhance the development of sociology's knowledge and methods. An applied science develops procedures that are central to it. These procedures come from at least three sources. As Deutscher points out, we must "mine our own discipline" and make the best of a rich heritage. Other disciplines are a second source of tools. Many fields are rich with techniques and practices; to be effective, applied sociology must respectfully borrow outside the field. Finally, new tools can be created as they are needed in the effort to solve practical problems.

Society's need for applied sociology is significant--the social environment calls for an applied orientation. While basic sociology is not supportive or understanding of an applied orientation, audiences in the larger society are indeed receptive to us. In an era of consumer demands, accountability mandates, and continuous quality improvement processes, academic disciplines are being asked to show their worth. Outside academia, social problems without solutions abound. Business, government, health care, and others are eager for answers.

Support for applied programs will grow. Concern for the development and accreditation of applied sociology programs is evident. Sociology departments are implementing applied programs in response to social demand. But there are questions about what constitutes an applied program. Calls for model programs and learning standards are numerous. Graduates of these programs will need to demonstrate that they can actively apply the knowledge and skills learned.

Visions of a Future Where There Is No Consensus

Interdependence or independence from the discipline. While we contend that an identity for applied sociology has been established, we can not say there is a consensus on the nature of the relationship with the discipline. Writers in this volume tend to support a seamless association between basic and applied sociology. Agreement on the vehicle for achieving this is not so clear. Can a single professional organization, for example, support both the basic and applied perspectives? Or, will we find applied sociology and sociological practitioners conceptually linked to the discipline, but organizationally separate? The direction we should take as sociological practitioners is not clear.

The survival of sociology. The fate of sociology is in question. While the articles in this volume support the value of the discipline, it is not clear whether sociology will survive. If graduates of our applied programs lose (or fail to claim) their identity when they enter the marketplace, if the public continues to have little understanding of what we do, and if the value of the discipline is not recognized, will sociology as a discipline end? This, indeed, is the ultimate challenge facing sociology as we enter the next millennium. Sociology is in a process of transformation. All in all, we are optimistic that the practice of sociology will continue to emerge as a force that will actively change society and the discipline of sociology itself. As such, this volume is a valuable resource for departments currently supporting applied programs as well as departments interested in starting applied programs. In addition, students in applied sociology courses, professionals interested in understanding the utility of sociological knowledge and methods, and applied sociologists who want to know more about their history can all benefit from this work.

Stephen F. Steele
Joyce Miller Iutcovich

CONTENTS

Part Three: Social Change and Intervention in Applied Sociology

Part Four: A Vision for Applied Sociology

APPENDICES

PART ONE:

APPLIED SOCIOLOGY'S PAST
AND FUTURE

INTRODUCTION

The past two decades have marked a dynamic period for applied sociology. This period saw the development of the Society for Applied Sociology (SAS) as well as other sociological practice organizations. The events that led to the reemergence of sociology's applied side and the role played by these sociological practice organizations is detailed in the first article by Joyce Iutcovich. Iutcovich analyzes these events as they have occurred within a process of professionalization. In doing this, she first traces the origins of sociology's applied side to the earliest sociologists who were interested in social progress and reform. Second, she identifies and discusses the key issues related to the practice of sociology, both in the past and today. Third, the initiatives of the Society for Applied Sociology and other sociological practice organizations are documented to highlight the efforts of practitioners to gain professional status. Finally, the effectiveness of these efforts in creating a professional occupational identity for applied sociology is evaluated. This original piece adds to our understanding of the struggles and challenges faced by today's sociological practitioners. It also documents much of the history of the Society for Applied Sociology, which has yet to be chronicled elsewhere.

As the founder of the Society for Applied Sociology (SAS), Alexander Boros provided a *call to action*. In the SAS founder's address, *Sociology: A Workable Myth,* Boros argued that for sociology to be accepted as a science and for it to prosper, it must validate its knowledge and theories through practice experiences. In his address, Boros outlined the forces, both inside and outside sociology, that spurred the development of applied sociology and SAS. He recognized that policy makers lacked confidence in sociology as a discipline that could bring useful information for good decision-making. Declining enrollments in sociology in the mid-1980s also indicated a need for change. He reckoned that sociology did not bring theoretical muscle to bear on pragmatic issues. Application and practice can establish that sociology is, indeed, the "workable myth."

In discussing this, Boros identified a number of challenges that must be met head-on before a viable applied connection can be realized. These are challenges facing the entire discipline, not just the basic or the applied side. In short, "improving the applied connection is and will always be a continuing responsibility of the entire discipline." These challenges can be grouped into three categories:

1) challenges related to the design, function, and marketability of applied sociology programs in the academy;

2) challenges related to the development of applied methodologies and the creation of codes/standards for applied work along with the promulgation of these through expanded and respected literature, and

3) challenges related to bridging the gap between the discipline's basic and applied sides.

When Alexander Boros delivered this address he saw applied sociology taking important new steps on a long road. Development of applied sociology was the responsibility of the discipline as a whole. He was encouraged as he enumerated indicators of change that reflected the emergence of applied sociology as a force: more applied papers listed on programs of the various annual sociological meetings, pro-practice developments within the American Sociological Association, an increasing number of sociologists working outside of universities in applied settings, and, the emergence of applied organizations with national and international memberships. Yet, central to realizing its future, applied sociology could not be merely a temporary measure to solve sociology's problems. Rather, it was important for applied sociology to be a valid representation of sociology's restructuring. Boros provides not only a snapshot of where sociology has been in the last decade, but also outlines where it could be if sociologists address its *applied connection*.

But, can we be successful at it? What would it mean to be a successful applied sociologist? The concept of success is rarely uttered in the same breath as sociology. Mark Iutcovich tells us that in order to experience success we must first define it. For Iutcovich, success occurs "whenever the action of individuals or collectivity receives positive rewards because such actions are regarded as important to the group or the larger society."

Iutcovich outlines the criteria necessary to know success.

First, success is culturally relative...in short, it has no meaning unless it is "placed in a genuinely historical and/or social/cultural context." As such, sociology may be situated, even marketed, in a culture to reveal its value. Sociology fails when it is not defined to have social worth. The value of sociology varies across cultures from Norway to Japan, from Israel to India. Being valued largely depends on the receptiveness of the audience, which may vary across subcultures and groups of clients. To depend only on the academic community for criteria of success eliminates large segments of society, segments which may be viewed as clients from one perspective and in need of sociological assistance on another.

Second, the objects of success vary markedly over time. A "famous person" becomes famous because he/she is defined so. This is not to discount the psychological value of self-worth, but the self is inextricably intertwined with the society. "Heroes" become personal manifestations of group's concept of success. Products, actions and collectivities all may find success across time. For Iutcovich, sociology succeeds when it meets social needs and its value is thus recognized and defined as such.

Taken together, this first set of articles establishes a context for applied sociology's reemergence in the past two decades and provides a sense of direction for its future.

1 Professionalization of Applied Sociology: The Role of Sociological Practice Organizations*

JOYCE MILLER IUTCOVICH
Gannon University
Keystone University Research Corporation

For a field to be identified as a profession, having a strong association and monopoly of function are key features (Carr-Saunders and Wilson 1933). Practitioners who desire to be a profession come together in associations and they work with political authorities to establish a legal monopoly over the pursuit and practice of that occupation. As a process that takes place through time, an occupation becomes a profession by: 1) making the occupation a full-time pursuit; 2) linking training of workers to a special training institute; 3) establishing an association; 4) obtaining a legalistic monopoly over the sphere of work; and 5) developing a code of ethics that regulates the professional behavior (Wilensky 1964). Most importantly, a prolonged specialized training in a body of abstract knowledge and a collectivity of service orientation distinguish a profession from the trades--electricians, plumbers, etc. (Goode 1960). Furthermore, professions have been extended autonomy or self-direction by a society that recognizes the value and reliability of an occupation (Freidson 1970).

Gaining this status as a profession, however, does not happen without significant effort on the part of individuals seeking professional status. In recognizing this, the story of the Chinese bamboo tree is instructive. The Chinese plant the seed; they water and fertilize it, but the first year nothing happens. The second year they water and fertilize it, and nothing happens. The third and fourth years they water and fertilize it, and nothing happens. The fifth year they water and fertilize it, and sometime during the course of the fifth year, in a period of approximately six weeks, the Chinese bamboo tree grows roughly ninety feet.

This paper was written specifically for this volume; special thanks are extended to John Kennedy, Dora Lodwick, Harry Perlstadt and Stephen Steele for their review and comments on an earlier draft of this paper.

The question posed is, "Did it grow ninety feet in six weeks or did it grow ninety feet in five years?" The answer, of course, is that it grew ninety feet in five years, because if they had not watered and fertilized it each year there would have been no Chinese bamboo tree.

The development of applied sociology is like the bamboo tree. The seed was planted at the beginning of sociology, which is typically traced to Western Europe during the mid-1800s. Early sociologists were concerned about social progress and reform. Since then, the notion of a practical sociology has been watered and fertilized over the past century and a half--although there may have been some spells of draught in the interim. Some might argue that we are still in the "watering and fertilizing" phase--perhaps ready to move into the "period of approximately six weeks" when rapid growth occurs. Regardless of the phase we're in, just as with the bamboo tree, it will take persistence over the long haul before we see the fruits of our labor.

What is the history of this "watering and fertilizing"? What have been the significant events in this history? Who have been the important leaders in the effort to bring recognition to sociology's applied side? What specific role has the Society for Applied Sociology and other sociological practice organizations played in this most recent phase of development--the past 20 years? Have these efforts resulted in sociology gaining professional status as opposed to being recognized only as a learned society?

To shed light on these questions, we will first review the origins of sociology's applied side and identify the key issues that have been raised over the years as related to the practice of sociology. Second, we will detail the most recent phase of development (from the late 70s to today) exemplified by the establishment of the Society for Applied Sociology and other sociological practice organizations (ASA Section on Sociological Practice and the Sociological Practice Association)--an historical account that has yet to be documented.

THE ORIGINS OF SOCIOLOGY'S APPLIED SIDE

It can be argued that the origin of sociology, as a discipline, was grounded in the concern for making the world a better place to live. The earliest sociologists were interested in social progress and finding ways to put their knowledge to use within society. Thus, sociology's historical roots are in social reform. When sociology first came to America "it was akin to a crusade for social improvement...early college sociology courses were likely to be taught by Protestant ministers interested in various reform movements" (Lazarsfeld and Reitz 1975/1989:43) The first American Sociological Society meetings were attended by university teachers as well as sociologists in practice settings (Rhodes 1981). The first graduate department in sociology at Columbia University, created in 1894, carried a statement that clearly articulated the alliance between social reform and early sociology:

> It is becoming more and more apparent that industrial and social progress is bringing the modern community face to face with social questions of the greatest magnitude, the solution of which will demand the best scientific study and the most honest practical endeavor...it is in the city that the problems of poverty, of meandering, of intemperance, of unsanitary surrounding, and of debasing social influences are met in their most acute form. Hence, the city is the natural laboratory of social science. (Lazarsfeld and Reitz 1975/1989:44).

In sociology's first half century we see numerous references to applied sociology, clinical sociology, or sociological practice. As early as 1898 Edward Payson wrote *Suggestions Toward Applied Sociology*. Although this volume was unpretentious, its publication at that time was significant. Payson signaled a move in the direction of applied sociology and made the distinction between a) applied sociology as a body of usable sociological knowledge, and b) the application of the theory to the readjustment of social practices as well as the sociological analysis of proposed social changes (Shenton 1927/1989).

Perhaps best noted for his classical work in the field of applied sociology is Lester F. Ward, the first president of the American Sociology Society (Shenton 1927/1989). His work, *Applied Sociology,* did not appear until 1906, but his distinction between "applied sociology" and "pure sociology" commenced about 1898 or 1899. Ward stated that the terms "pure" and "applied" may be used in sociology as in other sciences and that pure science is theoretical while applied science is practical. Ward continually urged for the modification of social conditions, relations, and processes:

> ...applied sociology deals with the artificial means of accelerating the spontaneous processes of nature. The subject matter of pure sociology is achievement, that of applied sociology is improvement. The former relates to the past and to the present, the latter to the future...Applied sociology takes account of artificial phenomena consciously and intentionally directed by society to bettering society (1906:5-6).

A colleague and successor of Lester Ward at Brown University, James Q. Dealy, published *Sociology, Its Development and Applications* in 1920. Dealy spoke of the applications of sociology emanating from the theoretical principles underlying the phenomena. "If one...comprehends the principles underlying such phenomena, he would then be prepared to go one step further and to show how such principles may be applied in studies of social conditions, so as to produce modification in these in any desired direction" (Dealey 1920 as quoted in Shenton 1927/1989:21).

Similar to Ward's distinction between pure and applied sciences, Henry Pratt Fairchild of Yale wrote his *Outline of Applied Sociology* in 1916. He called attention to the interrelationships of social problems and endeavored to make general sociology available for their study.

The role of the University of Chicago during this period should not go unnoticed. Albion Small noted in his article "Fifty Years of Sociology in the United States (1865-1915)" that the University of Chicago had been a factor in promoting the sociological movement and "insured from the beginning mutual reinforcement between men who were primarily interested in the theoretical phases on the one hand, and the applied phases on the other, of sociological knowledge" (Small 1916/1989:15). Both Albion Small and Charles R. Henderson were the primary players in the sociology department at the University of Chicago. Henderson's center of attention was social betterment, while that of Small was the methodology of social investigation. Henderson devoted himself to the "investigation of concrete conditions crying for immediate relief" (Small 1916/1989:16). He used the terms "applied sociology" and "social technology" interchangeably.

In 1927 Herbert Newhard Shenton wrote *The Practical Application of Sociology: A Study of the Scope and Purpose of Applied Sociology*. He says that institutions will find general sociology useful for the determination of their objectives, but they will need a specially organized *applied sociology* to work out ways and means of achievement. To Shenton, the term applied sociology referred to a "systematically organized body of sociological knowledge which is practically useful for human, social, and societal engineering. It is not a new science but a development and exploitation of the practical possibilities of objective and quantitative observational sociology..." (1927/1989:28).

Shenton also noted that about the same time that the phrase *applied sociology* came into use in America, the term *practical sociology* was used as early as the late 1890s (as used by Richard Mayo-Smith and Carroll D. Wright). His uncertainty as to which of the two terms would prevail resonates in this statement: "Just which of the two terms, *practical* or *applied*, will ultimately prevail is probably a matter which will have to be determined by usage. Both may continue in good use." (1927/1989:24).

Clinical sociology--another of the labels used in reference to sociological work that has a practical orientation--came into use in the 1930s. The article on clinical sociology by Louis Wirth that was published in 1931 in the *American Journal of Sociology* provided "a rationale for clinical practice that recognizes the value of theory and the opportunity to combine theory and practice for the benefit of both" (Glass and Fritz 1982:3). Wirth's focus was on the significant role that sociologists, as part of an interdisciplinary team, were playing in the development of child guidance clinics and behavior research centers. He defines *clinic* in terms of modern clinical medicine where the emphasis is on the *case method* of the study of the individual, rather than by its emphasis on the pathological. Thus, clinical sociology "is a convenient label for those insights, methods of approach, and techniques which the science of sociology can contribute to the understanding and treatment of persons whose behavior or personality problems bring them under the care of clinics for study and treatment" (Wirth 1931/1982:8).

Wirth reflected that the function of the sociologist was *not* to replace the psychiatrist, the psychologist, or the social worker. Rather, it was "to enrich the resources of these clinics through the introduction of a point of view and a method which have hitherto been largely neglected" (Wirth 1931/1982:20). The major therapeutic task of the sociologist was the "modification and manipulation of the child's social world" (Wirth 1931/1982:20). According to Wirth, the positive contributions of the sociologist was characterized as the "cultural approach to behavior problems."

> If the sociological approach has any significance then the notion that behavior, whatever else it may be from other points of view, as a cultural product, is a crucial starting-point. The sociological approach to behavior rests upon the recognition that a person is an individual with status, and that personality is "the sum and organization of those traits which determine the role of the individual in the group." ...The cultural approach to personality does not rule out as insignificant the biological, the psychological and the psychiatric approach, but illuminates phases of behavior which can not be adequately understood in terms of the latter. Furthermore, if the behavior of the child is seen as a constellation of a number of roles, each oriented with reference to a social group in which he has a place, his organic and psychological traits are thereby not excluded as unimportant, but become capable of interpretation with reference to their social significance (Wirth 1931/1982:13).

This early emphasis of sociology on social reform and problems of society as manifested in industrialization and urbanization eventually evolved into what has been called the *social survey movement* (Young 1946). Major surveys were in the area of wages, housing conditions, social relations in the family, and attitudes. The dissemination of social science data in the early 1900s was found in three publications: *The Survey, Journal of Applied Sociology, and The Journal of Social Forces.* All three of these journals were edited by sociologists who endeavored "to make sociology practically useful and at the same time to enrich and perfect sociology generally" (Shenton 1927/1989:22).

The oldest and first in the field was *The Survey,* first published in 1909. It offered a "medium of exchange of practicable sociological information and for a medium of interpretation between the theories and the practitioners in the field of applied sociology" (Shenton 1927/1989:23). On its tenth anniversary *The Survey* appraised this function and provided a description of the application of sociology during those years.

Emory S. Bogardus of the University of Southern California published the *Journal of Applied Sociology* between 1921-1927 (in 1927 its name was changed to *Sociology and Social Research*). The *Journal of Applied Sociology* was a product of the Southern California Sociological Society. It was a distinct effort on the part of the department of sociology at the University of Southern California to develop an applied sociology. It was "an active agent for the promotion of research in applied sociology and the assembling and exchange of practically useful sociology" (Shenton 1927/ 1989:22).

The *Journal of Social Forces*, first published in 1922, emphasized social movement, action, processes, and forces. It sought "to contribute something in theory, something in application toward making democracy effective in unequal places" (Shenton 1927/1989:22).

PRIMARY CONCERNS OF THIS EARLY PHASE

It is clear from the historical account presented above that sociology's earliest roots lie in the practical application of its knowledge--one that focused on the social problems of the day, with an emphasis on finding solutions and making society a better place to live.

However, it is not to say that there were no areas of controversy during this early phase as related to sociology's practical applications. First is the concern expressed by Herbert Shenton in 1927 regarding the distinction between applied sociology as a scientific body of knowledge versus the application of sociology as practice, which he saw as a social art. This distinction was first made in 1898 by Edward Payson in his volume, *Suggestions Toward Applied Sociology*. Shenton, concurring with Payson, defines applied sociology as a "systematically organized body of sociological knowledge which is practically useful for human, social and societal engineering" (1927/1989:17). On the other hand, "those who actually apply sociology to the solution of social problems and the effecting of social change, are professional social workers and social artists" (Shenton, 1927/1989:17). Shenton goes on to say, however, that both functions of research and practice may be performed by the same person.

A second concern is whether applied sociology can be defined in terms of good and bad, better and pernicious. Ward's definition, also expressed by Henry Pratt Fairchild in his *Outline of Applied Sociology,* includes in his treatment of applied sociology the notion of ethics and social improvement. However, according to Shenton (1927/1989:27), "applied sociology cannot be limited to producing such changes as are better...A scientist (pure or applied) does not work out improvements. It may be used to work out changes which may or may not be in any ultimate sense improvements." Thus, early on there was controversy over the value of neutrality in sociological applications.

A third area of concern which is one that has not been fully resolved even in today's debates, relates to the use of the labels *applied sociology, sociological practice, and clinical sociology.* Although both terms--*applied* and *practical*--were used early on, *applied* was more generally used in the discourse related to the *use* of sociology. To a great extent, these terms are used interchangeably and do not have defined differences in their meaning. On the other hand, *clinical sociology,* as first used by Wirth, denoted a use of sociology in a therapeutic setting for the understanding and treatment of *persons* with behavior or personality problems. Therefore, its initial use describes a micro level application of sociological insights to solving individual behavior problems. It was in 1944 when a broader definition of the term *clinical sociology* came into use. A formal definition of *clinical sociology* appeared in H.P. Fairchild's *Dictionary of Sociology,* written by Alfred McClung Lee (1944). Over the years, what has evolved is a definition of *clinical sociology* that refers to sociological intervention in a variety of settings. It is "the application of a sociological perspective to the analysis and design of intervention for positive social change at any level of social organization" (Fritz and Clark 1989:10). With its expanded definition comes renewed concerns about what distinguishes *applied sociology* from *clinical sociology* and what is the more generic, umbrella term--*applied sociology* or *sociological practice*. In one way, the evolutionary development of sociology, as a profession, is captured through its definitional controversies. Concerns over definition are part of the process of identity formation and legitimation.

APPLIED SOCIOLOGY'S DORMANCY STAGE

It is not possible to "draw a line in the sand" to demarcate the point in which sociology shifted to an emphasis on theory and methodological techniques. Legitimacy as a science was a concern even in the early 1900s when there were ongoing debates between sociology's practitioners and the academicians. This dual orientation of developing sociology as a scientific discipline versus applying sociological knowledge for solving social problems has influenced the course of the discipline since its inception--albeit in varying degrees of importance. As early as 1905 in the organizational meeting of the American Sociological Society, the inclusion of practicing sociologists was debated. "The search for scientific legitimacy led many sociologists in the early decades of the society to want to put as much distance as possible between its historical roots in social reform and its aspiration to status as an academic discipline" (Gollin 1983:443). Furthermore, in the early to mid 1930s, there was concern over the role of science in the Nazi state, resulting in a call for the autonomy of science and the exaltation of "pure science" (Merton 1938).

However, somewhere after World War II the main thrust of sociology had shifted away from application and intervention to theory and statistical testing (Franklin 1979). The overarching concern had been to gain legitimacy as a science and "by the 1950s the battle for academic respectability had largely been won, and sociology entered a period of sustained differentiation in subject matter, theoretical tendencies, and methodological approaches" (Gollin 1983:443-444).

In the period between the Depression and mid-1960s applied sociology did not disappear--it just took a back seat to the overarching dominance of sociology as a scientific discipline. Debates about styles of sociological work (e.g., qualitative vs. quantitative), theoretical orientations, and methodological practices were paramount during this time period. Interestingly, for some of the prominent sociologists engaged in applied research at this time, much of the criticism directed toward them came, not from the *scientific center,* rather it came from the *qualitative left* who were concerned about "the conservative stance and trivial or inhumane uses of an increasingly potent social science" (Gollin 1983:444). Identifying concrete uses of sociology during this time period, however, became hard to document. In an effort to do so, Lazarsfeld, Sewell, and Wilensky produced an American Sociological Association sponsored volume entitled *The Uses of Sociology* (1967). This was an offshoot from Lazarsfeld's presidency of the ASA in 1962 in which his theme addressed sociology's applied side--a focus that created some consternation within the ASA since it was considered *a bit undignified* by members of the Executive Council.

RENEWED INTEREST IN APPLIED SOCIOLOGY

Since the early 1970s there has been a renewed interest in sociology's applied side, concomitant with increasing tensions between sociologists in the academy and those working in applied settings. What led to this re-newed interest? Some might say that similar to other times of societal stress--urbanization and industrialization, depression and war--sociology's relevance to the diagnosis and contributions to the solution of these prob-lems leads to greater public interest and support. The late 1960s and early 1970s saw increasing societal problems and turmoil with the Vietnam War, racial strife, urban disorder, and a heightened Cold War with communist nations. There was a dramatic increase in federal support for research and training during this period, along with growing demands for relevance and accountability for the federal dollars dispersed.

Others might claim this renewed interest was a result of declining employ-ment opportunities within the academy (Cartter 1971). With renewed inter-est in sociology as a discipline in the late 1960s and early 1970s there was, indeed, a large and growing surplus of trained sociologists, therefore leading to a crisis in academic employment. The concern over this is evidenced by ASA's formation of the ad hoc Committee on Expanding Employment Op-portunities (ExEO) that existed between 1976-1979. It issued two reports with recommendations for action related to the employment crisis--although these efforts were largely ineffective, with the ASA executive councils ignoring or just not able to act on the recommendations (Gollin 1983). This inaction on the part of the American Sociological Association to address the issues of marketplace, training, and relevance of the discipline, brought about alternative efforts. Groups of sociological practitioners came together to create organizational structures to support and protect their interests.

The interest groups later becoming organizations national in scope are the Society for Applied Sociology (SAS) and the Clinical Sociology Association (CSA)--renamed the Sociological Practice Association (SPA) in 1986. In addition, factions within the American Sociological Association formed the Section on Sociological Practice and the ASA Executive Office also responded with a number of initiatives directed toward its practice members.

An account of the activities and initiatives of these three groups is described in what follows. SAS's development is chronicled in more detail (with important documents included in appendices), since SAS's history has yet to be published elsewhere unlike that of SPA and the ASA Section. Together, these accounts highlight the common threads that weave the tapestry of the contemporary sociological practice movement.

SOCIETY FOR APPLIED SOCIOLOGY

In the spring of 1978 Alex Boros and a number of other colleagues from northeast Ohio (Harold Cox, Gurmeet Sekhon, and Al Bhak) met at the North Central Sociological Association (NCSA). Over dinner they discussed their concern about the lack of applied sessions at the NCSA meeting. After several informal meetings during the fall 1978, the Society for Applied Sociology was established. Alex Boros became the identified leader of this group and was eventually elected its first president in 1984 after SAS's incorporation as a nonprofit professional association.

In an effort to provide an open forum for the discussion of topics relevant to those utilizing the sociological perspective in community settings, SAS created its first newsletter in 1979--the *SAS Memorandum.* SAS's first public meeting was held during the 1979 NCSA meeting in Akron, Ohio. Sessions at this meeting included: Critical Issues in Program Evaluation; Generic

Shifts in Viewing Applied Sociology; Symposium on Enhancing Management's Utilization of Program Evaluation; The Application of Art and Science in Sociology; and On Educating Applied Sociologists. During these first few years, the members of SAS gathered for annual business meetings during the NCSA and they sponsored applied sessions at the NCSA conference. Thus, SAS's beginning was very much regionally based, although its membership eventually became national and international in distribution.

SAS's support of applied sociology can be described in terms of its initiatives in the areas of: formal organization, publications, annual meetings, awards, education and training, and code of ethics.

Formal Organization. On an evolutionary basis, functions necessary to maintain an association become formalized through the establishment of structures and processes to carry out necessary tasks. SAS's evolution from its founding can be viewed in this light. This formal organization process is reflected in the following:

➤ In 1984 SAS was duly incorporated as a 501c3 tax exempt organization.

➤ SAS elected its first officers in 1984; annually it has held elections with officer positions for president-elect, vice president-elect, secretary, treasurer and council members at large. (The officers and committee chairs of SAS since 1984 are identified in Appendix A.)

➤ The first set of bylaws were written in 1984 and passed by the SAS board in October 1985, with subsequent revisions in 1991 and 1995 (see Appendix B for the first and current set of bylaws).

➤ A paid administrative officer position was approved by the board in 1989; Sam Sloss served as the first Administrative Officer (1989-1994) and Richard Bedea served in this position from 1995-1996.

➤ A committee structure was established in the first set of bylaws in which board members served as committee chairs. Initially the committees were limited to a few that served the primary functions of the organization: Membership and Development Committee, Program Committee, Nominating Committee, Local Arrangements Committee, and the Editorial Board. Eventually, the committee structure evolved to one in which committee chairs are appointed by the current SAS president and committee chairs have the latitude to appoint their own members. The current list of committees consists of: Archives, Awards, Bylaws, Development, Ethics, Finance, Liaison, Membership, Nominations, Professional Standards and Accreditation, Program, Publications, and Student Committee.

➤ SAS became one of six sociological organizations loosely organized as the *Coalition for Utilizing Sociology*. The other organizations--all of which were concerned with the application/practice of sociology-- were the Sociological Practice Association, the Sociological Practice Section of the ASA, the Task Force on Applied Sociology of the Society for the Study of Social Problems, Sociologists in Business, and the Chicago Sociological Practice Association. The Coalition was not a separate, formal organization, but rather a network of member organizations formed to facilitate communication, coordination, and cooperation. It was initiated through the efforts of the American Sociological Association in 1990 and annually the group met during the ASA meeting. It was governed by a board consisting of the Chair/President of each member organization; the first coordinator for the group was Marvin Olsen from SAS. This group eventually ceased to exist and it has been replaced with an annual meeting (again held at ASA) of leaders from aligned sociological associations. Thus, the group that meets is broader in scope and includes such groups as the Association for Humanist Sociologists and the Association of Black Sociologists.

➤ In 1992/93 during the presidency of Stephen Steele, SAS developed its first formal strategic plan that included these goals:

◆ Clarify the mission of the Society for Applied Sociology
◆ Increase membership in SAS
◆ Improve the organizational and financial structure

◆ Enhance the stature of SAS and applied sociology.

Publications. As a vehicle for communicating about the work of applied sociologists, the Society for Applied Sociology has sponsored a number of publications:

➤ The first newsletter, *SAS Memorandum,* was replaced by *The Applied Sociologist Bulletin* in 1979. Kathern van Wormer, a student of Alex Boros at Kent State University served as its first editor until 1982 when Joyce Iutcovich assumed the editorship. Subsequent editors of the newsletter were Sonia Alemango (1984-86) and Francine Jefferson (1987). In 1988 Harry Perlstadt took over as editor and the name was changed to *The Useful Sociologist.* Following Perlstadt, editors of *TUS* have been Dora Lodwick (1990-1992); Susan Stein (1993-1995); and Sam Sloss and Sheila Anderson assumed the editor's position in 1996. The newsletter was originally distributed quarterly, however in 1993 it's publication was changed to three times per year. It still serves as a means to communicate about SAS news and initiatives, as a forum to discuss issues of concern to applied sociologists, and as a medium to make announcements about other applied and clinical groups.

➤ In 1983 Joyce Iutcovich and Harold Cox were appointed as the first editors of the official journal of SAS-- the *Journal of Applied Sociology (JAS).* They served as editors through 1990 (Volume 7) when John Miller and Robert Sanderson were appointed as *JAS's* new editors. As an annual publication (until 1995 when it was published twice a year), its first volume was published in 1984. It is "dedicated to the work of sociologists who seek to improve social life through the application of sociological perspectives. It also seeks to help develop basic sociology through the feedback of these application experiences. It provides expression to those who want to improve the effectiveness of training sociologists for applied roles of clinical practice, program evaluation, administration, and consultation" (Boros 1984:v). Traditionally, *JAS* has served as a vehicle to publish presidential addresses, and some of the addresses of SAS awardees or keynote speakers. It also includes specific articles focusing on sociological practice, applied research, and teaching applied sociology.

➤ In an effort to introduce an innovative format for sociological publications, SAS published *Social Insight: Knowledge at Work*. This magazine style format was the brainchild of Alex Boros from as early as 1991. It took a number of years and a few editors-in-chief before the first issue was published under the editorship of Mark Iutcovich--in the spring of 1996 just prior to the death of Alex Boros. This magazine uses a style and format geared to the lay public, while it is marketed to a variety of audiences--practicing sociologists, lay people who might use sociological knowledge, and students in sociology courses.

➤ The *Consultants Roster*, a booklet individually listing applied sociologists and their area of expertise, was initiated under the leadership of Stephen Steele and completed by Joyce Iutcovich in 1994. This booklet was distributed to not only SAS members, but as well to community groups and governmental bodies. The booklet was intended to be used by anyone seeking the expertise/skills that could be supplied by an applied sociologist.

➤ A SAS website and SAS listserv (APPSOC) were created in 1995 under the direction of John Kennedy. The website address is: http://www.indiana.edu/appsoc/. The listserv can be subscribed to by sending an e-mail message to: Majordomo@indiana.edu.

Annual Meetings. As a way to provide opportunities for networking with other applied sociologists SAS began to sponsor annual meetings a few years after it was established. The first annual meeting was held at Kent State University (KSU) in the fall of 1983. It was hosted by KSU with sessions held at the campus conference center. There were 140 participants at this first meeting; *The Applied Sociologist Bulletin* (Vol. 5, No. 1, Winter 1984) has a detailed write-up of this first annual meeting by Alex Boros, the co-chair of the conference. This first meeting included: 1) a national summit meeting of applied and clinical sociology organization leaders; 2) a panel of experts reporting on applied developments in other disciplines; 3) a series of applied projects by sociologists; 4) three workshops on how to apply sociology in problem-solving on community problems.

Subsequent meetings have gradually increased in size with approximately 200 participants attending the recent meetings. In recognizing the difficulty that applied sociologists working in the nonacademic settings have in attending professional meetings during the weekday, SAS deliberately scheduled its annual meeting to begin on a Thursday evening and continue through Sunday afternoon. For the most part, as an opening session on the first evening, SAS meetings have featured local business, political, and/or social service workers who discuss a community issue that they are experiencing. Other sessions have focused on concerns and *best practices* of the field; the meetings have also served as a vehicle for identifying resources for teaching, research, and practice endeavors.

Although these meetings have been held in all parts of the United States, it wasn't until the 7th annual meeting that SAS moved away from its North Central base (the Seventh Annual Meeting was held in Denver, Colorado). And it wasn't until the Fifth Annual Meeting (Lexington, Kentucky) that SAS held its conference in a hotel setting, rather than a university campus. The keynote speakers at these meetings have included some renowned sociologists engaged in applied research, both inside and outside the academy (e.g., Peter Rossi, Russell Dynes, Earl Babbie), as well as sociologists who have gained popular recognition via their nonsociological activities (e.g., Andrew Greeley who writes novels and Bertice Berry who is a comedienne). In addition, the SAS conference participants have heard from nonsociologists (e.g., Richard Lamm, the former governor of Colorado and recent opponent of Ross Perot in his 1996 campaign to be a U.S. presidential candidate). Only on one occasion did SAS attempt to have a joint meeting with another association. At the Eighth Annual Meeting in Cincinnati, SAS and the Association for Humanist Sociologists met together. (See Appendix C for details on location, theme, and keynote speaker at each of the annual meetings.)

Awards. In realizing the importance of recognizing significant efforts on the part of applied sociologists, SAS instituted a system of awards. The first awards committee was chaired by Marvin Olsen in 1986. The various awards were instituted gradually over the years. (See Appendix D for list of individuals who have received awards from SAS over the years.) The awards given by SAS include:

➤ *The Lester F. Ward Distinguished Contributions to Applied Sociology Award* is presented to a person who has made significant contributions to applied sociology over a period of time. This was the first award instituted by SAS; its first recipient was Amitai Etzioni in 1987.

➤ *The Award for Sociological Practice* is presented to an outstanding sociologist who has demonstrated how sociological practice can advance and improve society. It was first given in 1988 to Elizabeth Peele, from the Oak Ridge National Laboratory.

➤ *The Community Service Award* is presented to a person or organization in the community where the annual conference is held. The recipient of this award has made significant and noteworthy contributions to the community. This award was first given to Marijean Suelzle, a sociologist from Chicago who worked extensively with community groups. Organizations have also been recipients of this award; the first was Tender Mercies, a social service organization in Cincinnati that provided services to the homeless.

➤ *The Alex Boros Award for Contributions to the Society for Applied Sociology* is presented to a member of SAS who has served SAS with distinction. Approved as another award of SAS at the 1995 meeting, the first recipient of this award has yet to be named. The first to receive this award will be honored at the 1997 annual meeting.

Education of Applied Sociologists. Although professional workshops for applied sociologists have been offered at the annual meetings, these short training sessions are primarily geared to the practicing sociologist already in the workforce. In recognizing the importance of focusing efforts on the student in applied sociology programs, SAS also has initiated a number of efforts to either support students or address their educational needs:

➤ The *Student Committee* was first formed in 1990 under the presidency of Howard Garrison. Its first coordinator was Sonad Sabash. This committee supports and coordinates student activities and serves as a liaison between students and the board. It often organizes student sessions at the annual meeting and at the 1996 annual meeting in Atlanta, the first student paper award was given to Laura Nichols from the department of sociology at the University of Akron. Her paper was entitled "Preliminary and Prospective Evaluation of a Transitional Housing Program for Homeless Women and Children."

➤ The *Mentoring Program* was first initiated by Catherine Mobley, the student coordinator in 1995/96, under Dora Lodwick's presidency (see Appendix E for a copy of the guidelines for this mentoring program). In the first year there were twelve SAS members matched with students coming to the 1996 meeting in Atlanta. This program provides support and guidance to students as they begin their sociology careers. It encourages "a dialogue and relationship between those applied sociologists who are firmly established in the profession and those sociologists who are starting out" (The Mentoring Program of the Society for Applied Sociology 1996:1).

➤ The *Commission on Applied and Clinical Sociology (CACS)* was first established in 1995 under the presidency of Joyce Iutcovich, although initial efforts in this direction began earlier (1992/93) when Stephen Steele formed the Committee on Professional Standards and Practice and appointed Harry Perlstadt as its first chair. The CACS was established jointly by the Society for Applied Sociology and the Sociological Practice Association to develop, promote, and support quality sociological education and practice in applied and clinical areas. Its first meeting was held in Phoenix, Arizona in February 1995 during the mid-year meeting of the Sociological Practice Association. Members first appointed to CACS included Harry Perlstadt (Chair), Stanley Capela (Treasurer), Michael Fleischer, Joyce Iutcovich, Dora Lodwick and Kathy Trier (Secretary) from SAS; Beverley Cuthbertson-Johnson, David Kallen, Richard Knudten, Robert Rhodes, Mary Cay Sengstock (Vice-Chair), and Linda Weber from SPA. Initially, the Commission was formed with the intention of only establishing a registry of students graduating from applied and clinical programs. However, at the initial meeting of CACS, it was quickly decided that CACS would become an accrediting body. After the first couple meetings (held quarterly), CACS approved bylaws, incorporated and developed an agenda for action that included:

◆ A Commission-sponsored accreditation of clinical and applied sociological practice programs.

◆ A Commission-sponsored registry of baccalaureate graduates who have successfully completed accredited general, clinical, and applied sociology programs.

◆ Creation of links between program accreditation and state-sponsored professional registries, certification, and licensure.

◆ Creation of a clearinghouse for dissemination of program models and resources to departments interested in developing clinical and applied programs.

Code of Ethics. An important criteria for being considered a profession is to have a code of conduct to guide the behavior of the members of the group. Codes of ethics serve to protect the welfare of individuals with whom a group of professionals work. This establishes trust between the professionals and public that are recipients of the services of the professionals.

Although the American Sociological Association drafted its first Code of Ethics in 1970 as a result of some questionable research activities in the 1960s, the ASA code (and its subsequent revisions in 1984 and 1989) did not address the issues and situations confronting applied sociologists. (The current revision of the ASA Code which will be put to the membership for approval in 1997 has made considerable progress in incorporating the various roles of sociologists--research, teaching, practice, and service. This was made possible through the appointment of long-time SAS members Joyce Iutcovich and John Kennedy to the ASA Committee on Professional Ethics.)

Recognizing the need for a code of ethics that would service the practicing sociologist, SAS first established an ethics committee under the presidency of Marvin Olsen in 1987-88. This committee was chaired by John Kennedy. However, it wasn't until 1994 that the SAS board approved a code that would go to the membership for approval. This Code, developed under the leadership of Jim Wolf as chair of the Ethics Committee, was approved by the SAS membership in 1995. (See Appendix G for a copy of this Code of Ethics.)

SOCIOLOGICAL PRACTICE WITHIN THE AMERICAN SOCIOLOGICAL ASSOCIATION

Constrained by ASA's Executive Council, consisting largely of academic sociologists from large research universities where basic research and publication in scholarly journals is the norm, sociological practitioners have had little impact on the academic focus of ASA. There are still a significant number of sociologists who view ASA as a learned society, therefore issues of marketplace, accreditation, licensure, and certification, are remote from their interests and appear irrelevant to the future of sociology. Mixed messages, however, are delivered by the American Sociological Association. Since the late 1970s there have been a number of initiatives implemented in an attempt to address the concerns of sociological practitioners:

➤ The formation of the ASA Section on Sociological Practice in 1978 and Committee on Sociological Practice in 1979 (initially an ad hoc "Committee on Professional Opportunities in Applied Sociology).

➤ ASA Workshop on Directions in Applied Sociology, held in Washington, DC, December 4-6, 1981; this resulted in *Applied Sociology: Roles and Activities of Sociologists in Diverse Settings (1983),* by Howard Freeman, Russell Dynes, Peter Rossi, and William F. Whyte (eds.).

➤ ASA Teaching Resources Center has provided a number of publications over the past 15 years geared to the sociological practitioner: *Teaching Applied Sociology: A Resource Book* (1982 and 1993); *Embarking Upon a Career with an Undergraduate Sociology Major* (1982); *Mastering the Job Market: Using Graduate Training in Sociology for Careers in Applied Settings* (1982).

➤ ASA Committee on Sociological Practice initiated the development of a list of applied programs at the MA and Ph.D. level. Marvin Olsen compiled the first list in 1984; it was updated by Brian Pendleton and Jeanne Ballantine, in collaboration with the Society for Applied Sociology in 1989-90; and in 1996 an updated list including undergraduate programs was put together through joint sponsorship of the ASA Section on Sociological Practice, The Society for Applied Sociology, The Sociological Practice Association, and the Commission on Applied and Clinical Sociology.

➤ In 1983 the ASA Section on Sociological Practice gave its first award in practice and applied sociology to Jack W. Riley and Matilda White Riley. Subsequent awards have been given by the Section to Anne Knettles McCarrick, Arthur B. Shostak, Katrina Johnson, Albert Gollin, David Kallen, Robert Dentler, Ronnie Steinberg, and William F. Whyte.

➤ The first Distinguished Career Award for the Practice of Sociology given by the ASA was in 1986--it was awarded to Conrad Taeuber. Others receiving the award have been: John W. Riley, Paul C. Glick, David L. Sills, Elizabeth Briant Lee and Alfred McClung Lee, Charles G. Gomillion, Elliot Liebow and Matilda White Riley, Grace M. Barnes, Nelson Foote, Albert D. Biderman, and Albert E. Gollin.

➤ The ASA Teaching Services Program has sponsored workshops: in June 1982 a 5-day Workshop on Teaching Applied Sociology at the University of Wisconsin-Whitewater was held; in spring 1984 a 4-day Workshop on Applied Sociology Programs and Curricula: Career Opportunities for BA, MA, and Ph.D. Students was held in Sacramento, CA.

➤ The ASA Certification Program was established as a result of the Certification Committee's recommendation in the fall of 1984. However, in the early 1990s this program was discontinued for lack of interest in it. As of July 1989 only 65 sociologists (less than 1% of ASA's membership) had sought and been granted certification: 12 in Social Policy and Evaluation; 14 in Medical Sociology; 13 in Social Psychology; 12 in Demography; 7 in Organizational Analysis; 7 in Law and Social Control.

➤ The journal *Sociological Practice Review* (SPR) was initiated in 1988 with its first published issue in 1990; the ASA Executive Council, however, discontinued *SPR* after its 1992 issues indicating it did not have sufficient subscriptions to support it. Robert Dentler served as its editor.

➤ ASA initiated a Professional Development Program in 1988 with Steven Buff appointed as its first director, followed by Janet Billson in 1991. This program had as its initial purpose "to increase awareness of sociological practice in both the public and private sectors." Through this program, seminars for the US Department of Education and the Census Bureau have been held; corporate presentations have been made; and an initiative to broaden access to federal government positions for sociology graduates resulted in the manual, *The Federal Network: A Manual for Sociologists Seeking Employment Opportunities within the United States Government.*

➤ The ASA formed the Committee on Certification and Licensure in the late 80s and State Licensing Monitors have been identified with the express purpose of identifying pending legislation that is restrictive or discriminatory toward sociologists. A *State Licensing Monitor's Handbook* was prepared by Michael Fleischer outlining the tasks of the State Licensing Monitors.

➤ The ASA Teaching Resources in 1990 published *The Internship Handbook: Development and Administration of Internship Programs in Sociology*, edited by Richard Salem of the University of Wisconsin-Whitewater and Barbara Altman of the National Center for Health Services Research.

➤ The Sydney S. Spivak Program in Applied Social Research and Social Policy was established in 1991 with a $750,000 grant from the Cornerhouse Fund; Spivak was a successful businessman who acquired a Ph.D. and became a professor in midlife. The fund was established to: 1) strengthen the social sciences, especially sociology, and 2) enlarge opportunities for minorities.

➤ *The Directory of Sociologists in Policy and Practice* was published in 1996 at the urging of Amitai Etzioni (the 1994 ASA President). Similar to SAS's *Consultants Roster,* it is intended as a resource to help local, state, and federal agencies; nonprofit and profit organizations; and other groups identify sociologists with expertise relevant to their needs.

➤ The ASA Code of Ethics, in its substantial revision initiated in 1994 and completed in 1997, included several sociological practitioners on the committee and explicitly addressed the ethical concerns and issues associated with applied work.

Clinical Sociology Association

In 1978 at the ASA meeting in San Fransciso, the Clinical Sociology Association was formally established. This organization grew out of an earlier meeting of 10 people who attended a roundtable chaired by John F. Glass at the 1976 ASA meeting in New York City. This roundtable was entitled "Clinical Sociology: A New Profession" (personal correspondence with John Glass, 1996). Glass was named as the first coordinator for this new group and served in that position for 1979-1980. The co-coordinator was Charles Cleveland. Members of the first Steering Committee were: John Glass, Charles Cleveland, Roger Straus, Suzanne Powers, Clifford Black, Louise Klasic, Ronnie Braun, Jan Fritz, Barry Glassner, Jonathan Freedman, Hugh Gardner, and Hugh Floyd.

As noted previously, it was Louis Wirth in 1931 who first provided the rationale for clinical sociology. He recognized the value of theory and practice combined--for the benefit of both. But sociology's applied and clinical side faded into the shadows as the discipline shifted its focus on establishing its scientific credibility. As this occurred, sociology's audience became itself and it became increasingly isolated, "speaking to itself in a language only it understood" (Kallen 1995:19). It was in this context, along with sociology's apparent decline, that sociological practice re-emerged in the late 1970s.

Prior to the founding of CSA in 1978, Warren Dunham made a presentation at the 1972 American Sociological Association and said he wanted "to carve out a new field of clinical sociology." He, like Wirth, viewed sociology as a tool for the analysis of both society and the personality. His focus, however, was on the problem personality and he saw a role for sociologists working alongside of psychiatrists and psychologists. The position of Dunham reinforced Glass's interest in the development of the field. Glass had been working as a clinical sociologist for some time, which prompted his efforts to establish an organization that could further the efforts of clinical sociologists.

The efforts of the Clinical Sociology Association and its successor, the Sociological Practice Association (the change in name occurred in 1986), is reflective of the developments of contemporary clinical sociology. (See Clark, 1990 for a detailed history of contemporary clinical sociology.) The first set of tasks forces formed and their chairs were: Standards and Ethics (Clifford Black); Internal Organization (Jan Fritz); Education and Training (Suzanne Powers); and Employment Development and Public/Community Relations (Hugh Gardner). The goals established by CSA were (Clark 1990:102-103):

- ◆ To promote the application of sociological knowledge to intervention for individual and social change.

- ◆ To develop opportunities for the employment and utilization of clinical sociologists.

- ◆ To provide a common meeting ground for sociological practitioners, allied professionals, scholars, and students.

- ◆ To develop training, internships, certification, and other activities to further clinical sociological practice.

- ◆ To advance theory, research, and methods for sociological interventions in the widest range of professional settings.

- ◆ By October of 1978, the Executive Board of CSA issued a statement defining clinical sociology:

Clinical sociology brings a sociological perspective to intervention and action for change. The clinician is essentially a change agent rather than a researcher or evaluator. Clients may be individuals, groups, or organizations. The clinical task involves a redefinition of self, role, and/or situation, using a variety of techniques or methods for facilitating change. The value-orientation is humanistic, holistic, existential, and multidisciplinary.

Over the years, a priority of CSA/SPA has been in the area of publications. Individual members of the association have been encouraged to publish in different arenas and to identify their work as clinical (Fritz 1991). As such, the following that highlights the organizational activities of CSA/SPA since its inception reveals the level of importance they attached to publications:

➤ The first newsletter of the Clinical Sociology Association was edited by Roger Straus in the summer of 1978, just prior to the formal establishment of the organization at the 1978 ASA meeting in San Francisco. This newsletter is now called *The Practicing Sociologist* and it is currently edited by Duane Dukes at John Carroll University in Ohio.

➤ In 1979 Roger Straus edited a special issue of *American Behavioral Scientist* that was devoted to clinical sociology. In that same year Straus also published an article entitled "Clinical Sociology: An Idea Whose Time Has Come...Again" in the fall issue of *Sociological Practice*.

➤ The first textbook on clinical sociology was co-authored by Barry Glassner and Jonathan Freedman in 1979; it was titled *Clinical Sociology*. Jonathan Freedman had attended the 1976 roundtable at the ASA led by John Glass.

➤ A Code of Ethics was tentatively drafted in 1979, with a formal Code adopted in 1982 during Jan Fritz's term as president. This Code has been revised in 1985 and 1987.

➤ Training conferences offering continuing education units (CEUs) have been held since the early 1980s, with over 30 training conferences and workshops held since that time. The First Cooperative Conference in Clinical Sociology was held in Lewiston, New York in August 1981. It was organized by Jonathan Freedman, Judy Gordon, Janet Mancini, and Suzanne Powers. The three-day conference was "to bring together in a teaching/learning/sharing environment, a key group of clinical sociologists in order to learn what persons interested in the development of clinical sociology are thinking about and doing...thereby to increase synergy in this field generally and each others' skills particularly...and to build an organization" (Freedman 1981). The CSA's training conferences provide intervention skills for those who wish to enter or who are already working in clinical settings. Thirty-nine persons attended this first training conference.

➤ The annual journal of the CSA/SPA was initiated in 1982, *Clinical Sociology Review.* Its first editor was Jan Fritz, who has been succeeded by David Kallen, (1985-1991); Susan Brown Eve (1992-1993); and W. David Watts (1994-1996).

➤ An association sponsored volume, *Using Sociology: An Introduction from the Clinical Perspective*, edited by Roger Straus was published in 1985 (with a new edition in 1994). This edited volume is marketed to applied and clinical sociology courses at the undergraduate level.

➤ Collections of teaching resources for clinical courses were published in collaboration with the American Sociological Teaching Resources Center in 1984 and 1986 (*Clinical Sociology Courses: Syllabi, Exercises and Annotated Bibliography*, edited by Elizabeth Clark and Jan Fritz 1984; and *The Clinical Sociology Resource Book,* edited by Jan Fritz and Elizabeth Clark 1986).

➤ In 1985 Jan Fritz edited the volume *The Clinical Sociology Handbook;* this handbook includes abstracts of over 400 articles and books in the area of clinical sociology that had been published or presented in the fifty years between Wirth's 1931 article and 1981. The complete collection of the documents currently resides at Lauinger Library at

Georgetown University in Washington, DC. It is the only collection of its kind.

➤ The first annual meeting held independently from the ASA was held in 1986 in Thornfield, New York. In the following years, annual meetings have been held in June in LaCross, Wisconsin (1987); Silver Spring, Maryland (1988); Ann Arbor, Michigan (1989); Providence, Rhode Island (1990); Costa Mesa, California (1991); Pittsburgh (1992); Denver (1993); Atlanta (1994); Arizona (1995); and Washington, DC (1996).

➤ In 1991 Howard Rebach and John Bruhn edited *Handbook of Clinical Sociology.* This volume presents a representative selection of current practice activities and issues; presents a broad spectrum of the field; exposes readers to a variety of perspectives, general practice concerns, the practice of clinical sociology in specific settings, the work of clinical sociologists with special populations; and examines issues of identity and future directions of clinical sociology (Rebach and Bruhn 1991:xiii).

➤ Leadership in CSA/SPA has been through presidents appointed by the board. Presidents of CSA/SPA have included John Glass (1978-1980), Jan Fritz (1981-1982); Jonathan Freedman (1983-84); Elizabeth Clark (1984-1988); Robert Bendiksen (1989); Phillip Robinette (1990-1991); W. David Watts (1992-1993); David Kallen (1994-1995); Ray Kirshak (1996-present).

➤ In 1986 the journal *Sociological Practice* was acquired by SPA; This journal is thematic and its first SPA-sponsored volume, edited by Jan Fritz and Elizabeth Clark, reviewed the history and development of clinical and applied sociology. Subsequent volumes have been on *Community* (1990, edited by Alvin Lackey); *Dispute Processing* (1991, edited by Peter Maida and Maria Volpe); *Health Sociology* (1992, edited by Elizabeth Clark and Jan Fritz); *Gerontology* (1993, edited by Joyce Iutcovich).

➤ Certification in clinical sociology began during the presidency of Jonathan Freedman in 1983. The certification process is competency-based and a certification demonstration is required. The first demonstrations were held in Boston in March of 1984. Credentialed sociologists can use the designation "C.C.S." (for Certified Clinical Sociologist) after their name.

CONCLUSION

Throughout sociology's history, the discipline's acceptance of its applied and clinical side has waxed and waned. At times ambivalence existed, while outright antagonism has prevailed at other times. Hence, where are we now on the long journey to be recognized as a profession of applied and practicing sociologists? Do we meet the criteria that have been established if a field is to be considered a *profession?* Do we have a distinct status as a professional field in which there is a legal monopoly over its pursuits and practice? At this point in time, the answer is, "no."

Sociologists are not licensed or credentialed professionals providing service to the public. Society does not recognize the value and legitimacy of socio- logical practice. Indeed, sociologists themselves haven't clearly defined an abstract body of knowledge that is distinctly sociological over which they can lay claim. Given the nature of the discipline and the extent to which our knowledge and methods cross the boundaries of other social science disci- plines, this task may prove to be very difficult.

The recent efforts of both the Society for Applied Sociology and the Socio- logical Practice Association exemplify their struggle to gain professional status for sociology's practitioners. SPA initiated certification a number of years ago, but without the political connections to establish legal protection, the SPA certification has not become widespread. In 1996 the American Academy of Sociological Practitioners was established to certify sociolo- gists, primarily in the area of criminal justice specialists (*Footnotes* 1996).

Furthermore, the joint effort of SAS and SPA to develop accreditation of applied and clinical programs through the Commission on Applied and Clini- cal Sociology is a beginning to define the specialized body of knowledge and skills of sociological practitioners. But more needs to be accomplished-- accreditation of programs at different educational levels, state laws pro- tecting the rights of applied and clinical sociologists to practice, state licensure in specialized areas of practice, and recognition by the public as to the value and reliability of sociological practitioners.

Both applied and clinical sociology have emerged in recent years as interest groups as well as organizations of persons enmeshed in practice (whether residing in the academy or outside). The role these groups have played is one of generating awareness, legitimacy for sociology's practice side, establishment of organizational structures, development of codes of conduct, facilitation of communication and networking among like-minded persons, and development of educational standards. But at this point in time all three practice organizations--Society for Applied Sociology, Sociological Practice Association, and the ASA Section for Sociological Practice--are struggling. Their individual memberships have never exceeded 500. In reference to the Chinese bamboo tree--the period of rapid growth and development after years of watering and fertilizing has yet to occur.

A number of significant concerns still prevail--issues of certification and licensure, accreditation of programs, definition of the field. Certification offered through SPA has never really caught on. The ASA dismantled their program years ago for lack of interest on the part of sociologists to seek the credential. The accreditation of applied and clinical programs offers an opportunity for movement--but it is too early to tell whether accreditation will follow in the footsteps of certification and simply remain an option that exists for which there are few, if any, takers. And finally, there is still disagreement between and among members of the three practice organizations regarding the distinction between applied and clinical sociology. Members of SAS still contend that *applied* is the overarching term under which you have applied research and clinical practice (Boros 1980). They do not agree that intervention and change is the distinguishing characteristic between applied sociology and clinical sociology, since applied sociologists also engage in intervention and change activities (Iutcovich 1996). They also tend to pigeon-hole clinical sociology into the micro-level activities associated with therapeutic intervention in the troubled lives of clients (Boros 1980).

Undoubtedly, the next few years will be critical to the growth and development of sociology's applied and clinical side. It may be that the "spurt of growth after years of watering and fertilizing" will come with the accreditation of programs leading to the legitimacy of any state-level certification and licensure of sociological practitioners. This is essential for being recognized as a professional occupation. It is still too early to tell whether the joint efforts of the Society for Applied Sociology and the Sociological Practice Association will bring this about through the Commission on Applied and Clinical Sociology. However difficult the challenges, we can only succeed if we persist over time. It is important for us to remember that "the only lost cause is one we give up on before we enter the struggle" (Havel 1992:1).

REFERENCES

American Sociological Association. November 1996. "National Level Certifications Available to Sociologists." Pp. 5. in *Footnotes*. Washington, DC: American Sociological Association.

Boros, Alex. 1980 (1990). "Why Applied Sociology." *Footnotes* (May). Reprinted in *The Useful Sociologist* 11 (Winter): 4-5.

Boros, Alex. 1984. "The Society for Applied Sociology." *Journal of Applied Sociology* 1:v.

Boros, Alex. 1984. "The First Applied Sociology Conference." Pp.2-4 in *The Applied Sociologist Bulletin, Vol. 5, No.1,* edited by Joyce Iutcovich. Erie, PA: Society for Applied Sociology.

Carr-Saunders, A.M. and P.A. Wilson. 1933. *The Professions.* London: Oxford.

Cartter, A.M. 1971. "Scientific Manpower for 1970-1985." *Science* 172:132-140.

Clark, Elizabeth. 1990. "Contemporary Clinical Sociology: Definitions and Directions." *Clinical Sociology Review* 8:100-115.

Franklin, Billy. 1979. "Clinical Sociology: The Sociologist as Practitioner." *Psychology: A Quarterly Journal of Human Behavior* 16(3):51-56.

Freedman, Jonathan. 1981. First Cooperative Conference in Clinical Sociology. Conference Brochure. Jamesville, NY: Clinical Sociology Association.

Freidson, Eliot. 1970. *The Profession of Medicine.* New York: Dodd, Mead.

Fritz, Jan. 1991. "The Emergence of American Clinical Sociology." Pp. 17-30 in *Handbook of Clinical Sociology,* edited by H. M. Rebach and J.G.Bruhn. New York: Plenum.

Glass, John and Jan Fritz. 1982. "Clinical Sociology: Origins and Development." *Clinical Sociology Review* 1:3-6.

Glass, John F. 1996. Personal correspondence August 3.

Gollin, Albert E. 1883. "The Course of Applied Sociology: Past and Future." Pp.442-466 in *Applied Sociology,* edited by H.E. Freeman, R.R. Dynes, P.H. Rossi, and W.F. Whyte. San Francisco: Jossey-Bass.

Goode, William. 1960. "Encroachment, Charlatanism, and the Emerging Profession: Psychology, Sociology, and Medicine." *American Sociological Review* 25:902-914.

Gouldner, Alvin W. 1956 (1989). "Explorations in Applied Social Science." *Social Problems* 3 (3):169-181. Reprinted in *Sociological Practice* 7:26-42.

Havel, Vaclav. 1992. *Summer Meditations.* New York: Alfred A. Knopf.

Iutcovich, Joyce. 1996. "Defining Sociological Practice." Presentation at the Annual Meeting of the Society for Applied Sociology, October 17-20, Atlanta, GA.

Kallen, David. 1995. "Some History of Clinical Sociology and Sociological Practice, Part I." Clinical *Sociology Review* 13:1-23.

Lazarsfeld, Paul F. and Jeffrey G. Reitz. 1975 (1989). "History of Applied Sociology." *An Introduction to Applied Sociology*, Chapter 1. New York: Elsevier. Reprinted in *Sociological Practice* 7:43-56.

Lee, Alfred McClung. 1944. "Sociology, Clinical." P. 303 in *Dictionary of Sociology,* edited by H.P. Fairchild. New York: Philosophical Library.

Merton, Robert K. 1938. " Science and the Social Order." *Philosophy of Science* 5:321-27.

Rebach, Howard M. and John. G. Bruhn. 1991. *Handbook of Clinical Sociology.* New York: Plenum.

Rhoades, Lawrence. 1981. *A History of the American Sociological Association 1905-1980.* Washington, DC: American Sociological Association.

Shenton, Herbert Newhard. 1927 (1989). "Applied Sociology." Excerpts (pp.28, 31-32, 99-108) *The Practical Application of Sociology: A Study of the Scope and Purpose of Applied Sociology.* New York: Columbia University Press. Excerpts (pp.28, 31-32, 99-108) reprinted in *Sociological Practice* 7:17-25.

Society for Applied Sociology. 1996. "The Mentoring Program of the Society for Applied Sociology." Arnold, MD: Administrative Office of the Society for Applied Sociology.

Small, Albion. 1916 (1989). "Fifty Years of Sociology in the United States (1865-1915)." *The American Journal of Sociology* XXI (May): 721-864. Excerpts reprinted in *Sociological Practice* 7:15-16.

Ward, Lester F. 1906. *Applied Sociology: A Treatise on the Conscious Improvement of Society by Society.* Boston, MA: Ginn and Company.

Wirth, Louis. 1931 (1982). "Clinical Sociology." *American Journal of Sociology* 37:49-66. Reprinted in *Clinical Sociology Review* 1:7-22.

Wilensky, Harold. 1964. "The Professionalization of Everyone." *American Journal of Sociology* 70:137-158.

Young, Pauline. 1946. *Scientific Social Surveys and Research, Part I.* Englewood Cliffs, NJ: Prentice Hall.

2

Sociology: The Workable Myth*

ALEXANDER BOROS
Kent State University

Along with other contemporary articles, this paper recognizes the many problems which are attributed to declining enrollments and a loss of confidence by policy makers. The analysis here differs in determining that the root of these difficulties stem from incomplete validation of sociological theories. Pragmatic tests are missing. The discipline has to make better use of applied sociology tests in real life settings. In order to overcome decades of neglect, sociologists will have to work together in meeting fifteen challenges before a viable applied sociology component can develop and assume its theory-testing role. Improving confidence by others in the validity of our propositions with applied pragmatic tests will also help solve our enrollment and employment problems. To receive widespread support by society, a science must be considered useful.

For the last decade, an increasing number of sociologists have expressed their concern for the future of sociology. There are, indeed, a number of disturbing signs of misfortune. The decline of university teaching positions has restricted job mobility of professors and narrowed entry level openings for new Ph.D. sociologists. There is a widespread drop in sociology majors throughout the country. Public support for sociology research projects has been subsiding. The subsequent lowering of morale among many disappointed sociologists is moving the discipline toward an organizational crisis. Certainly, no one will disagree that sociologists are at a turning point. What is to be done?

I believe that attention to these conspicuous signs of discipline has ignored the most vital issue that confronts our discipline. It is one of our oldest issues, one that perplexed Durkheim, Ward, Parsons, and all sociologists dedicated to discovering social explanations which correspond with social facts. Is sociology valid? Is sociology's claim as a science but a myth?

* Founders Address, Second Annual Meeting of Society for Applied Sociology. Covington, Kentucky, October 12-14, 1984. Copyright Society for Applied Sociology. Reprinted with permission from the **Journal of Applied Sociology**, Volume 2, 1985.

Applied sociologists have long faced the issue of validity when using socio-logical perspectives in solving problems of social life. In application work, we are held accountable for the value of our consultations. Our advice and reports cost practitioners money. They want--often up front--proof that our sociological insights are valid and accurately correspond with their work situation, since they are held responsible for any program failures later.

I am convinced that if sociologists can make an unequivocal case that sociological theories are valid, we will then go a long way to solving our derived problems such as: decline in academic employment opportunities, drop in sociology majors, reduction of public support, and lowering of mo-rale within our discipline. This is not essentially a public relations problem. The issue of validity is very real, requiring dedicated effort. We will in-crease our usefulness to society only by demonstrating our worth.

I will now briefly review the scientific foundation of sociology that is relevant to the issue of validity. Then, I will clarify the importance of employing the pragmatic criterion for validating sociological conceptual frameworks. Based upon the potential benefit of applied sociologists for basic sociology, there will be a discussion on how this applied connection can improve the soundness of sociological perspectives. I will close with a review of hopeful trends in the acceptance of applied sociological achieve-ments.

STRUGGLING TO BECOME SCIENTIFIC

Starting at the turn of the century, the development of sociology included debates about the relationship between applied work and basic scientific theories. One group of sociologists believed in the cooperative contribu-tions of both applied and basic researchers in producing a valid and useful sociology (Ward, 1906). To provide a publication outlet for this integrated approach, Emory Bogardus founded and managed the *Journal of Applied Sociology* from its inception in 1922 until its termination in 1927. During the same period, a major drive to promote an independent scientific sociol-ogy was made by a group of sociologists that led to a memorandum distrib-uted during the 1931 Annual Meeting of the American Sociological Society (Rhoades, 1981). From this period on, the majority of sociologists sought acceptability in academia by stressing the objective research aspects of basic sociological theories. With each decade, the basic sociologists in academia became more dominant and applied sociological interests waned. Sociology developed along the lines predicted by Ellwood:

> Every historical movement starts with some new enthusiasm, or hope, which reaches out in every direction and brings everything within the movement which may in any way serve its purpose. When the first enthusiasm is spent the movement settles down into fixed habits which are supported by strong traditions. Gradually, there grows up an orthodoxy regarding what the movement stands for, and, in order to hold their lines more securely, some leaders of the movement make the orthodoxy a very narrow one (1929).

By the 1950s the orthodoxy for sociology was narrowed down to the core of basic science objectives, eliminating applied interests as being outside of its purview. Applied sociologists became a minority within the discipline that they were instrumental in forming.

In the 1960s this basic orthodoxy came under attack by prominent sociologists such as Paul Lazarsfeld, C. Wright Mills, Alvin Gouldner, and Irving Horowitz. Olsen (1981) summarized their criticism:

a. Much of what passes for basic empirical research in this field is merely trivial data manipulation.

b. A great deal of our "theory construction" is really just meaningless categorizations and other mental gymnastics.

c. Pursuing pure science without any concern for its applied relevance is intellectually and morally indefensible.

d. The public will not continue for much longer to tolerate or support a field that makes no appreciable contribution to the welfare of society.

THE ISSUE OF VALIDITY

Actually, the issue of validity for sociological propositions has been a continuous problem in winning support outside of the discipline. Even though it is true that sociology expended in membership and influence during the 1960s and 1970s, this was a unique period of popular support for all social sciences that was atypical. It is my thesis that unless we fulfill the logical and empirical requirements of validity for our propositions, then the reputation of sociology as a viable and influential science in society will be always in jeopardy. The repression of applied sociology for the sake of a "pure" science has not produced an improvement in validity that was promised by the basic, academic sociologists from the 1930s. The issue of validity is more alive in the 1980s than ever--and more critical for a reexamination.

Not just sociology, but any science, involves tested, verifiable knowledge. In science, a fact is probably valid when substantial evidence exists to support it. Validity is never final or absolute, but relative to the amount and kind of evidence which substantiates it (Lastrucci, 1963). A student once asked me if I were looking for the truth? I answered that I didn't know what truth was and that I was merely looking for the **workable myth**. I elaborated by saying that all scientists are expected to work hard today to make yesterday's knowledge obsolete tomorrow. What we scientists believe in at any one time is tentative; it has mythical characteristics (Day, 1984).

How long the myth endures to influence society depends upon: (1) its believability in terms of other cultural elements; and (2) its workability in terms of its effectiveness in solving problems of life.

Ptolemy's model of the universe is an example of a famous myth--honestly conceived--that lasted from the second century A.D. to the sixteenth century (Boorstin, 1983). According to Ptolemy the earth was the center of the universe with the stars and planets moving in circular orbits around the earth. The fact that the velocities of the sun and planets were not uniform had to be overcome by the belief that the circular paths did not have their centers directly at the center of the earth. He stated that the planets, in addition to circling the earth, rotated in an epicycle, a secondary, smaller circle, and that this other motion was superimposed upon the principle form of motion. Although this scheme was complex, it did provide for some prediction of planet movements. The Ptolemaic theory was attractive to medieval theologians who wanted to believe that the earth did not move and that man was the central figure of the universe. The theory, supported by peer consensus, persisted even after Copernicus published his heliocentric theory in 1530.

The successful challenge of the Ptolemaic model was made by the great maritime explorers of the fifteenth and sixteenth centuries. To the practical sea captains sailing around the globe, Ptolemy's geocentric theory was not workable in their life and death struggles of reaching and returning from new continents (Hurd and Kipling, 1964). After thirteen hundred years, Ptolemy's myth of the universe was rejected because it proved to be useless to practical seamen.

As with the Ptolemaic model, how many theories in sociology are supported by peer consensus rather than vindication through verification of empirical predictions? One of the basic premises of science is the on-going pursuit to eliminate inadequate theories. Yet, Blalock (1984) in a recent book states that one of the major dilemmas in sociology is the nonelimination of inadequate theories. Without a controlled and efficient testing program, theories in sociology can become reified. In this sense, our theories may be like false epi cycles created to support the mythical sociological perspective of the social world. How do we know otherwise?

It is not that we are ignorant. Any textbook in research methodology discusses the common testing criteria of: content, construct, concurrent, and pragmatic. Anyone knowing the field of sociology is aware of how little the pragmatic criterion is actually used in research on real life settings. Subsequently, our bodies of scientific knowledge do not have the same public acceptance as do the sciences with strong pragmatic accomplishments, such as physics, chemistry, and biology. It was the practical development of the atomic bomb by physicists Teller and Szilard with the help of the mathematician Von Neumann that gave supporting evidence to the abstract, pure theory of relativity proposed by Einstein.

It is not that we have not had practical successes in sociology. Two methods which have been developed with the help of sociologists have greatly improved our powers of perception of social systems (Boulding, 1964):

1. The sample survey by which information can be drawn at relatively low cost from large populations with an approximate error.

2. Indexing information on social parameters in order to make such predictions as family size, school expansion, and racial integration.

Certainly sociology has been incorporated in the practical-oriented academic specialties of operations research, criminal justice, allied health, home economics, business, education, and community psychology. However, we have not been very successful in using pragmatic tests to help determine the acceptance or rejection of sociological theories. We have not exercised our own control over the practical use of our knowledge to test our theories. Who else should care?

MAKING THE APPLIED CONNECTION

A Workable Sociology

Even though from its beginning sociology was an interventionist discipline (Bailey, 1980), today's sociologists have to defend their craft against charges of irrelevancy for solving problems of social life. It is not until people are convinced that the products of sociology are relevant to their concerns that they will begin to worry about whether they are true. To be relevant, sociology has to be workable. Who could provide better feedback on the workability of sociological perspectives in producing social betterment than applied sociologists?

In its present operational mode, our discipline, along with other social sciences, has been found inept in practical problem solving for the following reasons (Special Commission on the Social Sciences, 1969):

1. Most professional social scientists are employed in academic institutions where their nonteaching activities are focused on basic theoretical research.

2. Empirical research tends to be exploratory, or for the purpose of testing theoretical propositions, rather than for practical problem solving.

3. Even when social science work is directed to application, it often produces fragments of knowledge that need to be joined with other fragments to present a program of action.

4. Social scientists fail to communicate effectively with laymen about their expertise.

5. When faced with a specific problem that has no ready-made conceptual answer, social scientists frequently retreat to the laboratory for more research and more facts.

To overcome these criticisms, it is obvious that applied sociologists are the best link between their discipline and the policy makers. However, Denzin (1970) identifies major limitations of current applied sociology in the connector role:

1. Much of applied sociology is not theoretical with little lasting impact upon the discipline.

2. Applied sociologists are apt to become supporters instead of critics of social policies.

3. The applied sociologist has little control over the work he or she does.

4. Applied research is often just data collection for "program justification."

In the fifteen years since Denzin published his critique, applied sociology has become more professional in outlook, with better opportunities within the discipline to provide feedback to colleagues on the workability of sociological propositions in real-life settings. Much more has to be done.

Facing the Challenges of Application

In order to overcome the underdevelopment of applied sociology, there are a number of challenges that must be met head-on with determination. Since these challenges are directed, in part, toward making sociology more valid as a science, they are the responsibility of the entire discipline. Strengthening the applied connection increases the opportunity for obtaining feedback on how well sociological theories correspond to the world of practical affairs. To get underway, I offer the following fifteen challenges that should be nailed to the door of our discipline.

1. How to benefit from the interventionist spirit of students?

Being an interventionist discipline to begin with (Popper, 1965), we can recruit applied-oriented students from such undergraduate courses as social problems, social inequality, criminology, collective behavior, medical sociology, and intergroup relations. Undergraduate applied sociology programs can be designed as a preprofessional program for these intervention-oriented students who then may choose further applied training in graduate programs. Our enrollment would increase as we meet the career needs of applied-oriented students. Potentially, the ability for sociology to expand employment in applied opportunities in industry, human services, business, and government is great, but it requires marketing a product.

2. How to bridge the gap between basic and applied sociologists?

A bridge of cooperation and respect between basic and applied sociologists has to be greatly improved. An illustration of the gap is found in Blalock's recent book which lists positive steps in solving major dilemmas in the social sciences without recognizing the importance of using applied sociologists in the testing and elimination of inadequate theories (1984).

Fortunately, other sociologists recognize the interdependence between basic and applied sociology. According to Merton, applied sociologists can help basic sociologists search out the determinants and consequences of diverse forms of social behavior through their various practical roles (1976). The potential useful information from applied sociologists, however, has been under-exploited (Gouldner, 1965; Gollin, 1984a). Zetterberg stated that the practical application of social theory forces theorists to be reasonably precise, to stay in close contact with reality, and to have more than a technical vocabulary to offer when talking about social events (1962). Even the invention of technological items such as the telescope, microscope, and the IBM card did as much to advance basic knowledge in astronomy, biology, and the social sciences as for the intended applied fields (Etzioni, 1983). On the other hand, basic research that has succeeded in clearing up previously confused concepts may have a direct impact upon a social problem not previously understood by applied researchers (Merton, 1976). In return, a sociological theory has applied implications if it makes proposals about reachable means to goals of a group whose interests transcend scientific and scholarly activities (Gibbs, 1979).

To make an analogy, sociology needs to stand on both basic and applied feet. Presently, it appears that our discipline is hobbling around on the "basic" foot while holding up the "applied" foot. It will take considerable effort to integrate the basic and applied approaches in sociology regarding the testing of theories. An excellent start has been made by Giles-Sims who developed a model for synthesizing social theory and applied research (1983).

3. How to institutionalize the specialty of applied sociology?

Our discipline has grappled with the problem of integrating applied and basic sociologists into the American Sociological Association since the beginning in 1906 (Rhoades, 1981). Anthropologists have had similar difficulties (Chambers, 1985). Throughout this period, validating sociological theories was handicapped by the lack of specialists who seek to apply them to social life. If we want applied sociologists to provide feedback on their experience in using sociological frames of reference, then they must be a recognized and respected part of the sociological enterprise. Some resistance stems from fears that widespread institutionalization of applied sociology could lead to oversell and subsequent condemnation of the discipline by policy makers (Street and Weinstein, 1975). Olsen has outlined a proposal for bringing about collaborative efforts between basic and applied sociologists to maximize effective interventions (1981). Ready or not, the discipline has already gone a long way in developing applied training programs (Freeman, et al., 1983).

Certainly, incorporating applied sociology in the training curriculum helps to assure that each new generation of applied sociologists can build upon the work of their predecessors.

4. How to provide certification and accreditation for applied sociology?

In the last decade, sociologists have accused the academic departments of criminal justice, allied health, home economics, and psychology with encroachment. The lesson that we can learn from these losses of applied courses is clear: use it or lose it. If we do not practice our sociology, other disciplines will. Complaints have been made by applied sociologists who claim that they are prevented from working by certification and restrictive state laws that have been enacted to protect other professionals, such as clinical psychologists and social workers.

To be protected at the departmental level, we need to develop accreditation procedures for applied sociology training programs. To protect our clinical sociologists and program evaluators in applied settings, we need to develop our certification procedures which would safeguard the unique practice skills of these specialists. Although there is considerable discussion about the value of accreditation and certification, the American Sociological Association has already begun the establishment of certification procedures of practicing sociologists (Huber, 1984). Beginning in 1986, ASA appointed six committees that will certify sociologists for the specialty areas of: Law and Social Control, Medical Sociology, Organizational Analysis, Social Policy and Evaluation Research, Social Psychology, and Demography.

5. How to continue developing effective applied training programs?

Accreditation and certification must be preceded by special training programs to prepare sociologists for applied work (Boros, 1984). Attaching one or two applied courses to basic sociological curriculums is not enough. We need to differentiate between training objectives at the undergraduate, masters, and doctorate levels. There are too many questions yet unanswered. What type of faculty should participate in this training? How should we evaluate the graduates of these applied programs? Should the training take place on-campus, off-campus, or both? The applied graduate has to be prepared for the day when the practitioner asks: "What do you know that is useful to me now?" The applied sociologist also should be prepared to answer: "What have I practiced which can be useful to my discipline?"

6. How to promote a literature on application experiences?

Unfortunately, the literature on applied experiences of sociologists is very limited. There were little encouragement or publication opportunities for applied sociologists in the mainstream journals of their discipline during the last forty years. It is imperative for training programs and applied practice that a comprehensive literature be developed on the use of applied sociological perspectives. The work of applied sociologists should no longer be ignored in textbooks of social problems, family and alternative life styles, and other courses. Neither should applied articles be confined only to our applied journals. We need a written heritage of applied sociology.

7. How to develop teachable practice applications?

Although our evolving literature should include materials on the execution of the various roles of applied sociologists, it is absolutely necessary that we provide information on the successful applications of our work as well (Olsen and Micklin, 1981). Clinical sociologists should describe intervention techniques which are useful at either the group or individual levels. Research and program evaluators must continue to codify the strategies used in consulting with agencies and firms. Administrators could recount the sociological skills found helpful in management problems. Applied sociological inventions that are effective should be delineated. In short, we need to establish what our applied skills are so that they can be taught to the next generation of sociologists. Otherwise, every sociologist must struggle alone in applied settings.

8. How to create a code of ethics for applied work?

The American Sociological Association has established a code of ethics for the basic research role (Long and Dorn, 1982). Although this code is suited to many of the applied research roles, there are enough differences to warrant a separate system of ethics for sociologists who are working in applied settings such as hospitals, industries, businesses, governmental offices, and human service agencies (Angell, 1967; Bokemeir and Carter, 1980; Chambers, 1985). Because applied sociology jobs are diverse, it will take a considerable time to develop an applied code of ethics.

9. How to improve rewards for application work?

Although some applied sociologists report that there are ample rewards for their professional work in applied settings, the majority frequently complain about being under-appreciated (Morrissey and Steadman, 1977). Some of the major criticisms are:

> a. Too often in academia, low status is attached to applied work done by sociologists.

> b. Criteria used by the discipline for judging the value of practicing sociologists are hardly ever based upon applied objectives and activities (e.g., published articles in mainstream sociology journals instead of agency monographs or technical reports).

> c. Agency directors, public officials, and business managers generally do not understand the potential of sociologists to help them solve their organizational problems, too often turning to graduates from business or public administration programs instead.

To rectify these conditions, much more can and must be done by academic sociologists who provide the image of sociologists not only for our majors but for all other students who take sociology courses. Disciplinary and professional sociology societies can work together to promote a more complete image of the numerous roles of sociologists, beyond the traditional ones of teaching and researching, to the general public through a deliberate public relations effort (Gollin, 1984b).

10. How to widen our communication circles?

Given the political events of the 1980s which led to the reduction of governmental funding for our research efforts, it ought to be clear that we must improve our communication to social circles outside of our own discipline.

We now face a public that may find our subject matter interesting but not needed for decision-making in the world of practical affairs. We need to respond effectively to critics who consider projects by social scientists not worthy of public support (Klein, 1982). Since we need supporters from all walks of life, it is imperative that we take the trouble to listen to concerns and definitions of their own situations by community members and offer them tangible, accountable solutions. Being thus responsive does not mean we are selling out.

11. How to maintain meaningful contacts with sociology graduates?

One of the best sources of societal influence and feedback rests with graduates from our training program (Adamek and Boros, 1983). Yet, how many departments can tell us whatever happened to their graduates from either undergraduate or graduate programs? We have foolishly ignored a valuable resource in representing our worth to groups outside of our universities. Meaningful contact could begin with our concrete help toward their search for suitable employment. We could later benefit from their feedback on the relevancy of their training to the workplace, as well as leads for the placement of interns and other job seekers.

12. How to develop theories of application?

Besides the development of theories of social life, we need to pay special attention to theories of sociological application as a unique form of social process (Strike, 1979). That is, we could examine the conditions under which certain types of sociological interventions, carried out in certain ways, produce certain kinds of outcomes. Interventions by sociologists can be and should be studied for improved sociological applications. This area, I feel, is our greatest challenge. We have made little effort to record our efforts at developing testable models of intervention.

13. How to produce methodologies for application work?

In order to be respected for the unique contributions of sociological perspectives, we must develop special, successful techniques of application for roles of planning, counseling, administration, and research. Program evaluation is already fairly advanced. I have found the cooperative team effort between researchers and community planners outlined in Lewin's Action Research Model (1948) to be appropriate to clinical sociologists who are seeking to produce social change in community organizations (Boros, 1979). What methodologies are useful to sociologists who are implementing administrative or counseling roles?

14. How to be professionally accountable?

To be in demand by policy makers, we have to accept the challenge of being professionally accountable for our application work. Unlike basic scientists who make their methodology and findings public for verification by other researchers, applied sociologists usually have organizational restraints placed upon them by the users of their services. Their work is often considered private and the property of their policy makers (Root, 1978). Therefore, we need to be imaginative in working out acceptable alternative ways to be held accountable to our practitioners, clients, and fellow sociologists. There can be no exemption from proving our worth to others.

15. How to evaluate and improve our success in meeting all of our challenges?

Periodically, there should be an overview of how well we are meeting the challenges in developing a respectable and useful applied sociology that satisfies objectives which are both disciplinary and professional by nature. A recent article by Freeman and Rossi (1984) is an example of this double accounting.

HOPEFUL TRENDS

Obviously, these fifteen challenges will not be met overnight. We are too far behind. Furthermore, improving the applied connection is and will always be a continuing responsibility of the entire discipline. Unfortunately, many sociologists as yet do not assume this commitment to develop a strong applied sociology component. There are a number of trends that suggest we are at last moving in a direction which is positive to applied concerns.

1. There is a growing manifestation within the discipline that applied sociology is a legitimate specialty:

a. In the last decade, there has been an increase in the numbers of applied papers listed on programs of the various annual sociological meetings.

b. There now exists special committees within the ASA to work on applied sociology concerns.

c. Beginning in 1986, there will be the first designated award by ASA for a distinguished career for the practice of sociology.

d. The ASA executive staff has been very responsive to the needs of applied sociologists, as can be readily ascertained in improved coverage of applied matters in the *ASA Footnotes*.

e. The ASA now regularly sponsors several workshops on the development of applied sociology training programs.

2. According to the 1982 *ASA Guide to Graduate Studies*, over fifty percent of all graduate departments offer applied programming for graduate students. The majority of sociology departments offer undergraduate internships in applied settings (Satariano and Rogers, 1979).

3. There is an increasing number of sociologists who are working outside of universities in applied settings (Manderscheid and Greenwald, 1983). They represent a potential for recruitment in applied sociology societies.

4. There are now several applied organizations with national and international memberships: The Clinical Sociology Association, the Applied Sociologists of Sacramento, California, the Chicago Area Applied Sociologists, the Practice Section of the ASA, and the Society for Applied Sociology.

5. There is an increased representation of applied sociology topics in the literature through readers, journals (e.g., *Sociological Practice, Clinical Sociological Review, and the Journal of Applied Sociology*), and

Eshleman's 1983 edition of *Sociology: An Introduction* which includes short summaries after each chapter of sociologists in applied roles. Applied sociologists are becoming visible.

CONCLUSIONS

One of Kuhn's noteworthy accomplishments was to discuss the epistemological problem of how one scientific idea succeeds another (Kuhn, 1962). In this paper I have been concerned how one segment of basic sociologists could impede the development of applied sociologists to the detriment of both. After eighty years, the validity of basic sociological theories is still a moot question. The growth of applied sociology has been stunted. A decline in the academic marketplace for sociology in the 1980s has produced shock to the discipline and forced a reexamination of organizational purpose.

Recognizing that our discipline is in a turning-point, I have argued that the solution should not start with the symptoms of our decline. Latching on applied options as a reluctant, temporary measure to solve current academic shortages in jobs and student enrollment is misdirected. Any restructuring of our discipline that does not start with the issue of validity will be short-lived. When the enrollment in academia meets the numbers to support the remaining faculty in fewer sociology departments, then will we return to the traditional departments that existed prior to the unusual expansion of the 1960s? What will happen to applied sociology as the quick fix? More importantly, what would happen to our need to improve our tests of validity for our sociological theories? Does anyone want to wait another eighty years?

By starting with the issue of validity, my proposal conceives the relationship between applied and basic sociologists to be mutually beneficial. This interdependence facilitates their cooperation on mutual matters. By working together on the fifteen challenges I have posted, all of sociology can benefit in the short and long run.

I am ending my presentation on a happy outlook. The future for sociology with a well-developed applied connection looks good. In accepting these fifteen challenges, we are helping to make sociology more valid to fellow scientists, more useful to society, and more acceptable to employers outside of academia. With effective promotion, we will need ten times more students to carry applied sociology into the marketplace of industry, business, human service, and governmental offices. These positive changes will undoubtedly raise our lagging morale as well.

It has been a long time since Robert Merton asked the discipline to turn its attention to the pressing problem of creating middle range theories. It is now imperative to mobilize our intellectual energies and produce an effective applied connection that will help test those middle range theories of sociology. Otherwise, will our own peer consensus be acceptable to the biologists, physicists, chemists, philosophers, and others who ask us the perennial question: "How do you know that you know?"

REFERENCES

Adamek, R. J. and A. Boros. 1983. "Training, work experiences, and professional identity of applied sociology M.A. graduates." *Sociological Spectrum* 3,1 (April-June): 159-179.

Angell, R. C. 1967. "The ethical problems of applied sociology." Pp. 725-740 in Lazarsfeld Sewell, and Wilensky (eds.), *The Uses of Sociology*. New York: Basic Books.

Bailey, J. 1980. *Ideas and Intervention: Social Theory for Practice*. Boston, Massachusetts: Rutledge and Kegan Paul.

Blalock, H. 1984. *Basic Dilemmas in the Social Sciences*. Beverly Hills, California: Sage Publications.

Bokemeier, J. and K. Carter. 1980. "Ethics in sociological practice: a survey of sociologists." *Sociological Practice* 3,2 (Spring): 129-151.

Boorstin, D. J. 1983. *The Discoverers*. New York: Random House.

Boros, A. 1979. "The role of action research in services for deaf alcoholics." *Journal of Rehabilitation of the Deaf* 12, 4 (April): 15.

Boros, A. 1984. "The applied connection for sociology." *Innovative Higher Education* 8, 2: 134-143.

Boulding, K. E. 1964. *The Meaning of the 20th Century*. New York: Harper Torchbooks.

Chambers, E. 1985. "Professional ethics and applied anthropology." In *Applied Anthropology*. Englewood Cliffs, New Jersey: Prentice Hall, Inc.

Day, M. S. 1984. *The Many Meanings of Myth*. University Press of America.

Denzin, N. K. 1970. "Who leads: Sociology or society?" *The American Sociologist* 5 (May): 125-127.

Ellwood, C. A. 1929. *Man's Social Destiny: In the Light of Science*. Nashville, Tennessee: Cokesbury Press.

Etzioni, A. 1983. *An Immodest Agenda: Rebuilding America Before the Twenty-First Century*. New York: McGraw-Hill Book Company.

Freeman, D. 1983. *Margaret Mead and Samoa: The Making and Unmaking of an Anthropological Myth*. Cambridge: Harvard University Press.

Freeman, H. E. and P. H. Rossi. 1984. "Furthering the applied side of sociology." *American Sociological Review* 49 (August): 571-580.

Gibbs, J. P. 1979. "The elites can do without us." *The American Sociologist* 14 (May): 79.

Giles-Sims, J. and B. Tuchfeld. 1983. "Role of theory in applied sociology." In Freeman, Dynes, Rossi, and Whyte (eds.) *Applied Sociology*. San Francisco, California: Jossey-Bass Publishers.

Gollin, A. E. 1984a. "Applied sociology can advance discipline." *ASA Footnotes* (January): 2.

Gollin, A. E. 1984b. "Publicizing sociological activities serves important function for the discipline." *ASA Footnotes* (December): 5.

Gouldner, A. W. 1965. "Exploration in applied social sciences." Pp. 522 in Gouldner, Miller, et al. (eds.), *Applied Sociology: Opportunities and Problems*. New York: Free Press.

Huber B. 1984. "ASA certification program accepted in principle." *ASA Footnotes* (October): 3, 8.

Hurd, D. L. and J. J. Kipling. 1964. *The Origins and Growth of Physical Science*. Baltimore, Maryland: Penguin Books.

Klein, G. C. 1982. "Let's not be lecturing on navigation while the ship is going down: On the creation of public interest sociology." *The American Sociologist* 17 (August): 120 -131.

Kuhn, T. S. 1962. *The Structure of Scientific Revolutions*. University of Chicago Press.

Lastrucci. C. L. 1963. *The Scientific Approach*. Cambridge, Massachusetts: Schenkman Publishing Company.

Lewin, K. 1948. *Resolving Social Conflicts*. New York: Harper.

Long, G. L. and D. S. Dorn. 1982. "An assessment of the ASA Code of Ethics and Committee on Ethics." *The American Sociologist* 17 (May): 80-86.

Manderscheid, R. W. and M Greenwald. 1983. "Trends in the employment of sociologists." In Freeman, Dynes, Rossi and Whyte (eds.) *Applied Sociology*. San Francisco, California: Jossey-Bass Publishers.

Merton, R. K. 1976. *Sociological Ambivalence*. New York: Free Press.

Morrissey, J. P. and H. J. Steadman. 1977. "Practice and perish? Some overlooked career contingencies for sociologists in nonacademic settings." *The American Sociologist* 12 (November): 154-162.

Olsen M. 1981. "Epilogue: The future applied sociology." Pp. 561-581 in Olsen and Michlin (eds.), *Handbook of Applied Sociology*. New York: Praeger Publishers.

Olsen, M. and M. Michlin. eds. 1981. *Handbook of Applied Sociology*. New York: Praeger Publishers.

Popper. K. R. 1965. "Social science and social policy." Pp. 32-41 in Braybrooke (ed.), *Philosophical Problems of the Social Sciences*. New York: Macmillan Company.

Rhoades, L. J. 1981. *A History of the American Sociological Association 1905-1980*. Washington, DC: American Sociological Association.

Root, K. 1978. "Is sociology relevant to the real world? Yes, but . . . "*ASA Footnotes* 6, 1 (January): 1-7.

Satariano, W. and S. Rogers. 1979. "Undergraduate internships: Problems and prospects." *Teaching Sociology* 6, 4: 355-372.

Special Commission on the Social Sciences of the National Science Board. 1969. *Knowledge into Action: Improving the Nation's Use of the Social Sciences*. Washington, DC: National Science Foundation.

Street, D. P. and E. A. Weinstein. 1975. "Problems and prospects of applied sociology." *The American Sociologist* 10 (May): 65-72.

Strike, K. A. 1979. "An epistemology of practical research." *Educational Researcher* (January): 10-16.

Ward, L. 1906. *Applied Sociology*. Boston, Massachusetts: Ginn and Company.

Zetterberg, H. L. 1962. *Social Theory and Social Practice*. New York: Bedminster Press.

Alexander Boros
1931-1996

Alexander Boros, founder and first president of the Society for Applied Sociology in 1985-86, represented the driving force behind SAS's growth and development. A professor of sociology at Kent State University from 1963 until his death in 1996, Alex earned a master's degree from Western Reserve University in 1962 and a doctorate from Case Western Reserve University in 1969. His tireless devotion to applied sociology and message that sociology is, indeed, a *workable myth,* will forever be remembered by his colleagues and other professionals in the field.

In the fall of 1978, Alex, along with Harold Cox and Gurmeet Sekhon, began discussing their çommon interests in applied sociology. After several meetings they decided to call themselves the Society for Applied Sociology (SAS). As the founding father of the Society for Applied Sociology, Alex left his mark on many of the initiatives of the Society--the establishment of the annual conferences, the development of the *Journal of Applied Sociology,* SAS's incorporation and election of officers (of which he served as the first president), and most recently, the magazine, *Social Insight: Knowledge at Work.* In 1989 Alex also received the Lester F. Ward Distinguished Contributions to Applied Sociology award from SAS. As a further honor, in 1995 SAS established, in his name, the Alex Boros Award for Contributions to the Society for Applied Sociology.

Applications and practice are powerful sources of validation of sociology's knowledge and theories, according to Alex Boros. He envisioned a sociology in which theory created through basic research could be tested in the field (e.g., "real life" settings) by applied sociologists. This message was echoed in much of his work. Alex's work focused on the development of services for those hearing impaired who are disabled with substance abuse. As a result of his pioneering efforts, Alex served as a consultant on the development of applied programs for the disabled in Austria, Poland, Hungary, Canada, Chile, Spain, Mexico, and London. Over the years, Alex obtained more than $2 million in public service grants from federal and state agencies as a consultant on the development of educational programs for agencies serving the deaf and people with multiple disabilities. He served his local community through countless public service hours dedicated to meeting the needs of the hearing impaired. A program that he designed and administered through Kent State University, Addiction Intervention for the Deaf (Project AID), was funded for over 10 years by the Ohio Department of Health.

This interest in rehabilitation and medical sociology led him to establish in 1969 what is believed to have been the first graduate program in applied sociology in the United States at Kent State University. Over the years he served his profession by working with and mentoring hundreds of sociology students. In the words of Joyce Iutcovich, a student of Alex and president of SAS in 1994-95, "for all his efforts, the Society for Applied Sociology will forever be indebted to him and carry his dreams forward into the 21st century. His dreams and visions of our future are what have kept us going." Other colleagues have been profoundly affected, not only by his scholarship, but as well by his nature as a human being. In his work as a professor where he developed applied programs, consulted with community agencies, worked with the deaf, mentored students, and engaged in scholarly research and writing, Alex never lost sight of his consistent commitment to the value of human beings and the need to preserve certain values.

Alex Boros's contributions in the area of rehabilitation and applied sociology are substantial. He has published in *Journal of Rehabilitation, Alcohol Health & Research World, Deaf People and Social Change, Journal of Applied Sociology, Clinical Sociology Review, Teaching Sociology, and Spectrum,* as well as other chapters in edited volumes.

3

The Sociology of Success: Fact or Fantasy*

MARK IUTCOVICH

Edinboro University of Pennsylvania

Keystone University Research Corporation

When I suggested to a colleague that my presidential address will be on the "Sociology of Success" she questioned the topic. Her statement was "You are not at an American Sociological Association conference to present a theoretical conceptual framework."

Fundamentally, the question was what would the applied sociologist gain by understanding the phenomenon of "success." What made me persistent and excited about such a topic was that there is such a vast literature relating to success, much of it offering recipes for success. For instance, one may find such titles as:

> How To Become Head of Your Firm Before Forty
> Successful Living Twenty Sure Ways to Job Success
> Personal and Professional Success for Women
> Concepts of Security and Success
> Women and the Fear of Success
> Success Values: Are They Universal or Class Differentiated?
> Equality, Success and Social Justice in England and the United States
> Childhood Background of Success in a Profession
> The Secret of Success
> New Thought: A Cult of Success
> The American Idea of Success
> The American Gospel of Success.

* Presidential Address, Fifth Annual Meeting of the Society for Applied Sociology, Lexington, Kentucky, November 6-8, 1987. Copyright, Society for Applied Sociology. Reprinted with permission from **Journal of Applied Sociology,** Volume 5, 1988.

There are also many more books providing simple advice on how to be successful. One may find similar of these types of articles in Readers Digest and in numerous other publications of popular repute.

These types of literature offer recipes for being successful. Some studies address specific relationships between individual position, background and success, but on the whole the literature does not offer a sociological approach to success. Success is viewed as being due to the individual actions, the consequences of which may be ulcers or even heart attacks.

This type of analysis does not enable us to develop strategies to be either successful as applied sociologists or as an organization. Moreover, it does not offer the necessary insight for consulting business, industrial enterprises, or agencies on how to be successful in their activities. Whenever we indulge in the type of analysis presented in the cited literature, we commit two sins: 1) the fallacy of reductionism, and 2) we follow more an ideological line of thought which concludes that the individual is guilty of glory or failure.

At this juncture, it is important to mention that throughout history many outstanding achievements by individuals and/or groups were not recognized until the historical and social circumstances changed. For instance, a body of work which today is regarded by the world as outstanding in English literature is the work of William Shakespeare. It should not be thought that Shakespeare's work was appreciated in his time. The condition of the time was that such work (i.e., acting and the theater) was not a respectable endeavor. In fact, the idea that Shakespeare was a genius did not materialize until almost a century after his death. Today a high school student cannot avoid studying at least one of Shakespeare's works. Thus, the glorification of Shakespeare did not take place until after his death. Only when the social condition changed did the larger public change its orientation and view the work of Shakespeare as a national treasure.

The success of an organization, discipline, product, or even an idea cannot be fully understood unless it is placed in a genuinely historical and/or social/cultural context. Here, we may ask why sociology as a discipline was once quite popular and/or successful and through time became less and less marketable. Indeed, answers were advanced such as: 1) ASA did not aggressively market sociological knowledge to the larger society, or 2) sociologists involved themselves in developing the so-called pure scientific knowledge and, therefore, ignored the applied side of the discipline. Thus, other disciplines captured certain areas in the marketplace which in practical terms belonged within the sociological expertise.

The cited answers all have their own merit and are sustained by the evidence presented. But to market a certain knowledge, or to understand why certain organizations and/or disciplines are more successful than others, we should focus on other dimensions and not just the psychological or the individual dimension and/or the organizational level.

Sociologists, in general, did not explore the problem of "success" in terms of social/cultural and historical conditions. In the article, "Reflection on the Annual Meeting," sociology has a prominent place in some countries, while in others it is ranked at the bottom of the scale. It is noted:

> At one end of the continuum is Norway, where sociology and the other social sciences are very much a part of the social policy making process with sociology in the ascendancy when welfare programs are expanding, while political science and economics dominate the process in times of fiscal restraint and budget tightening. At the other end of the continuum is Japan, where, according to Dr. Ken-ichi Tominaga, sociology occupies the bottom rung of the status ladder, despite the group-centered focus of Japanese economic life. Israel and India occupy positions in-between. Most surprising was the presentation by Dr. Stefan Novak of Poland. There, sociologists work both sides of the political aisle, and are respected by the government and the Church leaders. Moreover, according to Dr. Novak, his colleagues even sit down together afterwards to reflect in a civil manner on the policy-making process in which they were engaged on opposing sides *(Footnotes, p. 2).*

The point which I make is quite obvious in the quoted article. If we look at contemporary history we see the paranoid fantasies of McCarthyism

(Hofstadter 1967; Friendly 1967), the growth of pseudo-religious revival and even today's political inaction with Reagan's policies. All were successful and all were able to sell their beliefs and/or ideologies.

The same can be said of the PTL under Jim and Tammy Baker. Despite the scandal surrounding PTL, many of its faithful obviously still admire the Bakers. (Mike Royko has an article on this subject under the title "So Who's Perfect?" 1987.)

One might ask why Norman Vincent Peale (Hackett 1967; Hart 1950; Friendly 1967), who belonged to the Reactionary Committee for Constitutional Government, was extremely successful in selling his philosophy to an estimated 30 million Americans through weekly newspaper columns, national radio broadcasts and his own magazine Guideposts. His book, *The Power of Positive Thinking*, became the best-selling nonfiction book of modern times and ranked second only to the Bible in sales during the fifties. Indeed, Peale's success cannot be accounted from the individualistic point of departure.

The underlying rational for "success" is to respond to the receptiveness of the audience. Peale's and even Carnegie's use of religion as a device for success consciously or unconsciously exploited the social/cultural conditions of mid-century America, which church historian Martin Marty has described as "a revival of interest in religion." (1959, p. 15)[1]

The examples of the Bakers, Peale, and Carnegie dictate that success be analyzed in direct relationship to groups and/or subgroups within the larger society. As you know, a starting premise among most sociologists (including myself) is that "it is not men in general who think, or even isolated individuals who do the thinking but men in certain groups who have developed a particular style of thought in an endless series of responses to certain typical situations characterizing their common position" (Mannheim 1936, p. 3).

In following this line of thought, we can assume that groups and/or subgroups within the larger society will develop different reactions and perceptions regarding whatever is offered in the market knowledge, services or goods.

In the often-quoted words of Marx, "It is not the consciousness of men which determines their existence, but, on the contrary, their social existence which determine their consciousness" (1913, pp. 11-12).

Thus, in the larger society we find different modes of perceiving. These modes of perceiving are not randomly distributed, nor are the views adopted by any group as a matter of mere chance. Rather, as Mannheim postulates, it is more likely the case that "from whatever source we get our meanings, whether they be true or false they have a certain psychological-sociological function" (1936, p. 21).

In order to succeed, the individual consultant and/or applied sociologist should think in these terms. Whatever the position of certain groups, their thinking becomes so intensively interest-bound to a situation that they are simply no longer able to see certain facts which would undermine their sense of perception (Mannheim 1936). Only in this way can it be explained why it took Einstein ten years to convince his peers of his paradigm before his approach was finally accepted, mostly because of historical conditions of the Second World War (we needed the bomb).

In this presentation, therefore, we shall explore the phenomenon of success by focusing on:

1) Explanation of the methodological approach for this presentation;

2) Meanings of the term success; what should the sociological definition of success be;

3) The sources and functions of success;

4) The manifestation of success;

5) Some implications for the applied sociologist and the Society for Applied Sociology.

THE METHODOLOGICAL APPROACH

The methodological approach is an historical one. In order to support our arguments, we refer to historical events or conditions. Thus, the empirical manifestations are depicted from history. This approach also lends itself to following events through time and points out conditions which are favorable and unfavorable to certain actions by either individuals or collectivity.

THE MEANING OF THE CONCEPT

In Webster's dictionary (1964), the term success is defined as:

- result, outcome,
- a favorable or satisfactory outcome or result,
- the gaining of wealth, fame, rank, etc.,
- successful person as a recognition.

Thus, many meanings are given to the term success such as:

- whenever there is something accomplished,
- if a victory is obtained against an adversary,
- when there is compensation or recognition from the public.

The first of these meanings is very general and does not lend itself to a scientific investigation. The second comes from an individualistic point of view. The third refers to the interaction between the actor and the group and/or groups who accomplished a certain end.

Any activity of an individual and/or collectivity which is accepted and rewarded can be termed a success. The reward can be material or nonmaterial such as fame, decoration, prestige, popularity or money.

For a sociological understanding, "success" should be viewed as a social reaction to the action of an individual and/or collectivity. There are many instances in which the actions of individuals do not bring about a positive reaction from the public, and, therefore, such actions are disregarded, although they may be beneficial to the group, subgroup, and/or the larger society. Success can be defined as whenever the action of individuals or collectivity receives positive rewards because such actions are regarded as important to the group and/or larger society.

THE SOURCES AND FUNCTIONS OF SUCCESS

Once we have established what we mean by the term success, we can address the third aspect—the sources of success and its functions. As previously stated, success is directly related to the historical time and/or the socio-cultural conditions, and, therefore, should be seen as a social function. Success manifests itself in different forms as the characteristics of a society develop. Success varies from one society to another and should not be thought to always have a scientific and/or rational base. Throughout history success has manifested itself in mystical, superstitious, and irrational beliefs which, even today, are not completely eliminated from our highly complex and industrial society.

It can be said that successful actions reflect the social conditions. Also, because of the structural differences among types of activities (economic, technological, political, military, judicial, artistic, scientific, philosophical, religious, etc.), each sector has its own criteria for rewarding the activities of individuals and/or collectivities. Success varies from one sector to another. Moreover, success in one sector does not necessarily insure success in another sector or subsector. It can be said, therefore, that there is no such thing as universal success; rather, success varies directly with the division of labor and the characteristics of groups and/or subgroups.

Other analytical distinctions important to our understanding of success are:

1) Some person may be successful during his/her lifetime, but forgotten after his/her death.

2) Success may be more related to the product than to the person. For instance, the famous chemist, Lavoisier, unfortunately occupied a position as Fermier General (a tax collector) under the king. He was executed in 1794 during the time of the French Revolution.

3) The larger society and groups stress and create the conditions for certain activities and products which they deem important for survival and/or development. In this case the success is of the product and/or activity, and success is separated from the individual or collectivity.

4) Once the historical and social condition of each generation changes, the members of the society change their perception and develop different preferences and evaluative measurements for assessing success of an activity and/or product.

From our discussion it can be seen that it is not possible to have a "famous person" outside of a society. The supreme factor in determining success is the audience, which determines whether the action, product, etc., initiated by an individual should be valued.

It can be said, therefore, that there is no such thing as a "famous person" or "nonfamous person," but simply persons made up of flesh, blood and bones. The qualification of "famous" is a function of social values which are maintained by the larger society. In the final analysis, the enthusiasm of the public for certain activities such as poetry, art, science, religion, and any other product makes the person or persons successful.

Once we establish that the source of success is the collectivity/audience or groups, then we can establish the functions of success:

1) The heroes are essentially a particular manifestation of success—a diffused representation of the collectivity which is manifested through the individual.

2) Bestowing success on an action or product, the collectivity and/or society manifests its predominant values.

3) The social function of success is to advance the social values which characterize the society at the time.

THE MANIFESTATION OF SUCCESS

Success may manifest itself in various ways:

1) explosive—from anonymity to celebrity; or

2) incremental—by stages, which may manifest itself even after a person's death.

Explosive Success

An example of explosive success is Spartacus, who was the leader of the slave revolt. Plutarch describes the event in which Lentulus Batiatus established in Capua a training camp of gladiators who were prisoners of war. According to Plutarch (1959), seventy-eight gladiators started the rebellion, and they spearheaded the revolt. Indeed, all the events which took place is not our concern. It is sufficient to point out that under the leadership of Spartacus the rebels were able to defeat some of the most famous Roman generals. Spartacus became known throughout the peninsula and surrounding areas. Plutarch describes in detail this explosive success attained by Spartacus. The conditions at the time were quite appropriate for such a manifestation, and Spartacus was the spark which lighted the fire (Fast 1952).

However, explosive success refers not only to such manifestations as heroic action, heroic death, revolution, revolts, wars, etc. For example, an explosive success was achieved by the English writer Rudyard Kipling, considered by some the most outstanding poet after Shakespeare, although his success is not only due to remarkable talent, but also to the social condition of British imperial-colonial expansion.

Indeed an explosive success can manifest after the death of the person. An instructive example from many points of view is the case of Austrian Monk Mendel (1822-1884). Mendel in 1865-1869 experimented with the cross fertilization of peas with Hieracium. His achievement was not discovered until 1900, when suddenly it was elevated as a new theory of evolution and as the universal theory of heredity.

Incremental Success

Incremental success is the opposite of the explosive. It starts with difficulties and a continuous struggle from anonymity to recognition. The audience is not prepared to appreciate and sanction the product. It is contrary to the general expectations, and there is no congruency between what the audience expects and the individual action produces.

In 1744, Buffon, a French scientist, published *Theorie de la terre (A Theory of the Earth)*. In his book he presented a general conception of evolution which was opposed to the theological and creationist's conception. In the U.S. we have the Scopes trial or monkey trial.

In all these instances, the ideas of men were contrary to the traditional ideas recorded in the book of Genesis. Of course, these new ideas produced strong negative reactions. It is interesting that, at that time, the church and the faculty of theology at Sorbonne obtained from Buffon an apology and retraction of his theory.

A classical example of delayed or incremental success which one may find in the history of French literature is in the case of the writer Stendhal (1783-1842). Stendhal, by himself, acknowledged that he would not obtain any glory, fame or success until 1880. Remember he died in 1842. He was a very good prophet. It took roughly 50 years after his death for his writing to be appreciated. His ideas, penetrating psychological analyses of personal lives which are interwoven with the normative order of the time, made Stendhal one of the most prominent novelists in French literature. Indeed, I can go on in producing examples of either types of success, but I think both were sufficiently documented.

Another aspect of analytical importance regarding the phenomenon of success is the proper manifestation of success once it takes place. In some instances success may increase and decrease. The increase and decrease is more related to the social condition rather than to some magical force.

The problem is to ascertain the manifestations of increase and decrease of success. A logical and empirical possibility is to focus on such dimensions as intensity, duration, and diffusion. In other words intensity must ascertain if the action and/or product received great acclaim. Duration determines the length of time success lasts. Diffusion determines the degree to which the action and/or product is acknowledged by the larger society and/or group. From the combination of these three dimensions would evolve numerous variations, but essentially there will be a disjuncture or parallel relationship between the three dimensions. Indeed, a perfect parallelism cannot be found throughout history when all the three dimensions are in perfect congruence. An example regarding maximum intensity is the success accomplished by Alexandra Macedon (Alexander the Great), Jesus Christ, and William Shakespeare. I choose these three men as examples because they are of different domains and became famous for different reasons.

Alexander, besides being a conqueror, also liberated many nations from the Persian domination. He also introduced the Helenic culture (Jauquet 1926). His power and fame was widespread throughout the world of that time. After his expedition in India he showed his intention of forming one nation through the amalgamation of the Macedonians, Greeks, and the Persians. The year 324 BC was the highest point of his success, when at his wedding he paid off his soldiers and gave his important officers golden crowns. On June 13,323, he died. Not long after the Macedonian empire began to fall apart. Alexander's fame gradually faded away. Today he is thought as a hero for popular novels and in Hollywood pictures.

In contrast, the success of Jesus Christ has a completely different development. The intensity of success of a general is directly related to being alive. Death usually means a negative force in the maintenance of success. On the other hand, for the founders of religion there is a need for mysticism. In the case of Christianity the sacrifice and revival after the death of Jesus Christ has a dogmatic significance. Many theologians arrived at the conclusion that the mystical success surrounding Jesus Christ came only after his death. Without his death and revival, Jesus Christ would not have such an outstanding place in human history. Thus, Jesus Christ's success has been possible through the idea of revival from death, and the intensity of success reached a high point in the feudal period.

Shakespeare gradually achieved celebrity. His work became classic in the 1700s. After this period his fame gradually increased and in the 18th century reached the highest point of success. After 1875 his fame gradually decreased to some extent. Today, Shakespeare is regarded as an outstanding writer with international recognition.

In pointing out these three historical events, we can see the analytical distinction between different manifestations of success. Alexander Macedon's success was of an explosive type. In almost 12 years he became the conqueror of the old world and was thought to have divine powers.

Jesus Christ's success took place after his death and revival (resurrection). In his life he was condemned by the members of the society and was sentenced to death in a shameful way, being crucified with two thieves on each side. The success would not have manifested itself if the idea of resurrection had not been advanced.

While William Shakespeare's success had a very slow start and gradually increased through time, he was finally recognized as one of the most important figures of English literature. His success is outstanding since it has lasted through time and is diffused throughout the world.

The examples presented point out how the manifestation of success relates to the three dimensions (intensity, duration, and diffuseness). The successes of Jesus Christ and Shakespeare were accomplished only after their deaths; both are widely recognized and their successes are vivid. On the other hand, Alexander Macedon's success gradually faded away after his death.

SOME IMPLICATIONS FOR APPLIED SOCIOLOGISTS AND FOR THE SOCIETY FOR APPLIED SOCIOLOGY

Clearly, success is directly related to the interest, characteristics and historical conditions of the groups and/or larger society. Success is also related to the actuality of the historical conditions, and any action and/or product is evaluated in terms of the groups defined needs. Those defined needs should not be thought of as contributing positively to the group and/or larger society; they may, in fact, have serious dysfunctional consequences.

The different audiences within a society perceive and select actions and/or products in terms of their immediate interests. For example, I am reminded of an anecdote pertaining to Goethe and a Frenchman who visited him in the summer of 1830. Both of them were discussing important events which took place in France and which attracted the interests of most of the world. But after a while each of them realized that they were talking about different events. The Frenchman was talking about the downfall of the monarchy, Goethe was talking about the dispute between Saint-Hillaire and Cuvier pertaining to two different scientific conceptions. The Frenchman represented the political audience, while Goethe represented the scientific audience.

The same can be said about applied sociologists, because we are placed in different positions, and we should ask ourselves if we are prepared psychologically and otherwise to consult these subgroups that have some specific needs and thus achieve success in our endeavors. If we analyze the success of our organization—The Society for Applied Sociology—it can be considered as incremental success and at times having some setbacks.

With today's mass communications, we could accelerate the success of our organization and make known to different sectors within our society what we can do for them as an organization and as applied sociologists. We should remember that if our organization becomes widely recognized and successful, the members will gain as well. The success of a principal agent brings about a multitude of secondary successes.

When I looked throughout our Networking Directory I suddenly realized that our members have a variety of skills and knowledge which can meet the needs of diverse sectors. However, as an organization and as individual professionals with certain skills and knowledge, we must capitalize on and respond to the changing needs of the different sectors within society.

From our discussion it became clear that success as an organization or as individual professionals is not only in terms of our capacity, but how our action and/or product is perceived by different audiences. I am not discarding the importance of inventiveness, talent, effort, and even genius; rather, I stress the fact that all of them are subordinate to the demands of the audience, their criteria of selection, and their system of promotion and reward.

As you are well aware, the social conditions and values within society change through time, and we as students of the society should know how to watch for and adapt to such changing conditions, and devise appropriate services to meet the needs of the different audiences. At this juncture you can assess how sociological understanding of the phenomenon of success will help us as professionals and as an organization:

-Success may manifest itself in different forms and may not be directly related to the individual action, but to the product.

-In some instances reward may not be given to a very important action, but in time recognition may be achieved. If this is the case, then those applied sociologists who are frustrated because of slow or no recognition should be aware of those realities.

-In taking into consideration the three dimensions discussed previously, then we can understand how subgroups, groups and the larger society rewards actions and/or products.

For instance, an action considered important at a given time, but is not lasting, receives a big reward but will be temporal; a less significant action will get a small reward at the time, but will be of a lasting success; an action of local importance will get a local reward; a nationally recognized action will get a national reward and so on. Therefore, members of our society may be successful in different ways and should not consider that they never succeed in their work.

Another idea which should be brought to your attention is that success should not always be thought to have a rational basis because success may be achieved by individuals who indulge even in fraud, superstition, mystical, and irrational behavior. Therefore, in some instance success or even glorified achievements may have nothing to do with real contribution to the welfare of society.

The philosopher, Erasmus makes a distinction between real achievement and false achievement. The real achievement (contribution) sooner or later will become recognized and rooted and lasting while the false achievement has a short life span (Erasmus 1963a; Erasmus 1963b).

In today's society we assist in a situation in which there is a segmentation of success related to different types of activities and interests. Since certain activities and/or products became part of organizational settings and success cannot be imagined outside an organization, professional organizations are replacing the larger public opinion and the individual professional's actions are evaluated by the organization. This development also led to the institutionalization of success in different sectors of the society. This aspect should be food for thought to our society and members.

Applied sociologists might realize that success is not an isolated action by individuals, but is rooted in historical and socio-cultural conditions in spite of the fact that it has a psychological characteristic. Although the individual acts, his or her success is determined by the superstructure of the respective society. Success is not a fantasy, but it becomes one if we think in terms of individual action.

Unfortunately, in our society the stress on success from the individualistic point of view encouraged or led to an escapist attitude in order to obtain peace of mind and/or to avoid mental disturbances. Here applied sociologists should attempt to redirect their attention and replace fantasy with reality.

Approaching success from the individualistic perspective, anomie may take place in what Robert K. Merton (1963) has described as disassociation or disjuncture between the culturally stressed goals and the socially structured avenues for achieving the prescribed goals. The individual experiencing anomie finds himself incapable of managing the environment, and his confusion can lead to such mental disturbances as paranoia. Such individuals, frustrated in their desire to obtain success, develop delusions of grandeur and exaggerate their personal problems. They develop a sort of Messianic self-conception. Perhaps this is the reason that lately we have had some paranoid movements of secular or sacred orders as well as ultraconservative politics, and ultra-leftist movements.

The applied sociologist and the clinical sociologist have a fertile area of attempting to redirect the attention and replace fantasy with reality. Discussing success from a sociological perspective shows how success affects the individual, groups and even the larger society. Therefore, the field; the sociology of success—should be of interest to both the applied sociologist and the so-called purist sociologists. For, by focusing on the shifts in the criteria for bestowing rewards, we understand the mentality of the period or of a given group and structure in a society.

The sociology of success throws light on the question of how the interests and purposes of social groups come to find expression in rewarding individuals, activities and/or products. In my estimation one important way for us to understand groups, stratum, and/or a society is to focus on why recognition is accorded to certain types of activities and products, what rewards are given, and how rewards lead to the cultivation of such activities and/or products, and then we as professionals and as an organization will achieve success.

NOTES

1. In making my research on the problem of success, I came across Chenoweth's book, The American Dream of Success: The Search for the Self in the Twentieth Century, for the discussion on certain aspects, I am indebted to his writing.

REFERENCES

Allen, Philip J. 1955. "Childhood Backgrounds of Success in a Profession." *American Sociological Review* 20:186-190.

Allen, R.C. 1965. *The Secret of Success*. Louisville. KY: Best Books.

Chenoweth, Lawrence. 1974. *The American Dream of Success: The Search for the Self in the Twentieth Century*. Belmont, CA: Wadsworth.

DellaFave, L. Richard. 1974. "Success Values: Are They Universal or Class Differentiated." *American Journal of Sociology. 80:153.*

Dunlap, Jan. 1972. *Personal and Professional Success for Women.* Englewood Cliffs, NJ: Prentice-Hall.

Erasmus, Desiderius. 1963a. *The Praise of Folly.* Translation with introduction notes by Leonard Deare. Chicago: Packard.

Erasmus, Desiderius. 1963b. *The Enchiridion.* Translated and edited by Raymond Himelick. Bloomington, IN: Indiana University Press.

Fast, Howard. 1952. *Spartacus.* London: Bodley Head.

Friendly, Fred W. 1967. *Due to Circumstances Beyond Our Control.* New York: Vintage Books.

Griswold, A. Whitney. 1934. "New Thought: A Cult of Success." *American Journal of Sociology.* 40:309-318.

Hackett, Alice Payne. 1967. *Seventy Years of Best Sellers, 1895-1965.* New York: R. R. Bowker.

Hart, James D. 1950. *The Popular Book.* New York: Oxford University Press.

Hofstadter, Richard. 1967. *The Paranoid Style in American Politics.* New York: Alfred A. Knop.

Horn, John D. 1964. *How to Become Head of Your Firm Before Forty.* New York: Coleridge Press.

Huber, Richard M. 1971. *The American Idea of Success.* New York: McGraw-Hill.

Jauquet, P. 1926. *L'hellenisatine macedonien el l'orient.* Paris.

Kriesberg, Louis. 1951-52. "Concepts of Security and Success." *American Journal of Sociology.* 57:478-485.

Levine, A. and J. Crumrine. 1975. "Women and the Fear of Success." *American Journal of Sociology.* 80:964.

Lowen, Walter A. 1966. *Twenty Sure Ways to Job Success.* New York: Hawthorn.

Mannheim, Karl. 1936. *Ideology and Utopia.* New York: Harcourt, Brace & World.

Marty, Martin E. 1959. *The New Shape of American Religion.* New York: Harper and Row.

Marx, Karl. 1913. *Contribution to the Political Economy.* Chicago: Charles H. Kerr.

Merton, Robert K. 1963. *Social Theory and Social Structure.* Glencoe, IL: Free Press of Glencoe.

Peale, Norman V. 1956. *The Power of Positive Thinking.* Englewood Cliffs, NJ: Prentice-Hall.

Peterson, Eleanor M. 1968. *Successful Living.* Belmont, CA: Allyn & Bacon.

Plutarch. 1959. *Fall of the Roman Republic; Six Lives: Marius, Sulla, Crassus, Pompey, Caesar, and Cicero.* Translated by Rex Warner. Baltimore, MD: Penguin Books.

"Reflection on An Annual Meeting." 1987. *Footnotes* 15(7):2.

Rischin, Moses, (Ed.). 1965. *The American Gospel of Success.* Chicago: Quadrangle Books.

Robinson, Robert V. and Wendell Bell. 1978. "Equality, Success, and Social Justice In England and the United States." *American Sociological Review* 43:125-143.

Royko, Mike. 1987. "So Who's Perfect?" *The Times News Weekender* October 10: B-2.

Webster's New World Dictionary, Concise Edition. 1964. New York: World Publishing Company.

Mark Iutcovich

1929 -

Mark Iutcovich was the second President of the Society for Applied Sociology (SAS), 1986-87. He attended the first meeting of SAS at Kent University in 1983 and became actively involved in the development of the society.

Mark, with Alex Boros and James Hougland, organized the SAS meeting at the Edinboro University of Pennsylvania. In this meeting, Mark organized a special forum with the members of the community, the High School and political representatives. The topic was to express the opinion: "What Applied Sociology Can Do for You." With the support of the President of the university, (the university paid most of the expenses), a benefit of $4,500 remained with SAS.

Mark and Joyce Iutcovich offered the resources of Keystone University Research Corporation (KURC) to SAS whenever needed for publishing, mailing, and producing the magazine *Social Insight - Knowledge at Work.* Mark took over as Editor of the magazine in 1996 and the first edition of the magazine was published that summer.

During Mark's tenure as President, SAS membership increased, a successful conference was held in Kentucky, and student participation was increased. Although no longer a member of the SAS board, Mark has participated in all annual meetings, contributing to the welfare of the society, and served as the chairman of the Awards Committee in 1995. In 1997 he was the first recipient of the Alex Boros Award for Contributions to the Society for Applied Sociology.

His consulting and applied work has been in such areas as criminology, medical sociology and psychiatry, alcoholism, marketing, evaluation research, education, and political research. Mark has made many presentations at meetings/conferences in professional organizations such as: The American

Sociological Association, North Central Sociological Association, Pennsylvania Sociological Society, The Society of Applied Sociology, and the Society for Applied Anthropology.

Mark has published many articles in his area of research/consulting in such journals as *Sociological Focus, The American Sociologist, Journal of Applied Sociology*, and *Evaluation and Program Planning*. In 1987, along with Joyce Iutcovich, he published the book *Consulting as a Sociologist*, Praeger Publishers.

Mark received a Licentiate degree in sociology from the University of Bucharest (1950), an M.A. in anthropology from the University of Manitoba (1962), and a Ph.D. in sociology from Case Western Reserve University (1970). Mark is a full professor of sociology at Edinboro University of Pennsylvania. He is Director of Research for Keystone University Research Corporation and Northwest Institute of Research, Erie, Pennsylvania.

PART TWO:

APPLYING SOCIOLOGY: WHAT WE DO AND HOW WE DO IT

INTRODUCTION

Do applied sociologists really "do" sociology any differently than basic sociologists? Is there a paradigm shift such that human behavior is addressed distinctively by applied sociologists? The articles in this section show the nature of applied work and what the "doing" entails. Two major questions are addressed: What is it we do? How do we prepare for what we do?

What Do We Do?

Before we can engage in sociological practice, we must identify its purposes. Garrison saw applied sociology as a force for change in sociology and in society. Applied sociology can be an incubator for ideas that can help solve society's problems. Garrison supports sociology's usefulness by discussing three major purposes. First, applied sociology provides "intellectual tools" that serve as a "source to collect and organize data." While important, this is not a valuable end in itself. Rather, and secondly, applied sociologists extend their action by synthesizing "research for policy." We provide valuable and often unique insights to society's problems at many levels. Finally, Garrison identifies the highest use of sociology--i.e., "making sense of the world in which we live." Little is gained if applied sociologists shed no new light in understanding "human life in society."

Along the same lines as Garrison, Steele provides a definition of applied work. In short, he defines applied work as:

> Any use (often client-centered) of the sociological perspective and/
> or its tools in the understanding of, intervention in and/or enhance-
> ment of human social life.

Steele's definition reflects Garrison's purposes of applied sociology in a number of ways. First, sociology provides a distinct perspective that can be actively used to solve problems. Second, similar to Garrison, an applied sociologist uses sociological tools to understand social life. Third, applied work actively produces knowledge, change and enrichment of human social life. Important to all of this is that the work of an applied sociologist will be done for someone else--a client. In many ways, this aspect of the definition is most challenging. Client-centered work challenges the creativity, depth of knowledge and understanding, professional ethics, and interpersonal skills of a professional sociologist.

How Do We Prepare for What We Do?

Getting ready to be an applied sociologist requires not only a grounding in basic knowledge, skills, and values, but an action orientation, as well. Applied sociologists are oriented toward use of their knowledge and skills to solve real world problems. When we prepare students to use sociology, we develop the skills found in traditional sociology programs. So what's the difference? The difference lies in the utility attached to this knowledge. Applied problems demand a rigorous and creative application of the sociological perspective. Academic arguments over the legitimacy of qualitative versus quantitative methods often disappear in an applied setting. The real concern is which methods and techniques best solve the problem. Since problems in applied settings are frequently constrained by time, financial, political, and social factors, practitioners must resolve problems in less than ideal circumstances.

Jeanne Ballantine takes a comprehensive look at the preparation of applied sociologists. She sets the stage for her overview of applied training by investigating the external environment, jobs currently held by sociology majors, and employers' needs. Then, internal to the discipline, she examines the curriculum of applied sociology departments. Finally, she examines the "fit" between employer needs and program curriculum.

Where are sociologists employed? Sociology graduates do find employment. The real concern is whether they are employed "in spite of their training" or "because of it." Here the interface between applied programs and employer needs is critical. Ballantine suggests that sociology must "bridge a gap" between what we offer and what is needed if we are to be more effective in placing graduates. To this end she makes four important recommendations. First, programs must increase the connection between students and applied work (through exposure to "applied consultants" and intern placements). Second, programs must not "let our students fend for themselves." Rather, applied sociology programs must integrate applied skills throughout their curriculum. Third, we must "clear up misconceptions about sociology" among potential employers while enhancing our own self esteem. This is a tall order.

Also related to how we train sociological practitioners, Alexander Boros calls for a better understanding of subjectivity and its use in sociology. This includes more training in the process of "being subjective." He raises an important point. How do we work for a client and objectively investigate a problem? How do we maintain the essential distance from a problem without our personal views and emotions getting in the way? Boros contends that we can't... perhaps better said, "we shouldn't." Doing applied sociology is both an objective as well as a subjective pursuit—one with all the elements of emotion that both "interfere with" and/or "contribute to...professional work." Boros reminds us that science and scientific training have institutionalized objectivity and, in this sense, have removed us from the reality that we study. By "dissociating research from life" we are presumably seeing our research problems more clearly, without the clutter of "personal character, mental attitude, and feelings of the individual."

But, does this perspective help or hinder our efforts to understand human interaction? Boros addresses the problem of objectivity for sociologists. He drives us back to the central concern all sociologists need to ask: "Why are we doing...this...in the first place?" Too often the elements of human social life are ignored when extracted from the holistic environment in which they are grounded. Neither objectivity nor subjectivity can be excluded from sociological practice. Rather, we must deal with the question: "How can sociologists be more effectively subjective in the service of a relevant social science?"

4

The Uses of Sociology*

HOWARD H. GARRISON

Federation of the American Societies for Experimental Biology

Three hierarchically related uses of sociology—data collection, research synthesis, and interpretation—are described. A review of these uses of sociology offers a context in which to highlight the things that applied sociologists do well and an opportunity to suggest directions in which we need to move.

Academic sociology has been growing isolated from the central problems that confront our society. A large segment of the profession has been retreating from the issues of concern to the public and concentrating on increasingly remote and abstract areas of specialization. By virtue of its direct connection with major social institutions, applied sociology has the opportunity to correct this situation. In order to do so, however, we must break out of the circumscribed channels in which we have learned to operate.

In recent years, much of applied sociology has been narrowly focused on observation and description. While this has been a rational response to the conditions we have encountered as a profession, it is now time for applied sociologists to return to our historic role as an intellectual force within the discipline. By taking the initiative and generating new ideas and perspectives, sociological practitioners can ensure that sociology will be able to contribute solutions to the pressing social issues of the next century.

We have the ability to reorient the profession. Our strength is demonstrated by our numbers and our growing visibility. The appearance of the Society for Applied Sociology (SAS), the Sociological Practice Association (SPA), and other groups forced the American Sociological Association (ASA) to begin to direct its attention toward previously ignored constituencies. The

** Presidential Address, Ninth Annual Meeting of the Society for Applied Sociology, Annapolis, MD, October 31-November 4, 1991. Copyright, Society for Applied Sociology. Reprinted with permission from the **Journal of Applied Sociology**, Volume 9, 1992. I would like to thank William D'Antonio, Rehana Bacchus, Penelope Canan, Joyce Iutcovich, Lionel Maldonado, and the late Marvin Olsen for their comments and suggestions on an earlier draft of this paper.*

ASA launched a journal devoted to sociological practice. A section and a committee on sociological practice have also been established. In recent years, the association's newsletter, *Footnotes*, has featured the work of sociologists in business, government, and service organizations. New ASA initiatives undertaken with sociologists in government include efforts to promote awareness of sociology within the federal government and a new program to provide information on employment opportunities for government job seekers. These actions are a starting point, but we must also move beyond the organizational level and make our presence felt at the intellectual core of the discipline.

Sociology can be useful in at least three ways: as a source of intellectual tools to collect and organize data, in the synthesis of research for public policy, and as a way of making sense out of the world we experience. The first use is primarily descriptive, the second analytic, while the third requires interpretation. These uses are hierarchically related and represent increasingly difficult intellectual endeavors. The analytic uses are dependent on the descriptive tools and observations. Interpretations require data and analyses plus integration with other modes of understanding. Reviewing these three uses of sociology, I would like to discuss several things we do well and offer a few suggestions about ways in which we need to develop as individual practitioners and as a profession.

Intellectual Tools

Many of us apply the basic intellectual tools of sociology in our work and emphasize our usefulness as gatherers or evaluators of information. We accentuate our methodological skills in survey research, qualitative analysis, and quasi-experimental design. Most of my projects and much of the work reported in papers on our conference program are applications of these methodologies.

In many contexts, the emphasis on basic skills and practical utility is required because we are pioneers, reestablishing the legitimacy of sociology. The affluence of the post-World War II period and the baby boom gave rise to the golden era of academic sociology. During this period of expansion in higher education and abundant research funding, a considerable segment of the profession was drawn into academia and sociology lost touch with many of its more applied traditions. Many of us on the tail end of this era found ourselves having to reassert and reestablish the role of applied sociology, justifying our contributions in settings which the preceding generation of sociologists had abandoned.

Data collection methodologies enabled us to provide information and opened doors for sociologists in a wide range of organizations and milieus. We have made good use of these opportunities. As collectors and presenters of data, applied sociologists have helped to focus the public's attention on the key social problems of our era, from racial inequality to homelessness. Data on male/female earnings inequality illustrated that women earned 59 percent of the wages earned by males, and "the 59 cent dollar" became a symbol and rallying cry for many women's advocacy organizations. Statistics which we developed and reported on racial inequality in health, education, and earnings have also been used by civil rights groups to press for programs, legislation, and policy changes. The power of these data were recognized early on by opponents as well as proponents of change. Philip Hauser (1975) found that some of the congressional resistance to the inclusion of income and education questions on the 1940 census arose out of concern that the data might be used to promote racial equality.

Data from attitude polls also play an important role in our public life and have become a common feature of our culture, often prominently reported in newspapers and magazines. Social data, graphically portrayed, have become staple features in two of the most important media innovations of the last decade: the national daily newspaper, *USA Today*, and CNN, the cable television news network.

Through our emphasis on basic tools such as data collection, applied sociologists have had considerable success in the struggle for legitimacy. Our data and our studies are now an accepted part of "needs assessments" and program evaluations in a wide variety of situations. More must be done and we need to bring our intellectual tools into new contexts and settings.

Data collection, however, is only one of the uses of sociology and only one of the many contributions our discipline can make. It has been our strong suit in new and sometimes hostile environments, but not all that our discipline has to offer.

Moreover, restricting our roles to data gathering and description has negative consequences for us. We share key elements of our data collection methodologies with other disciplines such as statistics, anthropology, and psychology. By focusing on data collection, our unique sociological offerings are frequently lost in the emphasis of the common methodological core. In addition our niche as social methodologists is at risk as the growing sophistication of data collection turns to specialized subfields for research and operating expertise. Sampling statisticians now dominate the upper echelons of many survey organizations. Growing attention to the role of respondents as a source of survey error has increased the role of cognitive psychology in research on survey measurement (Groves 1989) and has recently brought cognitive psychologists out of the laboratories and into the ranks of many key survey agencies of the federal government.

Syntheses Of Research For Policy

We are able to offer much more than data and some conceptual terminology to describe it. At a higher level than measurement or description, applied sociologists synthesize findings from individual settings and develop general principles for guiding policy.

Our keynote speaker for the 1991 SAS conference, World Bank Senior Adviser Michael Cernea has described how social science knowledge in its raw, academic form was not sufficient to influence World Bank resettlement policy (Cernea 1990a). Once translated into operational procedures, however, it contributed to the success of several World Bank projects. The application of sociology not only helped improve World Bank programs, but it also enriched the body of sociological knowledge. Disciplinary gains included new research on quasi-experimental situations, an expanded body of empirical knowledge, identification of new issues and variables, as well as new data and analytic methods (1990a).

In order to expand our presence in the arena of public policy and social action, we need to bring our client-centered work into the mainstream of the profession. Paul Lazarsfeld, a pioneer in the application of sociology in new settings, stands out as an exemplar of this approach. Lazarsfeld developed many of his major theoretical and methodological contributions to social science from relatively circumscribed studies initially conducted for clients and he took great pride in the fact that his commercial studies generated articles for journals and insights for the classroom (Converse 1987).

Our role as actors in diverse social contexts gives us valuable perspectives and access to unique data. Working under tight deadlines, however, we are frequently under pressure to finish our work quickly and move on to the next project. We need to resist the temptation to conclude our work with the delivery of the final report to the client and make concerted efforts to integrate our findings into broader frames of reference. Only on rare occasions does a commissioned report make a direct impact on the profession or on public policy. The "Coleman Report" (Coleman et al. 1966) is perhaps the outstanding example of this. More often, however, the results of applied sociology become a "gray literature," known only to a tiny coterie of insiders. Upon finishing the evaluation of a program, we need to think about how insights from this project can be made available and useful to a wider audience.

Reanalyses can make seminal contributions to both theory and practice. The work of two distinguished participants at the 1991 SAS Conference provide excellent examples of how it is done. Michael Cernea (1991b) shows how project reports can be used to highlight theoretical or conceptual issues in *Putting People First: Sociological Variables in Rural Development.* In this book, he collected applied sociological analyses of development projects and made them available to an audience that might not have been aware of the original documents. Cernea's editorial analysis and commentary help to integrate the findings of these applied studies into a systematic body of sociological knowledge. Review articles summarizing the "gray literature" would be high on our agenda of things to do.

Diana Pearce, winner of our 1990 Sociological Practice Award, provides another example of how important secondary analysis can be. Her influential work on women and poverty reconceptualized issues, gave a voice to underrepresented members of society, and drew attention to a crucial dimension of poverty in contemporary U.S. society (see Pearce 1978; 1983; 1985). In her work with advocacy organizations such as Wider Opportunities for Women, Inc., the Institute for Women's Policy Research, and The National Coalition for Welfare Reform, she collected very little new data, and made her contribution primarily through reanalyses of data collected by other researchers.

Making our work available for further synthesis will help to bring sociology back into policy formulation, but this alone will not be sufficient. We must actively engage in public debates as citizens and participants, and not just wait patiently for the *New York Times* to call us for a quotation. Individuals who created strategies for social change that profoundly altered the course of the twentieth century, such as Mahatma Gandhi and Martin Luther King, Jr., developed their ideas through direct participation in the social movements of their day. In the future, as in the past, the most influential social theorists will be those who draw their inspiration from direct applications and social actions. The most important policy debates of the 1990s and the 21st century will not be those which are confined to the ivory towers. As a science of society, we must develop and test our ideas in constant interaction with our subject matter.

We must orient our research toward the major issues of the day and translate our findings into the terms in which those issues are being debated. As models of this approach, I would like to suggest the articles which political scientist Andrew Hacker occasionally writes for *The New York Review of Books*. Taking a few tables from recent Census Bureau publications or summarizing ideas from monographs written by scholars for specialized audiences, Hacker (1990,1991) provides challenging and useful ideas on the central issues affecting society. As a quantitative sociologist and user of multivariate statistical techniques, I am tremendously impressed by how cogently he is able to develop his argument using one or two percentage tables.

As a society, we face enormous social problems. Old approaches and remedies have proven ineffective. In this era of limited resources and urgent needs, we cannot afford to be inefficient, and we must not squander our opportunities. We need to make policy decisions carefully, basing them on a thorough understanding of problems and issues.

Making Sense Out Of The World In Which We Live

The third and highest use of sociology is the enrichment of our understanding of the world in which we live. The great artistic talents that inspired our most profound insights into the human condition— Shakespeare, Tolstoy, Hugo, and Cervantes—have made this kind of contribution. So have some of our best sociological thinkers: Erving Goffman, Robert Merton, C. Wright Mills, and Orlando Patterson. Moreover, as sociologists, these titans of our profession have provided a framework for understanding social forces as they effect human lives. They have addressed major issues from a sociological perspective, making individual experiences more understandable by linking them to broader social dynamics.

This is not a simple task. Our lives can be interpreted in many ways. Some interpretations can be derived from our experiences as individuals and attributed to our individual thoughts and actions. Throughout much of human history, religious world views provided a dominant source of explanation for human events. The sociological perspective, however, requires analysis and reflection. Like many other scientific principles, it may not be readily grasped by the unaided or untutored eye. It may be rediscovered by perceptive thinkers, but it is most efficiently taught.

In our various spheres of activity we are all teachers, even those of us who never set foot in a classroom. All organizations must train new and advancing staff. Those of us in research operations train subordinates in social science methods. In addition, we train colleagues, clients, and subject area specialists in methods of analysis and interpretation. This is more difficult than teaching in a classroom setting. Instead of wide-eyed undergraduates, this aspect of sociological practice frequently involves skeptical clients and professionals from diverse backgrounds. It requires more mastery of subject material and better communication skills than are typically seen in the classroom. A practitioner doesn't get a 16 week semester to present his or her material. In the settings in which many of us work, an audience can be irretrievably lost in a matter of minutes.

Arthur Shostak, winner of our 1991 Lester F. Ward Distinguished Contribution to Sociology Award, made this point in his address to our conference (Shostak 1992). He advises sociologists interested in working with organized labor to observe the proper protocol, use the appropriate forms and styles of communication, and develop a detailed understanding of the relevant issues and concerns.

In teaching, as in research, we must strive to go beyond the basics of data collection and analysis. We are bearers of an important intellectual tradition. We must perpetuate the higher level insights of our profession and strive to develop a sociological perspective in our staff, co-workers, clients, and fellow citizens.

What elements of this sociological perspective should we teach? My choice comes from *The Sociological Imagination* by C. Wright Mills. While this work contains some severe criticisms of applied sociologists, Mills makes some insightful statements on the uses of sociology and the practice of our craft. According to Mills (1959), the sociological imagination teaches us to see ourselves as biographies in a historically conditioned social structure. The individual perspective is not lost or denied, but located within a framework that includes other causal dynamics. In *The Sociological Imagination*, Mills also identifies a teacher's main job as revealing to students how a self-disciplined mind works. "The art of teaching is in considerable part the art of thinking out loud intelligibly." (Mills 1959, p. 79). Role models for such activities are extremely rare. As a graduate student at the University of Wisconsin, however, I had the opportunity to be exposed to one of Mills's own mentors, Hans Gerth.

Gerth's approach to sociology was encyclopedic. One of his lectures might include references to Japanese theater, Chinese history, the Old and New Testaments, Romantic Literature, and classical music. Sometimes a lecture would range over so many topics it would be difficult to follow. On other days, the ideas struck like thunderbolts and the ancient Greeks, Confucius, Beethoven, and Max Weber would come together in a brilliant crescendo. Diverse and varied aspects of human society would be described, organized, and interpreted. This is the most profound use of sociology: increasing our understanding of human life in society. As practitioners striving to understand real and concrete problems, we need to remember this and strive to reach the highest goals of our profession. We need to emulate the approach taken by the founders of our field. It is a very high standard, but one that is still being reached.

A contemporary model of this type of social analysis is provided by Nicholas Lemann, a journalist. In his examination of Black migration from the Mississippi Delta to Chicago, Lemann (1991) combines personal narratives, social history, demographic statistics, archival data, and sociological concepts to create a stimulating reappraisal of the antipoverty programs of the 1960s. Stories of individuals and families are placed in historical and cultural contexts. These experiences are interpreted in light of social changes and political decisions with the result that the poignancy of the individual experiences is not lost in the discussion of social forces, and the social dynamics described are greatly enriched by the biographical detail.

Lemann opens his discussion of Chicago in the 1960s with a vignette describing the Haynes family, one of the several families whose history he has traced from their origins in the Deep South. This very personal narration is followed by a historical discussion of the events surrounding Martin Luther King, Jr.'s decision to focus the Southern Christian Leadership Council's northern activities in Chicago. Another biographical sketch, this time of the Henry family, once again directs attention to the human consequences of the conditions confronting the urban migrants. Next, a discussion of policy decisions made by the Office of Economic Opportunity (OEO) in Washington, D.C. leads into a short chronicle of the Model Cities Program in Chicago. Alternating between personal and institutional histories, Lemann deftly incorporates demographic statistics, illustrating the structural nature of the changes described on the individual and institutional levels. Much later—after developing detailed biographical, historical, and demographic portraits of his subject—Lemann introduces theoretical concepts to explain the events he has carefully described. Beginning with the "classic" studies of American minority groups such as those of Myrdal and Riis, Lemann turns to contemporary social scientists such as Wilson, Gans, and Brimmer. Also included are quantitative sociologists Featherman, Hauser, Kasarda, and Jencks, authors whose methodological sophistication often prevents their work from being presented to general audiences.

In Conclusion: A Challenge

We must set goals for ourselves that take our insights beyond the narrow confines in which we work. We need to search for ways to pull ourselves out of our routines; we need to grow.

Those of us who are dyed-in-the-wool empiricists need to create a theory. Civil servants need to state an opinion (even if it has to appear anonymously). Academics need to step off campus, shedding their disdain for the bureaucratic and commercial settings in which the majority of the population labors.

The inspirational use of sociology that helps us to comprehend our world and its interrelationships is the highest use of sociology. Our aspirations as sociologists should be to use our tools for the enrichment of our understanding of the world in which we live. We must continually push our work one step further, always striving to move from data collection and synthesis of research to interpretation. C. Wright Mills (1959) advised intellectual craftsmen:

> ...[b]efore you are through with any piece of work, no matter how indirectly on occasion, orient it to the central and continuing task of understanding the structure and the drift, the shaping and the meanings, of your own period, the terrible and magnificent world of human society in the second half of the twentieth century (p. 225).

Mills's view of the classical social analyst is the application of sociology at its highest level.

REFERENCES

Cernea, Michael M. 1990a. "From Unused Social Knowledge to Policy Creation: The Case of Population Resettlement." Development Discussion Paper No. 342. Harvard Institute for International Development. Harvard University.

———1990b. "Knowledge from Social Science for Development Policies and Projects." Pp 1-37 in *Putting People First: Sociological Variables in Rural Development*, edited by Michael M. Cernea. New York: Oxford University Press.

Coleman, James S., Ernest Q. Campbell, Carol J. Hobson, James McPartland, Alexander M. Mood, Fredric D. Weinfeld, and Robert L. York. 1966. *Equality of Educational Opportunity*. Washington, DC: U.S Government Printing Office.

Converse, Jean. 1987. *Survey Research in the United States: Roots and Emergence 1890-1960*. Berkeley and Los Angeles: University of California Press.

Groves, Robert M. 1989. *Survey Errors and Survey Costs*. New York: John Wiley and Sons.

Hacker, Andrew. 1990. "Transnational America." *New York Review* November 22:19-24.

———1991. "Class Dismissed." *New York Review* March 7:44-46.

Hauser, Philip M. 1975. *Social Statistics in Use*. New York: Russell Sage Foundation.

Lemann, Nicholas. 1991. *The Promised Land: The Great Black Migration and How it Changed America*. New York: Alfred A. Knopf.

Pearce, Diana M. 1978. "The Feminization of Poverty: Women, Work, and Welfare." *Urban and Social Change Review* 11:28-36.

_____1983. "The Feminization of Ghetto Poverty." *Society* 21:70-74.

_____1985. "Toil and Trouble: Women Workers and Unemployment Compensation." *Signs* 10:439-459.

Mills, C. Wright. 1959. *The Sociological Imagination*. New York and London: Oxford University Press.

Shostak, Arthur. 1992. "Applied Sociology and The Labor Movement: On Bargaining." *Journal of Applied Sociology* 9: 11-28.

Howard H. Garrison

1949 -

Howard H. Garrison was president of the Society for Applied Sociology during 1990-1991. He attended Eastern Michigan University and the University of Michigan as an undergraduate, and he earned his doctorate in Sociology at the University of Wisconsin-Madison. From 1976 through 1979, he taught and conducted research at Virginia Commonwealth University in Richmond.

Howard began his career as a sociological practitioner in 1979 when he took a position as a social science analyst with the United States Commission on Civil Rights (USCCR). His principal projects for the USCCR involved statistical studies of unemployment and inequality and drew upon his graduate education in social stratification and statistics. Later he conducted investigations of Federal employment and training for the National Academy of Sciences.

Howard's first formal contact with the emerging applied sociology community came in 1981 with an invitation to write the "Racial Inequality" chapter of Marvin Olsen and Michael Micklin's book, *Handbook of Applied Sociology*. He later contributed a chapter to Joyce and Mark Iutcovich's *Consulting as a Sociologist*. His work on the American Sociological Association's Committee on Ph.D. Certification in Social Policy and Evaluation Research introduced him to Alex Boros and, through Alex, the Society for Applied Sociology (SAS).

From 1986 through 1993, Howard worked for a Washington area consulting firm, Aspen Systems/Applied Management Sciences, developing and directing surveys and studies of science policy for the National Science Foundation, the National Institutes of Health, the American Psychological Association, and the Civil Engineering Research Foundation. Other major clients included the U.S. Department of Education, the Health Resources and Services Administration, and the Department of Justice.

During this period he served as Vice President and President of SAS. As Vice President of SAS, Howard organized the program for the 1988 annual meeting held in Chicago, one of the first efforts to move the Society beyond its original base in the Ohio Valley. He served as President of SAS in 1990-1991. During Howard's term of office, the Bylaws Committee prepared an updated version of the bylaws that was approved by the SAS board and was adopted by the membership. Work was also initiated on a SAS code of ethics. Howard established responsibilities for the newly created position of SAS administrative officer. A new membership directory was begun and procedures for maintaining membership records were developed during his term as President.

In 1993, Howard established the Office of Policy Analysis and Research for the Federation of the American Societies for Experimental Biology (FASEB). In 1996, the office was combined with the Office of Government Liaison to form a new department, the Office of Public Affairs. As director of the new office, Howard works with the leadership of ten research societies to develop programs and policies in support of investigator-initiated research in the basic biomedical sciences. Major activities include government relations, coalition building, electronic communication, and publication.

Since he served as SAS president, Howard has had articles published in *The FASEB Journal, Scientometrics, Evaluation Research, Dental Materials,* and *Archives of Internal Medicine.* He directs an annual review of funding for biomedical and related life sciences research and has created a series of articles for general audiences describing the benefits of biomedical research.

5

Market Needs and Program Products: The Articulation Between Undergraduate Applied Programs and the Market Place*

JEANNE BALLANTINE

Wright State University

The articulation between undergraduate applied programs and the market place is analyzed in several parts: where sociology graduates are employed, what employers are seeking in employees, what undergraduate programs are providing, the match between employer needs and program products, and suggestions and recommendations on bridging the gap in order to obtain employment for sociology graduates. Survey data on employment, needs of employers, and departmental programs are summarized, and recommendations for applied undergraduate programs are made. Several models are reviewed, and content suggestions are included.

INTRODUCTION

Almost daily I hear the question, "What can I do if I major in sociology?" When our graduates seek jobs, employers ask what a sociology major can do to help the organization. Part of the reason for these questions is the lack of information we as sociologists present to students and potential employers. It is the articulation between the two worlds of employers and educators I wish to address in my comments (Parilla and Stewart 1990).

The following comments are divided into four parts, each of which sheds light on the issue of articulation between academics and employers. First, it is important to know what jobs our majors hold. Second, what skills and knowledge are employers seeking? A number of studies have been pub-

* Presidential Address, Eight Annual Meeting of the Society for Applied Sociology, Cincinnati, Ohio, October 12-14, 1990. Copyright, Society for Applied Sociology. Reprinted with permission from the **Journal of Applied Sociology,** Volume 8, 1991. I wish to acknowledge the help of Amy Karnehm, graduate student in Applied Behavioral Science at Wright State University, in data analysis from the ASA/SAS survey.

lished; results from two of these will be summarized. Third, it is important to know what applied programs and courses sociology departments offer. In this part, a summary of a recent study, cosponsored by the American Sociological Association and the Society for Applied Sociology, describes several models of applied training programs. Fourth, the relationship between the needs of employers and training in undergraduate applied programs is discussed. A modest proposal for bridging the gap between employers and sociology programs is presented.

The terms applied sociology and sociological practice are used in this paper interchangeably (Ruggiero and Weston 1991) to refer to "sociological knowledge and action oriented toward intentional social change to achieve desired goals" (Olsen and DeMartini 1981). Undergraduate training programs in applied sociology "provide a collective identity, a sense of career and a feeling of difference from other sociologists--usually academicians" (Deutscher 1981a; 1981b; 1984). In the working environment this often means "using the data, methods and insights of the discipline to help managers achieve their objectives." (Wenner 1991, p.7).

I. Where are sociology graduates employed?

The number of undergraduates receiving degrees in sociology has been on the increase in recent years (D'Antonio 1990). It behooves us to know the job prospects for these majors: What is the employment picture and what are employers looking for?

As an introduction, the Figures 1 and 2 show what 1985-86 sociology graduates did in 1987 and the general position titles held by graduates with BA degrees. These figures show that sociologists are employed in many settings--government, business, social service, education. In 1989, approximately 20% of ASA members were employed outside academia (Figure 3), and Manderscheid (1983) estimates that the total number of sociologists within ASA and non-members in applied settings in 1990 could be as high as 35% (Freeman et al. 1983).

Review of the job titles sociologists hold (Figure 4) gives us another piece of information--for what jobs are undergraduate sociology majors being hired.

Figure 1
What 1985-86 Graduates In <u>Sociology</u> Did In 1987

Eighty-six percent were in the labor force

Unemployed	7%
Employed part time	17%
Employed full time	62%

Sixty-three percent of those working were in jobs generally requiring a degree:

Sociologists	1%
Elementary and secondary school teachers	5%
Social workers	15%
Recreation workers	1%
Counselors	4%
Therapists	2%
Managerial	18%
Other professional specialty	9%
Other technical and non retail sales	8%

Thirty-seven percent were in other occupations:

Administrative support occupations	23%
Service occupations	9%
Retail sales	4%
Craft operative and laborer	1%

Occupational Outlook Quarterly, Summer 1990, p.31.

Figure 2: Position Titles
Practitioner Roles

Organizational Researcher in Industry, Government, or other Service Organization

Divisional Staff Position (Human Resources, Industrial Relations, Public Relations, Organizational Planning, Community Relations, Marketing)

Research or Consultant Practitioner Working as an Independent Professional, Trainer, or Field Employee

Manager
a. Independent Research or Consulting Firm
b. Staff Function in a Manufacturing or Service Organization

Owner
a. Independent Research or Consulting Firm
b. Manufacturing or Service Organization

Academic Roles

Teacher
Academic Researcher
Mediator and/or Arbitrator

Miller, Delbert C., ed., "The Industrial Sociologist as Teacher and Practitioner: A Career Bulletin for Graduate Students," American Sociological Association, Professional Development Series, (revised 1992).

Figure 3: Place Of Employment

Two-year college	3%
Four year college	13%
Four-year university	65%
Government (all)	5%
Private (professional or not)	10%
Self-employed	3%
Other	1%

"Membership Profile" (based on total membership of 11,281) ASA members in April 1992, data provided by ASA.

Figure 4
Job Titles of Sociology Bachelor's Degree Recipients

PROFESSIONS

Social Work
Social Worker (e.g., Social Caseworker; Social Worker, County Social Services)
Medical Social Worker

Counseling
Vocational Rehabilitation Counselor
Family Counseling (e.g., Coordinator of Family Counseling; Family Counselor, Hospital)
Other (Field Counselor; Addiction Counselor; Social Rehabilitation Counselor)

Education
Elementary/Secondary Teacher
College Teacher
Learning Disability Tutor

Continued on page 110

Researcher
>(Assistant) Research Director
>Research Associate
>Research Assistant
>Other (Data Coordinator; Evaluation Assistant; Psychometrician;
>>Research Technician: Statistical Analyst)

Legal
>Lawyer,
>Other (Conciliation Court Paralegal: Legal Assistant)

Writing/Publishing,
>Editor
>Writer (e.g., Freelance Writer; Staff Writer; Technical
>>Writer, Insurance Company)

Nursing
>Head Nurse; Staff Nurse; Registered Nurse;
>Psychiatric Nurse; Nurse's Aid

Computer Programming
>Computer Input Operator

OTHER PROFESSIONS

Management/Administration
>Manager; Retail/Convenience Store
>Management Analyst
>Other (Vice President; Vice President of Operations; Partner,
>>Well Drilling Company; District Sales Manager; Manager
>>& Supervisor of Group Home; Marketing Manager;
>>Program Coordinator, YWCA; Director, Chiropractic
>>Clinic; Personnel Management Specialist; Management
>>Trainee)

Continued on page 111

Sales

Retail Sales (e.g., Salesperson; Automobile Salesperson; Sales, Health Food Store; Cosmetics Salesperson; Consultant, Bridal Sales; Cashier; Inventory Control; Credit Assistant, Department Store)

Insurance

Underwriter/Adjuster; Liability Claims Examiner

Other (Real Estate Agent; Assistant Sales Auditor; Account Manager; Sales Leader; Account Representative, Computer Software)

SERVICE OCCUPATIONS

Crime Control and Criminal Justice

Parole/Probation Agent/Officer

Juvenile Parole/Probation Officer

Police Officer (e.g., Deputy Sheriff; Highway Patrolman; State Trooper; Special Agent, FBI

Correctional Service Officer, Prison

Other (Industrial Security Investigator; Loss Prevention Officer; Youth worker, Juvenile Detention)

Community Service

Social Services Director

Volunteer Work (e.g. Volunteer Coordinator; Volunteer & Public Education Coordinator, Crisis Center)

Day Care/Child Care Worker

Other (Safety Coordinator; Independent Living Trainer, Home for Girls; Behavior Manager, Development Achievement Center; Information Specialist)

Health Related

Assistant Activity Director, Nursing Home; Health Facilities Evaluator; Assistant, Family Planning Clinic; Nutritionist Assistant; Fire Paramedic; Coordinator of Staples, Tri-County Dental Program; Public Health Analyst

Continued on page 112

Government
> Planning (e.g. Senior Planner, County Government; Assistant Planner
> Other (Data Review Technician, Social Security Administration; Licensing Worker; Civil Service Test Examiner; Budget Analyst)

Other Service Jobs
> Restaurant Service (e.g., Bartender Waiter Waitress)
> Other (Public Relations; Customer Service Representative; Messenger/Page; Loan Processor; Outreach Worker; Professional Singer)

Clerical
> Secretary
> Bookkeeper (e.g. Bookkeeper/Typesetter, Newspaper; Bookkeeper/Secretary)
> Receptionist (e.g., Secretary-Receptionist; Communications-Receptionist
> Administrative Assistant, Law Office

Construction and Trades
> Trades (e.g., Petroleum Landman)
> Construction (e.g., Construction Worker)

Miscellaneous
> Technician, Optometrist's Office;
> Farmer/Rancher; Legislative Assistant

Number of Cases on Which Percentages Based: 759

Huber, Bettina J. 1984. "Career Possibilities for Sociology Graduates." Washington, D.C.: American Sociological Association.

Figure 5

Corporate Affiliations of Sociologists in Business Members

Personnel	1%
Pharmaceutical	2%
Government	2%
Brokerage	2%
University	3%
Advertising	4%
Media	4%
Freelance	6%
Utilities	7%
Professional Associations	8%
Insurance	10%
Market Research	11%

"What Sociologists Can Do for Business." 1988. *Sociologists in Business.* January 5.

The business sector employs sociologists in several key areas: human resource management; public relations; marketing; management; organizational planning; research in organizational settings, including factories, banks, retail stores, hospitals, and restaurants; and mediators and arbitrators. These business settings take advantage of areas of sociological expertise and practical application of sociological skills (Figure 5).

The federal government classifies sociology jobs into specialized areas of demography, law and social control, medical sociology, organizational analysis, and social psychology ("Maintaining Competence in the Federal Workforce in the 1990s and Beyond"). The most common federal positions fall into the categories of research, administration, and planning and evaluation; the position titles give clues as to positions for which sociologists are hired and include research analysts in labor force and manpower, population, social science, and statistics; contract and grants officers, human resource directors, personnel managers, and project directors; and policy analysts, program evaluators, rural development analysts, and urban and regional planners.

The next step for sociologists concerned about the opportunity market is to "sell" the products undergraduate programs produce. We need to know what employers need, where jobs are, expand those markets, and develop new markets.

II. What are employer needs?

To answer this question we see that studies of competencies sought by employers yield a list of general skills, many of which are available from sociological training and other liberal arts curricula (Deutscher 1981a, 1981b, 1984). It includes the following (Brown 1987):

> Ability to work with peers.
> Ability to organize thoughts/information.
> Self-motivation.
> Ability to plan effectively.
> Willingness to adapt to needs of an organization.
> Ability to interact effectively in group situations.
> Self-confidence regarding job responsibilities.
> Ability to handle pressure.
> Ability to clearly conceptualize problems.
> Effective problem-solving skills.
> Effective leadership skills.
> Ability to listen to others.

Many of these skills and competencies desired by employers are an integral part of sociological training. Figure 6 combines findings from two studies of employers' needs and sociological programs.

By knowing what positions are available and what employers are looking for, we have information essential to planning applied programs. Next we consider results from a survey of applied offerings in undergraduate programs to determine what is included.

III. Survey of Undergraduate Sociology Programs with Applied Content.

The third part of these comments focuses on what applied content sociology programs are offering. In the winter/spring of 1990, the American Sociological Association and Society for Applied Sociology conducted a joint survey of sociology departments to determine the types of applied programs at the undergraduate and graduate level. Preliminary descriptive results include a sample of 265 respondents from undergraduate institutions. Of these 265, 184 offer from one to eight undergraduate courses or internships in applied sociology. The applied courses most commonly offered, in order of frequency, were research (field research, methods, data analysis offered by 22%); general applied sociology course (16.3%); and public service (planning, policy, and personnel services offered by 8.2%). Other course offerings in applied/practice sociology included human services, social work, criminal justice, and education.

Fifty-seven percent of the institutions reported that an undergraduate program in applied sociology was available to students. These programs were primarily offered as an option or concentration, with only a few institutions offering a separate major. The number of students in applied programs seldom exceeded 50. Several respondents stressed the importance of small size which allows them to "give individualized attention and provides a strong learning experience for students." The following table summarizes the types of programs offered:

Optional Track	24
Concentration	14
Separate major	14
Minor	5

Number of students = average per program of 12
Number of faculty = average per program of 2.5

At least 20% of those colleges and universities offering undergraduate courses in applied sociology plan to add new courses within the next three years. Thus, some programs are planning to expand. This is consistent with the trend that began in the 1980s; "limitations of the employment market have resulted in the sprouting of a forest of seedling applied sociology programs" (Deutscher 1984, p. 3). The problem is that many of these attempts to add applied sociology to the curriculum are not well integrated into the existing program and do not stand alone (Seem 1990).

Analysis of qualitative data on programs showed that offerings fall into three main models, parallel to those reported by Howery in *Teaching Applied Sociology* (Howery 1984).

Model I: Sociology departments offer one or more courses in "applied sociology" or "careers in sociology." Data from the survey indicate that this is the most frequent applied experience offered by departments; 158 institutions reported offering between one and three applied courses. This requires minimum change in the traditional curriculum and is usually accomplished by faculty member(s) adding one or more courses to the existing curriculum.

Model II: Sociology departments offer tracks or concentrations in substantive areas of sociology. This model was found in 38 institutions in the survey. The most frequently offered areas were criminal justice, family studies, and applied research. A few departments offer certificate programs in applied sociology.

Model III: This involves internships or field experiences. Of the institutions represented, over 80 offer such an experience. Internships covered a broad range of experiences, from applied sociology to human services, and research--especially field research and social work/sociology internships.

An additional model that was apparent from the data analysis showed institutions including applied components in existing courses. Little change takes place in the curriculum, but it does require some faculty to revise their courses. Revisions most frequently involve faculty integrating skills, field experiences, or research into their course requirements (Seem 1989).

With information concerning positions held by graduates, skills needed by employers, and programs for undergraduates, we can now discuss the articulation between the work world and academic world.

IV. Articulation between Employer Needs and Program Products

A recent joint American Sociological Association and Association of American Colleges (AAC) study of undergraduate sociology curricula-- *Liberal Learning and the Arts and Science Major: Reports from the Field*--reported on the importance of developing in students a sociological perspective; sociology should ...help students become more skilled and adept in using sociological perspectives in their personal and social lives....This includes an understanding of different types of social struc-tures and the idea that we can test propositions and models related to these structures.

This perspective remains at the core of most traditional and applied sociol-ogy programs. The recommendations also suggest course sequencing for general sociology programs: introductory sociology, method/statistics, theory, substantive courses, and "senior seminar." As we focus on training of un-dergraduates for the job market, the report stresses that the sociological perspective must remain paramount.

The question is whether the academic and applied foci can be combined successfully in undergraduate curricula. Some argue that the traditional undergraduate sociology program should focus on providing students with a solid grounding in theory, methods, and substantive sociology, and teach students to think and reason; the implication is that "applied" experiences could dilute the academic seriousness of sociology as a discipline, and that applied sociologists may prostitute themselves by selling "to the highest bidder" (Deutscher 1984, p. 2; Olsen 1987).

The debate about the proper socialization experiences for students has not abated. I argue that the focus on the developments in applied sociology curricula do not detract from traditional curricula, and in fact can enhance students' learning of traditional curricula (Ballantine, 1989). Supporting this view is the belief ...that the collective body of sociological knowledge will benefit from the further merger of theory and practice. This belief rests upon the premise that sociological theories are more adequately constructed, tested, and refined when they are grounded, applied, and evaluated in real-life settings (Seem 1991, p.64).

The idea of providing applied experiences to undergraduate students with the hope of increasing their skills and marketability, among other goals, has spread rapidly in the United States and Canada. A number of under-graduate programs have jumped on the bandwagon as shown by the data.

Several factors are behind the motivation of departments to increase applied experiences: 1) the fluctuating job market; 2) limited funding sources; 3) the trend toward problem solving and use of social settings outside academia for research; and 4) the realization that sociology can make a difference to society.

1. The job market for undergraduate sociology majors has increased in applied settings, up 25% between 1980 and 1990. Freeman (1983) predicts that, although the job market in general is decreasing, demand in applied areas will increase, especially in the government sector in medical health services and business.

2. Some funding sources have dried up, causing sociologists to expand their horizons in attempts to find support and outlets for knowledge and research. With the increasing encroachment of other disciplines and licensure requirements in what were formerly fertile grounds for sociologists, new approaches to placing graduates are needed (Johnson et al. 1987, p. 362).

3. The interest in applied sociology is consistent with the emphasis on teaching critical thinking and problem solving. These skills are high on the list of qualifications desired by employers, along with abilities to communicate and produce reports via written and oral mediums, analyze statistical data, design surveys, work with a team, make deadlines, and administrate and supervise (Weston 1984); also important are knowledge of the public or private sector, work experience, and other sociological skills. Students with training in these areas will be at an advantage in the job market. In addition, internships provide practical experi-

ence in a setting where students learn to use these skills.

4. Sociologists contribute to solutions to societal problems through their substantive expertise, research, and evaluation abilities. By training students in these areas, they can be effective actors in society.

V. Bridging the Gap between Employers and Sociology Programs.

In order to meet employer needs, develop the sociological perspective, and provide applied training, articulation is proposed. We need an isometric relationship between skills and knowledge, and systematic integration of applied content into the curriculum.

Departments need to set goals for their curricula and for the type of graduates they are trying to produce.

> Effective design of sociological practice curricula is more than tinkering with traditional curriculum....[it] requires that traditional content be integrated with ethical decision making, other sociology related skills, and supervised student practice (Seem 1991, p. 64).

Several recent articles discuss steps for completing this process. Program changes should flow from these goals rather than being added piecemeal.

Once goals are established, changes might take any of the following forms: added courses with applied content, recommended courses in other disciplines such as business and public administration that, combined with sociology, enhance the organizational knowledge of students; illustrations and examples in courses from real-world social and organizational processes; internships; (op. cit., Johnson et al. 1987) and skills such as communication, research methods, and sociological knowledge.

After each department has evaluated its current offerings and set goals, it can integrate applied components relevant to the goals. The following are some specific examples of skills which can be integrated into the curriculum:

I. Communication skills:

a. Class papers, projects: these can take the form of actual agency reports or evaluation reports to give students practice in communications relevant to applied settings.

b. Structured discussion groups for problem solving: students receive experience in group team work and in group dynamics.

c. Memo and grant writing: students are presented with problems to address or actual grant applications.

d. Oral presentations: students can be assigned to present research or evaluation reports or case studies. Again, group presentations foster team work.

e. Deadlines for reports and presentations: adherence to deadlines is valuable preparation for applied settings.

II. Critical thinking and problem solving:

a. Set up problem-solving situations in conjunction with course subject matter and discussion groups.

b. Survey design and other methodological techniques: set up practice situations in which to apply methods.

c. Data analysis: have students practice how to analyze and present data for lay audiences.

d. Clear conceptualization of problems: practice these skills in classroom and exam assignments.

III. Research/Statistics:

a. Data analysis: have students practice analysis of qualitative and quantitative data.

b. Computers: prepare students to use various statistical packages (SPSS, SAS).

c. Interface with statisticians: help students prepare instructions for statisticians.

IV. Formal Organizations and Group Dynamics Skills:

a. Work with teams/peers: practice group work to solve problems.

b. Administrative, supervisory, and leadership skills: work on problem solving, case studies, and give students opportunity to direct team efforts.

V. Program Development:

a. Develop and evaluate policy options: give students practice in discussing the merits of various options.

b. Develop project goals: give students hypothetical agency problems and have them develop goals.

VI. Using Sociology and Active Learning:

a. Translate sociology into practice.

b. Apply sociology to business and other settings.

c. Develop knowledge of public and private sector: course work and internships.

d. Adapt to organization needs: internships, interviews with leaders.

VII. Conclusions and Recommendations

I recently chatted with a colleague who is working in government service and who formerly trained undergraduate applied sociology students. She said we fail to teach students the politics of practice: how to do social policy and get organizations to change. Few if any texts can provide this knowledge. How can we address this issue? Two effective methods of reality training areas follows:

◆ Bring in applied consultants to work with students;

◆ Place students in internships to work in real settings.

We should not sit back and let our students fend for themselves. We can provide them with professional materials such as the ASA Code of Ethics and the ASA publication, "Careers in Sociology" (ASA, 1991). By knowing market needs and integrating applied content and skills into our curricula, we can "sell" our products in the marketplace and infuse these structures with doses of sociology. In time, acceptance of sociology graduates should grow.

If we can successfully integrate skill training along with substance material, we will have come a long way toward meeting employer needs and providing our students not only with training but also with experience for successful entrance into the market. Before we can convince others of our value, we must value applied work ourselves. Our next step should be to clear up misconceptions about what sociology is and convince more employers to value our products.

In conclusion, some view sociologists as advocates rather than as scientists or analysts. In their conversations they associated sociologists with socialism, social engineering, preferential hiring with reverse discrimination, and costly public programs which encourage malingering and dependency (op. cit. Wenner 1991).

However, in some fields, such as crime and delinquency, racial and ethnic relations, organizational behavior, and family and community "[sociology] is well established" (Wenner 1991, p. 7).

Indeed, then, careful planning of practice curricula; integration of sociological knowledge, ethical decision making and other practical skills, teaching practice which emphasizes active learning, respectful communication, and responsible behavior within a learning group; and student transformation and empowerment are cornerstones of effective sociological practice education (Seem 1991, p.66).

REFERENCES

ASA Membership Profile, August 1990.

Ballantine, Jeanne H. 1989. "Developing Applied Content in Sociology Courses." *Journal of Applied Sociology* 6:89-94.

Brown, William. 1987. "Identification and Application of Competencies for Applied Sociologists." Paper presented at the Southern Sociological Meetings, Atlanta. Georgia.

Brown, William. "Careers in Sociology." ASA, 1991.

Brown, William, John Washington, and Allyn Stearman. 1985. "Teaching Competencies Important to Non-academic Employers." *Teaching Newsletter* 10(1).

D'Antonio, William. 1990. "Recruiting Sociologists in a Time of Expanding Opportunities." in T. C. Halliday and M. Janowitz, eds. *Sociology and Its Publics: The Forms and Fates of Disciplinary Organizations*. Chicago: University of Chicago Press, 1992.

Deutscher, Irwin. 1984. "The Moral Order of Sociological Work." *Journal of Applied Sociology* 1(1):1-12.

_____.1981b. "Social Needs vs. Market Demands." *Sociological Focus* 14(3):161-172.

Freeman, Howard E., R. Dynes, P. Rossi, and W.F. Whyte (Eds.) 1992. *Applied Sociology*. San Francisco: Jossey-Bass.

Grzelowski, Kathryn and Jim Mitchell. 1985. "Applied Curriculum Can Enhance Liberal Arts Learning." *Footnotes* 3(9):5-6. Washington, D.C.: American Sociological Association.

Howery, Carla B. 1984. "Models and Examples of Some Applied Sociology Programs at the B.A. Level." *Teaching Applied Sociology* 33-59. Washington, D.C.: American Sociological Association (under revision).

Huber, Bettina J. 1984. "Career Possibilities for Sociology Graduates." Washington, D.C.: American Sociological Association.

Johnson, Doyle Paul, W. Brown, J. Hage, T. Lyson, D. Orthner, S. Paulson, G. Squires, and R. Wimbirley. 1987. "The Challenge of Training in Applied Sociology." *The American Sociologist* 18(4):356-368.

Liberal Learning and the Arts and Science Major: Reports from the Field. Washington, D.C.: Association of American Colleges, 1991. Ch. 11.

"Maintaining Competence in the Federal Workforce in the 1990s and Beyond." Washington, D.C.: American Sociological Association, Sociologists in Government and Professional Development Program.

Manderscheid, Ronald W., and Mathew Greenwald. 1983. "Trends in Employment of Sociologists." Pp. 51-63 in *Applied Sociology*, edited by H. Freeman, R. Dynes, P. Rossi, and W. F. Whyte. San Francisco: Jossey-Bass.

Miller, Delbert, ed. Feb 1988. "The Industrial Sociologist as Teacher and Practitioner: A Career Bulletin for Graduate Students." Washington, D.C.: American Sociological Association Professional Development Series.

Occupational Outlook Quarterly. Summer 1990, p.31.

Olsen, Marvin E. and Joseph R. DeMartini. 1981. "Predoctoral and Postdoctoral Training in Applied Sociology." Paper presented at ASA Workshop on Directions in Applied Sociology, Washington, D.C., December.

Olsen, Marvin E. "The Process of Applying Sociology." *Journal of Applied Sociology* 4:1-12.

Parilla, Peter F. and Brad J. Stewart. 1990. "What Can I Do with a Sociology Major?" Presented at annual meetings of Midwest Sociological Society, Chicago.

Seem, John. 1989. "Constructing Sociological Practice Curricula." *Wisconsin Sociologist* 27: 18-28.

_____.1990. "Designing Applied Courses." *Teaching Sociology* 17:471-475.

_____.1991. "Sociological Practice Education: Curricula Design and Teaching as Practical Sociology." *Sociological Practice Review* 2(1):64-67.

Ruggiero, Josephine and Louise C. Weston. 1991. "Working Definitions of Sociological Practice: Results of a Recent Practitioner Survey." *Sociological Practice Review* 2(1):59- 63.

Wenner, Lambert N. 1991. "From Gown to Town: A Decade in Applied Sociology." *Sociological Practice Review* 2(1):1-8.

Weston, Louise. 1984. "Specifying the Skills Employers Seek." *Teaching Applied Sociology.* Washington, D.C.: ASA Teaching Resources Center.

"What Sociologists Can Do for Business." 1988. *Sociologists in Business.* January 5.

JEANNE BALLANTINE
1944-

Jeanne H. Ballantine was president of the Society for Applied Sociology in 1989-1990, following Jim Hougland and Marvin Olsen. She received her graduate degrees at Columbia University (1967) with a specialty in political sociology and Indiana University (1970) with a specialty in sociology of education. Marvin Olsen encouraged her to become involved in the newly formed organization, SAS, and she attended her first meetings at Kent State University and Edinboro University of Pennsylvania, and has attended most years since that time. She became involved in the committees of SAS, helping with program planning, membership, preparing documents for SAS, and other activities and committees.

Several major events occurred during Jeanne's tenure as president: the administrative officer position was defined and the first administrative officer, Sam Sloss, selected; new journal editors were selected; the secretary and newsletter editor positions were separated; an institutional membership category was established; lists of volunteers were provided for committees; and the dues structure of SAS was changed. In addition, the newsletter took on a new, very professional look. One of the most significant accomplishments during this time was the coordination of the committee structure and regular reports from committee chairs.

Cooperation between SAS and other organizations included joint meetings with the Humanist Sociologists in Cincinnati, providing people to organize applied/practice sessions at regional and other sociology meetings, and work on joint projects with ASA Sociological Practice Section and ASA Teaching Resources Center. Marvin Olsen was coordinator of the Coalition for Utilizing Sociology, involving SAS and five other organizations in joint efforts to promote applied sociology.

A survey of applied programs was initiated in conjunction with the American Sociological Association. This survey, compiled by Jeanne Ballantine,

Brian Pendleton, and Carla Howery, has been updated again in 1996 by the Sociological Practice Section of the ASA. It is available through the ASA Teaching Resources Center.

Jeanne has worked primarily in academic settings. She helped organize her department's applied masters degree program in 1975, a program which is still going strong and produces successful graduates who take positions primarily in graduate schools to study for Ph.Ds, and in the area's social service sector. She has taught courses in the master's program, supervised both practice and theses, and otherwise been active in administering the program.

Most of Jeanne's publications have been in the areas of sociology of education and teaching sociology. She has also contributed to the ASA Teaching Applied Sociology handbook and other applied journals and publications.

6 BEING SUBJECTIVE AS A SOCIOLOGIST*

ALEXANDER BOROS

Kent State University

Several examples are given to illustrate how sociologists cannot avoid making subjective judgments in carrying out their work. A case study of seven turning-points in one applied sociology project is presented to show the consequences of being subjective. Objectivity as a problem for sociologists is discussed. The lack of training in being subjective to enhance sociology work is emphasized. A brief review is made of early sociologists commenting on the subjective side of sociology. The article concludes with a list of recommendations on how to improve the balance between subjectivity and objectivity in doing sociology.

INTRODUCTION

I gave careful thought to how I should present this first Presidential Address of the Society for Applied Sociology. If I were to follow the tradition of scientific organizations, my talk would ideally focus on a new research frontier and be objectively reported. There is also a well-respected convention for the audience to listen to these addresses in a detached and formal manner.

Actually, this old custom of formally reading stark scientific reports first became prominent with the founding of the Royal Society of English Scientists in 1662 (Boorstin 1983). The Royal Society's first President was William Brounckes. One of the Society's aims was to eliminate emotional comments, poetic utterances, and vague generalities during organized sessions. Other scientific societies followed the pattern. Concomitantly, audiences learned to respond with appropriate respect.

* Presidential Address, Fourth Annual Meeting of the Society for Applied Sociology, Indiana State University, Terre Haute, IN, September 26-28, 1986. Copyright, Society for Applied Sociology. Reprinted with permission from the **Journal of Applied Sociology,** Volume 5, 1988.

Even now, scientific societies expect Presidential Addresses to be devoid of humor, case histories, and untested subjective interpretations. You are probably assuming I will uphold these honored and time-tested traditions by delivering an objective talk without emotional distractions.

However, I am going to astonish you by violating custom. You will hear no familiar rendition of research data and sociological theories. Instead, the topic I have chosen has to do with feelings--not those of the people we study--but our own feelings as we carry out our sociological work. Without ignoring the intellect, I intend to express my feelings while evoking your emotions.

The frontier I consider worthy of my Presidential Address is the issue of how the emotions of sociologists can interfere or contribute to their professional work. My insights are relevant to both basic or applied sociologists. I hope to make my points clearer by communicating subjectively.

The emotions of scientists has been a controversial subject over the centuries. People often stigmatized scientists as being ivory tower thinkers who had difficulty making contact with the emotional reality of others. Some observers also suspected that scientists have trouble failing to contact their own feelings, as well (Podgorecki 1986).

Fortunately, now and then, a few sociologists have expressed their own feelings in public. The Polish sociologist Podgorecki (1986) published a book of his daily experiences over a one year period of time. The account describes his feelings and thoughts as he reacted to a political conspiracy aimed at eliminating his applied research institute in the University of Warsaw. Fortunately, his detailed narrative also included subjective expressions to other events in his life. It was interesting for me to follow the introspections of a total person, with no separation from personal or professional insights. Intellectual and emotional responses to daily events were intertwined as they are for us all in real life. During his 1974 plenary address at the International Sociological Association in Toronto, Canada, Horowitz (1975) revealed his feelings about the responsibilities of his discipline in confronting issues of life and death of societies.

After receiving a Certificate of Merit from the 1968 meeting of the District of Columbia Sociological Society, Stuart A. Rice (1968) reflected very subjectively upon the circumstances that led him to become a sociologist. The twists and turns he took from 1907 included political activism, confrontations with Professor Giddings at Columbia on objectivity, and applied research in human services. These three sociologists are illustrative of the possible insights into sociologists at work which have inspired my address.

Despite my emphasis upon subjectivity, my presentation is logically ordered to make several points. The next section will examine "Objectivity as a Problem" for the preparation of sociological work. Next, I will present examples of the undeniable role of subjectivity in my own "Community Intervention" projects. The nature of "Subjectivity in Sociology" will be examined historically. I will then discuss the need for a more effective use of subjectivity in the section "Working Toward a Better Balance."

OBJECTIVITY AS A PROBLEM

There cannot be any doubt that the predominant emphasis both in undergraduate and graduate education is and has been upon the development of "objectivity" in problem formulation, research procedures, data analysis, and formal presentation of findings.

The mainstream approach in sociology since 1950 has been the preparation and pursuit of basic knowledge. According to Parsons (1959), the establishment of scientific journals and objectivity is the working code of our profession. Even today, improving objective methodology of research rather than social relevancy of findings continues to be stressed in our most prestigious journals.

As with most of you, a considerable part of my training was aimed at separating my subjective side from sociological work. I tried to practice objectivity as I was taught. Lately, I am questioning that singular approach. Four personal encounters raise doubts in my mind about the misplacement of subjectivity in our discipline.

First, I was directing a research project on informal patient interaction within a rehabilitation hospital. One of my graduate students was assigned the task of discovering how patients utilize different sources of information to cope with hospitalization. He was to interview patients and take an inventory of personal possessions kept in their rooms.

While in my research office one day, I heard a voice over the hospital intercom request in code:

"Dr. Strong, Dr. Strong report to room 212." The message meant that physical force was urgently needed in the room where my student was assigned for the morning. I ran into the room and found my student busily recording papers the patient had discarded in her wastebasket. In the same room, a female patient was threatening suicide on the window ledge, while two orderlies were attempting to rescue her. When the emergency was over, I took my student back to my office and asked him what happened. He said he was carefully taking his inventory of the patient's belongings with permission when she began to cry and threaten suicide. I asked why he didn't try to intervene. The student replied that he didn't think he should get involved in matters outside of his research assignment. Puzzled, I asked the student what he thought was the purpose of our research project. He answered: "To examine hypotheses of patient self-help." I asked what else. He said: "To arrive at a theoretical model for informal patient interaction." I asked what else. The student seemed baffled but replied: "To test out a new methodology of studying informal interaction." Finally, exasperated I asked why we were doing the research in the first place. After a long pause, the student mumbled: "I guess to help people." "That's right," I said. "You had a chance to help a frightened woman in that room today, and you blew it."

It would be reassuring, if I could assume that such a mistake was done by one irresponsible student. I can't help wondering how often we sociologists may be flagrantly ignoring chances to lend a helping hand to people while we are gathering data on problems of inner city crime, homeless people, child abuse, and marginality among Native Americans living outside of their reservations. If people cooperate in our studies as respondents and subjects, does it not behoove us to offer our expertise to the community when applicable?

My second example, somewhat different, stems from a visit I made to assist a student finish his graduate applied sociology project. He required assistance in writing a grant proposal to provide training that would prepare two pre-school cerebral palsy children to pass a state admission test for public schooling. If the two children could pass the test, they would be eligible for public schooling he offered through his agency.

School was canceled the day I arrived because of a heat wave. He gave me a fast tour of his empty facilities. I noticed a helmet stand, upon which there were little helmets hung from pegs. On the front of each helmet there was a child's name printed in large letters. He told me that all his disabled students had to wear protective helmets to prevent injury from frequent accidental falls. When I asked about two empty pegs, he told me they were for the two pre-school students he hoped to admit to his program.

We sat down to work on separate assignments. He sat opposite from me at a table. While I studied the state laws, he drafted the design for the training program. After several hours, I wearily pushed the books away from me and said: "I am sorry, but it can not be done." He kept writing and never looked up. I repeated my disappointment. Still, he gave no answer. Out of frustration I shouted at the top of my voice: "It can not be done. The laws will not allow us. Give it up!"

Finally, the student looked up and walked across the room. He picked up the helmet stand and carried it to our table, placing it opposite from me. He sat down and began to write again. I stared at the helmet stand and began to read the names of Tom, Billy, Tina, Mary, and all the others on the helmets until I came to the two empty pegs. I do not remember how long I looked at those empty pegs, but sometime during that night I picked up the state guidelines and studied them again. After more hours, I stopped reading and said: "I know how we can meet the requirements of the state laws." I left for home, hoping my contribution would help.

I saw the student three months later when he came to Kent State University to be examined on his applied project. As soon as we met, he said: "The grant proposal was funded!" In my mind's eye I again saw the helmet stand, but this time it had no empty pegs.

Sociologists need to better understand how our own emotions can drive our sociology work. Even in basic research, the thrill of discovery rewards the persevering scholar.

My third example also involves one of my applied graduate students. I was asked by the director of an agency to describe the characteristics of detached men renting rooms on the sixth floor of his building. He was disappointed in their lack of participation in all agency activities, excluding meals.

I carefully observed them for several weeks as they came to the large dining room each day for their meals. They came down the elevator in groups without talking to each other. They sat down to eat and were speechless again. After each meal, they returned to their rooms and remained there alone. My participant observation brought no new insights.

I decided to interview them, but I found out little. Group discussions fared no better. No matter what traditional technique of data collection I used, I still was unable to depict these men as real personalities with individual histories and experiences. I gave up.

One of my graduate applied students volunteered another method. She received permission to locate a small social service office on the sixth floor where the detached men lived. Her door was the only one that remained opened. The men stayed behind their own doors until mealtimes. Next to her door, she nailed a note pad with a pencil for messages. She made a sign that said: "I am here to help you. Come on in." If someone were too shy, he could write it on the note paper and put in under her door at night.

Without waiting for their response, she proceeded to ask the men to help her plant flowers in window boxes. Little by little, men assisted her with the building of the boxes and the planting of the seeds.

Some men came into her office to chat the time away. Others brought in their problems that needed solving. As time went on, she became very involved in their lives. The men still sat speechless in the dining room, though.

The intern worked in that makeshift office for two months. She kept a daily log of her activities as part of her internship.

When her internship was over, I read her log. The men on the sixth floor slowly emerged in the log as people with problems and regrets. They talked about their years away from families. One wanted his citizenship papers straightened out. Others needed help with welfare forms. Some wanted help to write letters to family members they have not seen for years. I could not believe that I was reading about the men I had been attempting to study for several months. These were candid pictures of colorful people. I was touched by the last entry.

The intern was writing about the day she closed her office for good. She said good-bye and introduced the staff person who would now take her place. Each man, in his own way, dropped by to offer thanks. She was about to close the log, when someone slipped a note under her door. She read the note and entered it in her log. The note said: "Good-bye." I detected what might have been tear drops on this last page of the log. Apparently, getting involved is a two-way street.

We sociologists need to realize that some information about the inner worlds of people is not available with objective methods of data gathering. When she helped them with their problems, she also opened the doors to communication. She was able to interpret their actions because she shared many of their feelings. One advantage we sociologists have over physical scientists rests with what we share with our subjects. Although physical scientists cannot empathize with their inanimate subjects of study, we can subjectively reach out to ours.

My fourth example of being subjective in doing sociological work comes from an experience I had with a basic research project carried out on the topic "Social Stratification of the Dead" (Boros and Miller 1976,). We wanted to ascertain if social class affected the handling of the dead. Part of the study included a random sample drawn from death certificates. Burials between and within cemeteries were compared by social class indexes. I visited each cemetery in our study to describe the settings and interview each cemetery superintendent.

While walking around in one cemetery, I stopped at a freshly dug grave. I noticed an envelope resting next to a rock beside the mound of dirt. Out of curiosity, I picked up the letter and read: "Dear Dad." The envelope was sealed. I wanted to open the letter even though I felt it was wrong to do so. I argued with myself that the letter couldn't be private if it were left in this public place. On the other hand, I knew it was not written for me to read. With relief I put the letter back on the grave. However, for several days afterwards, I was still tempted to read that letter. The urge only subsided when the area was hit by a heavy downpour of rain, and I concluded that the letter was ruined by the rains and the winds.

How often do sociologists face similar ethical issues in seeking support for a cherished hypothesis? How often are they aware of these choices? Are we prepared to deal openly with our feelings on these matters?

LAG IN THE METHODOLOGY OF SUBJECTIVITY

The Prevailing Tradition Linked to Max Weber

If asked, other sociologists can undoubtedly give examples of similar problems in being subjective with their work. I contend that there is a serious lag in our understanding and use of the methodology of subjectivity. The stumbling block seems to rest with our adherence to a position by Max Weber, who demanded a value-free sociology. In Weber's own words: "I am ready to prove from the works of our historians that whenever the man of science introduces his personal value judgment, a full understanding of the facts ceases" (1946, p.146). Confusion over Weber's contribution of the subjective "verstehen" method did not help (Abel 1948; Wax 1967).

According to Gouldner, the consequences of Weber's position adopted by our discipline was that subjectivity and objectivity became separate activities (Gouldner, 1962). Subsequently, sociologists developed sophisticated procedures for enhancing objectivity in research, while avoiding or neglecting the separate but equal development of subjectivity as a way of understanding and using social facts.

A Growing Backlash

Gouldner argued that a value-free sociology was impossible and suggested several solutions (Gouldner 1962). Becker (1967) suggested that a value sensitive sociologist should ask: "Whose side are we on?" Myrdal (1968) concluded that sociologists have become expert at "disassociating research from life." Despite strenuous training in being value-free, physicists have had to reexamine their strict position after the atomic bomb was dropped on Hiroshima. When Bronowski--one of the atomic scientists--was shocked by his 1945 visit to the aftermath of the atomic bombing of Nagasaki, he wrote an influential book on science and the use of human values (Bronowski 1956). Ordinary people are also beginning to increase their criticism of social scientists for gathering information--on human misfortunes without offering to assist those whose problems they have uncovered. Lately, Native Americans are raising the issue of anthropologists disregarding the respectful handling and proper re-burial of bones from ancestral graves.

Defining Terms

Re-examination of the relationship between subjectivity and objectivity is long overdue. Clarification is impeded by lack of consensus on the meaning of the terms. Omitting the philosophical debates, I define objectivity as that which is presented to consciousness, as opposed to the consciousness itself. On the other hand, subjectivity refers to the personal character, mental attitude, and feelings of the individual. It is important to examine how these intellectual and emotional activities are related in the professional roles of sociologists.

The Sociologist as a Person

To better understand the role of subjectivity, it is necessary to do case studies of sociologists making decisions that involve their feelings.

What would one find if the life of Max Weber, for example, were analyzed outside of his intellectual pursuits. If you want to see a subjective side of Weber, read his reflections on his visit to America in 1904. As a relief from his years of illness, he remarked of his trip to America: "Stimulation and occupation of the mind without intellectual exertion simply is the only remedy" (1975, p.304). According to his wife and biographer, Weber reacted to the complicated New York City of five million diverse peoples and horse driven carriages at the turn of this century by looking out his hotel window and declaring: "It smells of horse manure" (1975, p.281). That is being subjective!

Perhaps, the long awaited advance in developing a methodological understanding and professional use of subjectivity will come from applied sociologists whose values cannot be ignored or hidden. In the following case study of my personal involvement with community intervention projects, I will illustrate the subjective turning-points to show how my personal reactions affected the dynamic development of research strategies. At each turning-point--some major and some minor--I will pause and ask you to imagine what you would do and feel before I recall my reaction at the time. In this novel way, you could try vicariously to be subjective as sociologists.

COMMUNITY INTERVENTION: A DEMONSTRATION

In telling my account, I am omitting the objective, statistical data we sociologists usually present. The intellectual side of my project will be the topic of other papers for another time. Instead, I will describe only those events that triggered off an emotional response from me that affected the development of my applied project. What follows, then, is a demonstration of one sociologist reporting on being subjective during seven turning-points in assisting the deaf community of Cleveland, Ohio solve problems. These turning-points varied in importance and intensity.

Turning-Points

1. Deaf Leadership Project

My interest in community intervention work started in 1970, when Cleveland deaf leaders asked me to help them organize an advocacy group to promote needed social services for their deaf community (Boros 1987). My applied graduate students and I helped the deaf leaders plan and implement several advocacy projects that successfully won the admiration of agency leaders. On one such project, the deaf leaders asked our help to plan and implement a state-wide deaf expo in Cleveland, Ohio. It was to be a three day event in a huge exhibition room and auditorium of a large downtown department store. We met with the deaf leaders each weekend for nine months to plan the expo. It was difficult to reach deaf Ohioans because only a few of them could be contacted by telephone. Public notices of the deaf expo were presented on television, newspapers, and posters in every bus serving Greater Cleveland. On the day before the expo, our exhausted planning group finally relaxed. We had done our job well. Deaf exhibitors were already on their way to the exhibition center from all over the state. Prominent national speakers were scheduled to fly in for speaking engagements. The Lieutenant Governor and Mayor were speakers.

Then, I received an emergency call from the public service director of the department store. She told me that a strike closed down their loading docks. Deaf exhibitors would not be allowed to unload their exhibitions for the deaf expo.

What would you have done?

Since there was no way that we could contact and stop deaf people from going to the store, I called the public affairs representative of the union and asked for special permission for our deaf people to cross their picket lines. He said no one was ever allowed to cross their picket lines! I told him that I supported his position but I called to offer him our help. I patiently explained what might happen the next morning. Deaf people would arrive at the docks and not understand the picket procedures. Frustrated, they would still try to pass the pickets. There might be shoving and pushing. Some deaf people may get hurt. Because of the wide publicity for the deaf expo, there would be television cameras present. Newscasters would be there to report on the events. Bystanders might also miss the meaning and importance of the pickets. The union official was silent, then he said he could call me back. Within ten minutes he called and said: "O.K. 'Youse' guys can cross our picket lines, but 'youse' guys better be deaf!" The deaf expo went on to be a great three day success.

2. Deaf Alcoholism Workshop

I was asked by two agency counselors to produce a workshop on the problems of treating deaf alcoholics. Several of my applied graduate students and I obtained the resources to put on a national workshop to be held in Cleveland, Ohio. The deaf leaders objected to the title: "Dimensions in the Treatment of Deaf Alcoholics." They said that the words alcoholism and deafness should not be together on the same line, since many people would think alcoholism is especially problematic in the deaf community. These deaf leaders said that they have been subjected to the stigma "deaf and dumb" for centuries; they did not want a new stigma of "deaf and drunk." They asked that the workshop be promoted without mentioning deafness.

What would you have done?

I explained to the deaf leaders that professionals need to know the nature of a workshop before deciding to attend. Without the help of professional counselors, deaf alcoholics would continue to be untreated. I reassured them that the promotion of the workshop would be only among professionals and the deaf community. The workshop was done and received participants from 15 states and Canada. A monograph was printed and distributed (Boros and Sanders 1977) which led to the development of alcoholism programs in Ohio and other parts of the country.

3. Double-need Assessment Project

After the workshop, we presented several grant proposals to local agencies for the creation of an advocacy program to help Cleveland deaf alcoholics obtain responsive treatment that would be interpreted in the manual language. However, we could not get any funds until we established a need. We could not receive any money to do a needs assessment study because the alcoholism counselors did not believe that there were enough deaf alcoholics to warrant special programming. When a deaf alcoholic jumped off the sixth floor roof of a treatment center for homeless alcoholics to his death, his suicide note read: "This place is like all other places I have been to, no one can communicate with me. Good-bye."

Based on this one misfortune, I was able to obtain funding for a one year study of the number of deaf alcoholics in Cleveland, Ohio. The director said the money was only available to determine the extent of alcoholism among deaf people. The restriction eliminated my wider goals of advocacy and in service training.

What would you have done?

I said the director's restriction placed me in an ethical dilemma I could not accept. I would not find deaf alcoholics only to count them. There were no facilities in Cleveland that could respond to both the psychosocial aspects of their deafness and their dependency upon a manual language. Instead, I offered my original plan of doing a double-need assessment. I would seek to answer the following research questions:

> a. How many deaf alcoholics needed treatment?

> b. Could agencies adequately respond to our clients with our special in service training and consultations?

My original proposal was funded as requested.

4. Deaf Leaders' Reaction to Alcoholism Project

I was officiating as President of an Ohio Deafness and Rehabilitation Association meeting when several deaf leaders walked into the room and demanded to be placed on the agenda. I agreed to let them speak. An influential deaf Ohioan leader held up a recent newspaper with a headline that said: Professor Alex Boros Receives Funds to Help Eighteen Hundred Deaf Alcoholics. He complained that most readers will believe alcoholism is an extensive problem among deaf people, since no headline ever singles out alcoholism among "hearing people." Apparently, the public relations department of my university discovered I was funded and used my estimate of the number of deaf alcoholics who needed our service for their news release to local newspapers. I looked at the angry deaf leaders and knew that without their support I could never be successful in outreach work within the deaf community.

What would you have done?

I hired the outspoken deaf leader waving the newspaper as a part time deafness consultant to my project. I explained that his job would be to represent deaf people and assist us in serving them responsively. He took the job and was very helpful in obtaining support for our work among deaf people. It was one of the most helpful decisions I made on that project.

5. The Ohio Grand Deafness Ball

Not all of my turning-points were serious crises. Several months later, I presented a talk on the dangers of alcoholism to a large audience of deaf people who were attending a biennial conference of their own Ohio Deafness Association. Their grand ball concluded the conference later that night. I attended the ball as a guest, sitting at a table near the bar. Everyone was dressed in their finest. While I carried on a conversation with people at my table, I noticed a group of excited men in a heated exchange. They hurried out of the ballroom and came back with baskets of potato chips, placing one basket on each table. The men formed a group and then watched people eating the potato chips. The men seemed disappointed. Finally, they looked at me. Others began to look my way. Something was wrong, and I felt it involved me.

What would you have done?

I got up and went to the bar and ordered a glass of beer and brought it to my table. It did not take too long before people from all around the ballroom left their tables to order drinks. Everyone finally was relaxed. The group of men were relieved. They needed the sales from the bar to help pay the costs of the Ball. Apparently, they thought I would not approve of their drinking after my talk on the dangers of alcoholism.

6. National Grant for an Action Research Model

I wrote a grant application to the National Institute of Alcohol Abuse and Alcoholism (NIAAA) for testing hypotheses on community intervention strategies using Kurt Lewin's action research model. The three year project would have cost $750,000 and could have been adopted by the Ohio Department of Health if proven successful. My grant went through the usual peer review and was approved for funding. Ronald Reagan was elected President and his administration eliminated the whole department from which my funds were to come.

What would you do?

I wrote a service-oriented grant proposal to the Ohio Department of Health and was funded to develop a demonstration project on how disabled people could be better served by alcoholism agencies. Although my original re-search interest took on a secondary importance in the state funded advo-cacy program, I learned a great deal about how the network of agencies function and resist change. I was part of the network.

7. Defunded by the Cleveland Office

I was jointly funded by Akron and Cleveland offices of the Ohio Division of Alcoholism to do an advocacy project for disabled people of Northeast Ohio. One year after this combined funding, the Cleveland office decided they would withdraw their share of support for the second year. I appealed to the citizen advisory council of the Cleveland office. Reluctantly, they invited me to their monthly council meeting at noon. They did not provide an interpreter as I requested, nor did they move the council meeting to an accessible building so that one of my own board members who uses a wheelchair could attend. I carried the wheelchair user up several stairs and brought my own manual interpreter for a deaf alcoholic female client of ours.

We arrived at the hearing one half hour early. Council members passed by us to the closed meeting. Three hours later, some of the council members were already leaving. We were still not invited in. Finally, after three and half hours of waiting, we were invited to testify. We entered the conference room and noticed that only a few members were left and that they had eaten a catered meal while we were waiting outside. Although I was angry at their flagrant violation of the Ohio Sunshine laws that require open public meetings, I proceeded to make my appeal with an interpreter signing my words to the frightened deaf woman who accompanied us. She feared she would lose the services which rescued her from a mental institute and alcoholism. While I was talking, I noticed the council members appeared to be indifferent to the facts of my appeal.

What would you have done?

Without offering any explanation to anyone, I reached over and grabbed the two hands of my interpreter and prevented her from communicating to the deaf client. Surprised, the interpreter struggled to be free and the deaf woman was shocked. I turned to the council members and shouted at them to look at the deaf woman and see how long they could see her suffer without communication. I declared, angrily, that by cutting our funds they were cutting her communication with us permanently. I shouted several times: "Look at her, look at her."

I finished my presentation and left. We were funded for three more months. Fortunately, my project continued to be supported by the Akron office. Four months later we received a call from a Cleveland hospital about our deaf client from the appeal hearings. She wanted to see us. Without our special service, she resumed her drinking and in despair attempted suicide by swallowing her crucifix.

Reflection

Looking back at these seven minor and major turning-points in doing an applied sociology project, I find implications for the individual sociologist as well as our discipline. At the personal level, I realize that there were many different decisions possible at each turning-point which would have affected my project differently. I rarely had ample time to prepare for action.

Any decision entailed a subjective reaction. The process also involved the emotions of others in the situation. If my project derailed because of a faulty reaction on my part, staff and clients would also suffer. Even though I experienced feelings common to any person adapting to changing social conditions, it became obvious that my sociology training did not prepare me for handling my own emotions while doing professional work.

Subjectivity also has implications for our discipline. Community intervention by involved sociologists could provide valid data on how social organizations resist change by outsiders. Many of these insights could be compared to similar ones gained in the Chicago Area Studies by sociologists doing community liaison and mobilization work (Carey 1975). Some significant data may be only available through a sociologist's empathy with people caught in the "hurting edge" of social life. Even role-taking necessitates emotional involvement for accuracy. It is possible to communicate these emotional reactions in special narrative ways. The importance of subjectivity for sociology would be better understood if case studies on sociologists making decisions would be analyzed. It thus should be possible to develop and incorporate a methodology of subjectivity in our sociology training programs which would be as valuable as is the current preparation for objectivity.

SUBJECTIVITY IN SOCIOLOGY: THE HEART OF IT ALL

Without proper attention paid to our meaningful use of subjectivity, our discipline has a methodological deficit. Since sociology has drifted away from our reform-oriented beginnings to develop our objective side (Rhoades 1981), have sociologists failed to develop the capacity to feel in their work (e.g., like fish caught in dark underground caves have lost the capacity to see)? Readers may find it difficult sometimes to realize that the abstract theories and frequency tables appearing in some of our most prestigious journals actually refer to real people.

Perhaps, we need to reexamine our roots during the turn of the century in order to rediscover the heart of sociology. The early articles in the first several volumes of the *American Journal of Sociology* expressed strong feelings about what sociology should become. Small, one of these founding sociologists, was especially subjective in many of these early issues and other writings. He criticized sociologists for using algebraic and geometric formulations of life relations while ignoring reality in actual human experiences (Small and Vincent 1894).

Even a few decades later, subjectivity still played a valuable part in the views of sociologists. Smith (1930) stated with strong feelings:

When I took my oral examination for the Ph.D., I had acquired fifty-seven systems of sociology and the hundred and fifty-seven theories of society then in vogue. I could drool glibly about what Spencer and Comte, Giddings, Ward, and Tarde thought about collective behavior.... Then, I stepped out, so to speak, in quest of this thing I was supposed to understand--this thing named human life, human society. I got in with the organized uplifters and monkeyed around in the slums. I consorted with doctors and nurses, and saw life, with bleeding lips and tired eyes, sitting in the clinics and hospitals and madhouses.... It came to me with a shock that human society, as described by the classical sociologists, was a Platonic idea, a conceptual idealization, having about as much correspondence to the fire and sparkle, the tears and blood of real life... as to a pregnant skunk (pp. 102-103).

Lynd (1939) wrote a little later:

However great a part pure curiosity and the disinterested desire to know may have played in the acquisition of scholarly knowledge and natural science, it has been the interested desire to know in order to do something about problems that has predominantly motivated social science, from the Wealth of Nations down to the present (pp. 114-115).

After spending twenty-seven years doing various applied projects, it was both refreshing and inspiring for me to discover that there were other sociologists also experiencing similar feelings as my own. These subjective reflections by early sociologists should be researched and analyzed. Contemporary sociologists could then put their own work in better perspective. These early sociologists are not obsolete because their voices are distant. They expressed feelings about the vital issues that continue to be at the heart of sociology and always will be. We need to tune into their wave length and turn up the volume. There is nothing wrong with replaying their messages until we get them right.

WORKING TOWARD A BETTER BALANCE

Regarding the issue of subjectivity, the obvious conclusion from the writings of early sociologists and reflections from my own case study of seven turning-points in my project is that we need a better balance between subjectivity and objectivity in all our work roles as sociologists. **A science of human behavior that is only intellectual without a heart is not workable!**

If it were possible to have given this Presidential Address to the Royal Society of English scientists of 1662 who advocated objectivity in all of their deliberations, they would have already left the room disappointed. They would have seen no need to develop and use a methodology of subjectivity. However, if they would have stayed, I'll tell you what they would not have heard me say to an audience of applied sociologists.

> 1. They would not have heard me say that we should undo the advances that we have made in developing a sophisticated methodology of objective research techniques.

> 2. They would not have heard me say that our sociological research and training gains should be abandoned.

> 3. They would not have heard me say that our progress in developing more reasonable theories of social life should be undone.

If these positivist English scientists would have stayed in this hypothetical situation, they would have heard me give the discipline of sociology the following recommendations:

> 1. Examine the actual and relevant subjective activities of sociologists working under different conditions through the case studies of daily logs.

> 2. Discover the nature and strength of essential emotional commitments of contemporary sociologists to the development of a sociology that is relevant to social betterment.

3. Determine if our conceptualizations are unduly intellectualized, such as the concept of "taking the role of the other."

4. Study how emotions play a part in our own creative processes.

5. Examine how emotions affect the morale of our discipline from generation to generation.

6. Develop methods in ascertaining how the feelings of sociologists affect the discovery and analysis of social data.

7. Learn how to train sociologists to be sensitive to the use of their own feelings in improving the validity and social relevancy of their work.

8. Originate communication techniques to complete the cycle from personal sociological experiences to scientific data and then back to personal and understandable conclusions for different audiences.

To implement these recommendations, our discipline must make a considerable investment of both intellectual and emotional resources to upgrade the methodology of subjectivity to be comparable with our advances in objectivity. We need to answer the turn-of-the-century question: "How can sociologists be more effectively subjective in the service of a relevant social science?" Far from reaching the ideal of pure objectivity, a number of studies in North America, Britain, and France have shown that real science proceeds by "violating all the positivist rules in the name of getting some work done: cutting corners, appealing to authority, inserting personal opinion in place of certified knowledge all over the place" (Becker 1987, p. 26).

In conclusion, both objectivity and subjectivity are required of ourselves if we are to be effective sociologists. Neither one can be omitted. Because we concentrate on one, we should not lose sight of the other. We cannot wait any longer or society will accuse us of gathering data from the wastebaskets of social life while remaining aloof from serious problems of human misery that go unsolved.

Did I make my point? Perhaps it depends upon the perspective you take. I am reminded of the following story.

A boy was doing some batting practice by himself. His objective was to throw a ball over his head and then with both hands wrapped around the bat he wanted to hit the ball into a vacant field. The boy threw the ball up once and missed it. He threw it up a second time and missed hitting it again. Then, he threw the ball up the third time only to miss it again. A bystander said: "You are not a very good player, you just struck out." The boy replied: "Listen, Mister. I just pitched a no hitter."

REFERENCES

Abel, Theodore. 1948. "The Operation Called Verstehen." *The American Journal of Sociology* 54: 211-218.

Becker, Howard. 1967. "Whose Side Are We On?" *Social Problems* 14:239-247.

Becker, Howard S. 1987. "The Writing of Science." *Contemporary Sociology*. 16:25-27.

Boorstin, Daniel J. 1983. *The Discoverers*. New York: Random House.

Boros, Alexander and Ruth P. Miller. 1976. "Social Stratification of the Dead." *Intellect* 104:110-113.

Boros, Alexander and Edie Sanders (eds.). 1977. *Dimensions in the Treatment of Deaf Alcoholics*. Kent, OH: Kent State University.

Boros, Alexander. 1987. "Consulting with a Grass-Roots Community Group." Pp. 225-239 in *The Sociologist as a Consultant*, edited by Joyce M. Iutcovich and Mark Iutcovich, New York: Praeger.

Bronowski, J. 1956. *Science and Human Values*. New York: Julian Messner.

Carey, James T. 1975. *Sociology and Public Affairs*: The Chicago School.

Beverly Hills, CA: Sage Publications.

Gouldner, Alvin W. 1962. "Anti-Minotaur: The Myth of a Value-Free Society." *Social Problems* 9:199-213.

Horowitz, Irving Louis. 1975. "Science and Revolution in Contemporary Sociology: Remarks to an International Gathering." *American Sociologist* 10:73-78.

Lynd, Robert S. 1939. *Knowledge for What?* Princeton, NJ: Princeton University Press.

Myrdal, Gunnar. 1968. "The Social Sciences and Their Impact on Society." Pp. 145-187 in *Social Theory and Social Invention*, edited by Herman B. Stein, Cleveland, OH: Case Western Reserve University Press.

Parsons, Talcott. 1959. "The Profession: Reports and Opinion." *American Sociological Review* 24:547-559.

Podgorecki, Adam. 1986. *A Story of a Polish Thinker*. Koln, Germany: MVR Druck.

Rice, Stuart A. 1968. "Why I Wanted to be a Sociologist." *The American Sociologist* 3:284-285.

Rhoades, L.J. 1981. *A History of the American Sociological Association 1905-1980*. Washington, DC: American Sociological Association.

Small, A. and G.E. Vincent. 1894. *Introduction to the Science of Sociology*. New York: American Book Co.

Smith, Russell Gordon. 1930. *Fugitive Papers*. New York: Columbia University Press.

Wax, Murray L. 1967. "On Misunderstanding Verstehen: A Reply to Abel." *Sociology and Social Research* 51:323-333.

Weber, Marianne. 1975. *Max Weber: A Biography*. New York: John Wiley.

Weber, Max. 1946. "Science as a Vocation." Pp. 129-156 in *From Max Weber: Essays in Sociology*, edited by H.H. Gerth and C. Wright Mills. New York: Oxford University Press.

7

The Craft of Applied Sociology: Skills, Challenges, and Vision*

STEPHEN F. STEELE

Anne Arundel Community College
Applied Data Associates, Inc.

*This article reviews three themes: (1) the context of the skills
and abilities of the craft of applied sociology including a
definition "applied work" (2) forces in support and in opposition to the craft of applied sociology, and (3) immediate challenges to applied sociology. These themes are explored in light
of a corporate vision for SAS as well as applied sociology.*

Today we are here to celebrate the craft of applied sociology. A great
conference, growing enthusiasm, and growing numbers should lift our
spirits. What would Lester Ward think? In the preface to the second edition
of his Dynamic Sociology (1897), Lester Ward cited two criticisms
presented by reviewers. First, the book was judged to be "too expensive."
Second, a reviewer reminded Ward that the book had "sociology" in the
title. This tragic flaw was certain to spell the demise of his work! Apparently, Ward was not too troubled as the book retained the title; we do not
know exactly what happened to the price. I would like to think that Ward
would find the SAS Eleventh Annual Meeting supportive of his decision to
keep both "dynamic" and "sociology" in the title.

In addressing the craft of applied sociology, I will review three major
points. First, I would like to position the skills and abilities of our craft in
context and provide a definition of the work of applied sociology. I will just
call it "applied work." Second, I will address some of the forces in support
and in opposition to the craft of applied sociology. And, third, I will conclude by reviewing some immediate challenges to applied sociology. Explore with me for a few minutes the "Craft of Applied Sociology."

*Presidential Address, Eleventh Annual Meeting of the Society for Applied Sociology, St.
Louis, Missouri, October 14-17, 1993. Reprinted with permission from the **Journal of
Applied Sociology,** Volume 11, 1994.*

The Position of Applied Sociology: What is Applied Work?

So, where is applied sociology and just what is applied work? Using Lester Ward's work as a benchmark in the application of sociology, our craft has been an important element in American sociology for over a century. Today, applied and clinical sociology are growing enterprises. What is the nature of the applied work that we do? We often employ a tripartite vision of sociology: teaching, research, and practice (American Sociological Association 1991). However, these three components of professional sociology are neither mutually exclusive nor are they all encompassing. Applied sociology not only suggests practice, but also teaching and research, as well. Additionally, applying sociology suggests the process of using the sociological perspective, inclusive and exclusive of research. Conceptualized this way, sociologists involved in organizational development, management, and planning, are doing applied work. Both applied and clinical elements of sociology direct our skills toward problem understanding or intervention in which a client often identifies the research problem. In this realm, our strength is in the breadth of our vision.

Having said this, I believe we can define applied sociology in terms of the work that we do. For this presentation, allow me to define "applied work" as:

> Any use (often client-centered) of the sociological perspective and/or its tools in the understanding of, intervention in, and/or enhancement of human social life.

While the nature of applied work is often different than that of basic research work, it is no less rigorous. The setting in which applied work occurs produces a variety of challenges. Applied researchers often are valued for their ability to produce the best possible research findings or action in whatever setting the problem may lie. Research designs and techniques, strategic decisions or recommendations, and management decisions must be imaginatively adjusted or grounded in the client's environment with the focus on a practical, real-world problem. Theory is not excluded in these situations, but it is not the central reason for the work.

Rather, theoretical perspectives provide essential tools for analysis of the social setting and problems emerging from that environment.

What abilities do sociologists bring to the marketplace? Arguably, at least three abilities come in the "sociological package."

1. We really do maintain a unique perspective. Our macro perspective, our lack of tolerance for atomistic views, our focus on interaction versus individuals all distinguish us from most other social and behavioral sciences. Sociological theories are important "tools" in conceptualizing and, then, applying sociology. As a practitioner, I'm sometimes pleasantly surprised at my clients' amazement at the use of this perspective. To them it appears to be astonishingly different. To the extent that we can clarify and apply this view, we strengthen our skills.

2. The tools and skills that we use (and share with other fields) which allow us to "study society scientifically" are appropriate for the needs of this era (Babbie 1990). The unique and imaginative use of research methods combined with the sociological perspective, the use of statistics and related mathematics, and the ability to measure a concept and solve a problem empower a sociologist in the marketplace. When these are combined with computer skills, we generally offer an attractive resume.

Perhaps more important , and basic to our training is our understanding of interaction as a universal tool for analyzing or managing a variety of human settings. In an applied setting, of course, this does not mean rigid protocols in unrealistically controlled situations. Rather this means flexibility, creativity, and imagination in dynamic surroundings.

3. In a traditional "sociological upbringing," we were trained to be researchers who could expect to teach in a college or university. We are capable of capitalizing on both of these available skills. The false dichotomy between research and teaching is destructive. Professional time spent as a teacher provides valuable consulting and management skills. While applied sociologists may be engaged in a variety of technical projects including serious data gathering and analysis, much of our consulting and management time is teaching! This includes "socializing clients" and presenting results.

The charm and the advantage of these three items are their simplicity and their ubiquity. They are empowering and practical. While most sociologists have been trained in these basic skills, we often lack the perspective to apply them in the marketplace. Our training has been dominated by a value for basic science. This is only one hurdle in employing our craft. What are other forces in support of and in opposition to applied work, the craft of applied sociology?

Forces in Support of the Craft of Applied Sociology

Our craft is a dynamic one. Clearly forces exist that are both in support of and in opposition to the craft of applied sociology and we need to appraise them. Let's first turn to forces in support.

First, current social and political environments offer a market for our perspectives and tools. Hypothetically, social change should create a demand for applied work. In the United States, we have seen efforts to "reinvent government" (Gore, 1993) and the health care system (White House Domestic Policy Council 1993). The changing demographic nature of the United States and The North American Free Trade Agreement have obvious multicultural dimensions which beckon a sociological view. The velocity of local, national, and international change likewise invite applied work. In the words of Howard Garrison (1992), "we must orient our research [and our applied work] toward the major issues of the day and translate our findings into the terms in which those issues are being debated" (p. 5).

Second, let's face it, our craft is personally and professionally rewarding. Problem-centered work is active, exciting, challenging, and gratifying, often with immediate rewards. Applied sociology and practice actually can be financially rewarding. Variety, versatility, and imagination are inherently part of the process. Development of new "tools" is constantly required to operate in such an arena. We often benefit from the dynamic nature of cross-disciplinary problem solving and teamwork. We even can be pleased at the slow, but certain evolution of professional organizations which can adequately support us. While these forces are reassuring, they are not without opposition.

Forces in Opposition of the Craft of Applied Sociology

What are the forces that oppose us? Some are external and some are internal. I plan to review five of these, namely: competition from other fields, the isolationist nature of sociology, constraints of formal academic training, lack of supportive infrastructure, and, perhaps most important, our own pride and self-respect.

Externally, other professionals compete with us for, if nothing else, market share. At the very least, we need tools and training to successfully compete. Certainly, part of this problem lies in the fact that clients don't know who we are and that we could be of value to them. We face a variety of issues here: marketing sociology and licensure to name only two.

Internally, discipline-centered research dominates the field of sociology, and this, I believe, has had the effect of isolating us. We "talk to ourselves" more than we need to. This creates a self-fulfilling prophecy: we talk to ourselves in our own language, thus, nobody outside knows who we are. They can't speak our language, so they don't talk to us, so we keep talking to ourselves. We end up isolated from the world that we study. In many cases, it is not what we do but where we do it. Our focus is on interaction at all levels. What *could be more practical*? We must simply move off our island of isolation.

Furthermore, clients expect results and applied sociologists must present and defend their results, often to audiences which may vary broadly in composition. Doing applied work does not offer the luxury of communicating in the single language of the discipline, but must creatively adjust and translate findings as well as complex social theory into a variety of languages. On any given day, doing applied work may mean solving problems for and communicating with labor union members on the shop floor in the morning, with the company chief executive officer at lunchtime, with the housekeeping staff of a hospital by mid afternoon, and the hospital administrators at dinner that evening. (Incidentally, a day like this means heartburn!) The challenge of using sociology in worlds outside the academy is extraordinary.

And, what about our formal academic preparation? Formal academic training—even in applied sociology—often does not specifically address the problem-centered needs of applied work. The emphasis needs shifting. Sociology is both a general and a generalizing discipline. One of our strengths is our breadth. By narrowing our focus on discipline-centered problems, we lose the value of the perspective. Sociology might grow from the development of "General Practitioners" who are as comfortable with organizational downsizing, continuous improvement strategies, strategic planning, needs assessment, and evaluation as they are with esoteric views within a small piece of basic sociological research. Training the "General Practitioner" must span the entire higher education experience from freshman level undergraduate students to doctorate level graduate students. Quoting Jeanne Ballantine (1991):

> If we can successfully integrate skill training along with substance material, we will have come a long way toward meeting employer needs and provide (our) students not only with training but also with experience for successful entrance into the market (p. 16).

We need to broaden our repertoire of skills. While professional organizations in applied sociology are growing slowly, access to "tools" and training are not thoroughly available through networks or infrastructure. When an applied sociologist realizes that a problem is beyond her knowledge and skills base, a "referral" network of specialists does not readily exist to provide support. We often must go outside our field to find what we need. This in itself is not a problem if we can maintain our valuable identity. Finally, we need to take pride in that which we do. Our own "grumbling" about lack of professional respect can be one of our own worst enemies. We are reminded by Mark Iutcovich (1988) that "success affects the individual, groups and even the larger society" (p. 12). We must identify and revel in our successes. Personally, I have become tired of low energy nay sayers in the discipline. We have too much going for us to produce a pessimistic future for those of us who are currently in the field and students entering it.

Reviewing Some Immediate Challenges to Applied Sociology

What challenges face us? Answers to this question were provided in part by the collective genius of the members of the Society for Applied Society. Late in 1992, the Development and Planning Committee of the Society for Applied Sociology conducted a needs assessment of the organization's members. The respondents to the survey helped to focus the direction of this organization, but I believe, in many ways, they helped to focus the direction of applied sociology and sociological practice. Respondents identified at least four major challenges, namely: influencing public opinion and government policy on applied sociology, finding and listing jobs for applied sociologists, developing standards for applied sociologists, and expanding joint efforts with other organizations. I will review each of these challenges.

First, respondents cited the importance of influencing public opinion and government policy on applied sociology. This issue is not ours alone to consider, but that of all sociology. My impression is that American society maintains a rather "naive" approach toward sociology, in general, and applied sociology, specifically. The current national political administration in the United States appears supportive of social action, social problem investigation, and problem solution. We are in the right place to have an impact. We must formulate a strategy to present our strength and knowledge.

The second issue is clear: finding and listing jobs for applied sociologists with degrees at the undergraduate and graduate levels. This is another difficult challenge. The domain of possibilities is great. Finding work poses the question of professional identity. We need to translate our knowledge, skills, and abilities into existing and emerging "jobs" and pursue them as legitimate professionals. Yes, we can "be" teachers and sociologists, but we can also be strategic planners, market researchers, organizational development specialists, managers, and a host of other "job" classifications. We must develop an effective strategy to routinely locate, publicize, and fill positions with qualified applied sociologists.

And, how well do we do applied work? This appropriately leads us to the third challenge: developing standards for applied sociologists. Here, I believe, we are collectively thinking about something in addition to ethics. Beyond that which is "morally" right, we need to deal with that which is technically accurate. Far from "gatekeeping," we are searching for the qualities of dignity and talent that guide us as professionals. We must develop a strategy which deals not only with codes of conduct but also with excellence in initial and continuing education and training in our discipline.

The evaluation of applied work raises professional concern. Allow me to review four (admittedly self-generated) criteria which I believe relevant for evaluating applied work. The quality of applied work can be measured against the ability:

1. To identify a practical, client-centered problem, explored by an appropriate research or intervention design, grounded in the client's context;

2. To produce appropriate, rigorous analysis of findings, communicated at appropriate levels for the target client audience(s);

3. Where appropriate, to produce recommendations that follow clearly and appropriately from the data, communicated in practical terms;

4. And finally, to utilize the sociological perspective appropriately grounded in the language of the client's corporate culture.

Let's turn to the final challenge. Where do we go to get needed assistance?

The fourth challenge is that of expanding joint efforts with other organizations. As much as we might like to believe it, few problems are exclusively "sociologic." That doesn't mean that most issues won't be clarified at least a bit by a "good shot" of sociological perspective. But, the complexity of modern problems requires multiple perspectives and an assortment of talents to solve them. Our relationship with the American Sociological Association is excellent. We have begun to forge an association with the Applied Anthropologists as well as sociologists in the Coalition for Utilizing Sociology. Hopefully, we will see a future that includes a permanent tie between SAS and the Sociological Practice Association. We need to formalize our national and international efforts in this area.

Conclusion: A Corporate Vision

Let's conclude with a springboard for future action in the craft of applied sociology and the development of the Society for Applied Sociology. I will restate the SAS Corporate Vision (1992).

Throughout the near future a variety of organizations will compete for members and resources in applied sociology. When we include applied anthropology, geography, and psychology (as well as natural and physical sciences), we realize that we are not alone in the pursuit of making our discipline practical.

In the long run, the craft of applied sociology (as well as sociological practice and clinical sociology) are here for the foreseeable future. However, organizations that provide support for applied sociologists are likely to diminish in number. Duplication of purpose as well as lack of breadth will make membership in a variety of these groups redundant and economically unfeasible. Some groups will simply cease to exist, others will combine or form coalitions. In this environment, an organization and the craft it supports which has a clear mission, a solid organization, clear service to members and reasonable inclusiveness will survive and flourish.

In the short run, if applied sociology is to be a force in the field of sociology, we need to strengthen our organization and clarify our mission now. We must be prepared to encourage and accommodate large numbers of new members from a variety of areas: international, students, academic, non-academic.

Additionally, we must first "do what we do well," instill confidence in those doing applied work and those who wish to. We must clarify our purpose, be guided by our strengths, and have the courage to take calculated risks.

We must expand our base of support. Recruit new members and retain them by effectively assessing their needs and, then, providing practical, efficiently delivered services and support.

We must operate on at least three levels (as we say sociologically): micro, middle range, and macro. At the micro level, we need to be attentive to member needs. At the middle range, we need to be attentive to our organization. And, at the macro level, we need to be capable of developing appropriate coalitions and alliances while diffusing the craft throughout the society.

Finally, we must move through the 90s into the next century, strengthening our craft so we are capable of leadership in the present and future. We must take charge of our destiny. Applied sociologists, "heal thyself."

Some five years ago in his discussion of social change, SAS President Marvin Olsen (1989) said it this way:

> [A]pplied sociology can provide the knowledge to make these strategic decisions in an informed manner, and thus facilitate the process of intentionally created social change (p.12).

He then asked (and I once again ask): "Are we willing to undertake the challenge?" (p.12).

REFERENCES

American Sociological Association. 1991. *Careers in Sociology.* Washington, DC: American Sociological Association.

Babbie, E. 1990. "The Essential Wisdom of Sociology." *Teaching Sociology* 18:526-530.

Ballantine, J. 1991. "Market Needs and Program Products: The Articulation Between Undergraduate Applied Programs and the Market Place." *Journal of Applied Sociology* 8: 1-18.

Gore, A. 1993. *The Gore Report on Reinventing Government.* New York: Times Books.

Iutcovich, M. 1988. "The Sociology of Success: Fact or Fantasy." *Journal of Applied Sociology* 5: 1-14.

Olsen, M. 1989. "Strategies for Changing Society." *Journal of Applied Sociology"* 6:1-12.

Society for Applied Sociology. 1992. "A Plan for the Society for Applied Sociology, 1994-95." Strategic Planning Document.

Ward, L. 1897. *Dynamic Sociology, or Applied Social Science as Based Upon Statistical Sociology and the Less Complex Sciences.* 2nd ed. New York: Appleton and Company.

White House Domestic Policy Council. 1993. *The President's Health Security Plan.* New York: Times Books.

Stephen Floyd Steele

1947-

Steve Steele served as President of the Society for Applied Sociology in 1992-93. He has applied sociology's concepts and tools for over two decades. As a teacher, practitioner and leader, he has been an advocate for understanding the practical value of the application of social science. He first encountered sociology in the mid-1960s at Schoolcraft College, a community college in Livonia, Michigan. Full time employment at the Detroit Diesel Engine Division of General Motors, dedicated family life and part-time college, no doubt, were contributing factors to a practical view of sociology. Formal training in sociology continued at Eastern Michigan University. He finished his undergraduate degree and Masters work at EMU, taking a teaching position at Anne Arundel Community College in Arnold, Maryland in 1972. In a quarter-century at Anne Arundel his love for teaching and his commitment to undergraduate education and student development took an applied path with the creation of the Center for the Study of Local Issues (CSLI).

Established in 1978, the Center applies social science research in the county served by Anne Arundel Community College. Steve's early involvement in the Center's creation led to increased student access to applied sociology during the first two years of college. Since 1981, the Center has recruited a small group of outstanding students to learn social research methods through classroom seminars and assignment to a local research project for which the student intern has direct responsibility. As Director of the Center for the Study of Local Issues in the 1980s, he worked locally to enhance the problem-solving value of sociology, and nationally to promote the applied research center as a vehicle for local research. In the mid-1980s CSLI and the American Sociological Association co-sponsored three national workshops on starting local research centers. These successful conferences, augmented by numerous on-site presentations throughout the United States, drew national and international attention to the practice of social science.

Steve answered the call for leadership in the ASA and the Society for Applied Sociology. By the late 1980s he served as Chair of the Membership Committee of the American Sociological Association, and Chair of the ASA Section on Undergraduate Education. In this time period, Marv Olsen encouraged him to run for Vice President of the Society for Applied Sociology. As Vice President he guided the successful 1990 Annual Meeting in Annapolis, Maryland. Shortly thereafter, he served as SAS President in 1992-93. His presidency saw SAS membership top 440 members and the approval of a strategic plan. Meanwhile, responses to a SAS membership survey conducted by then membership chair, Anne Hendershott, fostered the development of an *ad hoc* Committee on Professional Standards and Accreditation, headed by Harry Perlstadt. Alex Boros and Mark Iutcovich laid the groundwork for *Social Insight* magazine in this time frame, and Steve introduced SAS to Richard Bedea, who would succeed Sam Sloss as the SAS Administrative Officer. Throughout his term, he focused the strengthening of applied sociology and sociological practice as forces in the discipline. In 1994 he was elected Chair-elect of the Sociological Practice Section of the ASA, serving as Chair in 1995-96.

In parallel activities in the 1990s, Steve and this research partner, Joe Lamp, began Applied Data Associates, Inc., a small research and consulting partnership. ADA was formed to assist organizations in the public and private sectors to gather information to address their concerns and solve their problems. ADA's goal has been to develop research, planning and evaluation products, and procedures that are clearly crafted for ease of understanding and use. Meanwhile, he continues his work at Anne Arundel Community College and has extended his teaching efforts to the graduate education level in the Applied Behavioral Science Program (in the Division of Business) at the Johns Hopkins University School of Continuing Studies.

PART THREE:

SOCIAL CHANGE AND INTERVENTION IN APPLIED SOCIOLOGY

INTRODUCTION

Social action, social intervention, and bringing about social change are all aspects of applied sociology. To be involved in applied work is to understand and carry out the process of change. The articles in this section address the change process and the role of the applied sociologist. There are a number of questions addressed. First, how do we bring about change? Marvin Olsen looks at the strategies for "intentionally created change." Second, should applied sociologists really be involved in the change process? Harold Cox reminds us that involvement in social movements and "efforts to improve social conditions" is central to the profession of sociology. Finally, are our research methods effective in assessing social change? Jim Hougland explores the value of properly executed sociological research for studying social change.

How Do We Bring About Change?

Social change is intrinsic to social life. We are in a dynamic, ever-changing world. To understand change is to understand life as "process." Whether we like it or not, unintended or "undirected" change will occur. What happens when we want to "grab hold" of change, when we want to guide it in some way and move it toward a desired outcome? Marvin Olsen addressed this important issue. He maintained that knowledge gained in applied sociology could give "humanity greater control over our collective social life."

Intentionally created social change occurs in at least three ways. Olsen identifies three "sets of strategies." Briefly stated, these strategies flow downward (social mobilization), upward (social confrontation), and inside (involvement strategies). Each strategy employs a different process for use. In social mobilization strategies, organizational, community, societal or other leaders launch change from their positions of power. *Social confrontation* strategies employ collective forces for change moving upward from those dissatisfied with existing conditions who want to change them despite resistance from system leaders. On a more cooperative level, involvement strategies attempt to integrate the downward and upward forces in an effort to mutually change social life. Olsen reminds us that change is difficult, hence, each strategy maintains intrinsic strengths and weaknesses. Yet, each may be appropriate in itself for use in the production of social change.

Olsen provides blueprints for the development and implementation of each strategy. We find that we can "direct the process of social change toward desired goals." Consistent with the perspective of applied sociology, he displays the methodical, rigorous use of sociological knowledge in the process of social action. He shows us the value in using our methods and perspective. Importantly, Olsen challenges us in his conclusion:

> Social science--and especially applied sociology--can provide the knowledge necessary to make these strategic decisions in an informed manner, and thus facilitate the process of intentionally creating social change. Are we willing to undertake this challenge?

Should We Be Involved in the Change Process?

Should applied sociologists take Olsen's challenge? Is the use of sociological knowledge and methods for informed social change inherent in being an applied sociologist? There is little doubt that Harold Cox would say, "Yes!"

For Cox, sociologists both inherit and actively cultivate skills that make "involvement in social movements and efforts to improve social conditions... legitimate activities for professional sociologists." Historically, sociology springs from roots of those who sought to address, understand and change injustices of the social system. It is an element of the discipline that is part of our past and our present.

The profession has the skills to take action. Sociology need not be knowledge for knowledge's sake. Not unlike the knowledge of medicine or psychiatry, the application of sociology is realistic and valuable. Cox presents evidence suggesting that application of a science may, in fact, reinforce its professionalism. Applied sociology supplies the structure for "identifying a problem, then investigating the problem with an eye toward its solution, and ends with recommending or taking the necessary action to resolve the problem." How can we know if the sociological perspective is a plausible, reasonable answer to society's questions? Through application, we test the "limits" of our theories.

In many respects Cox argues for more problem-centered sociology. Reminiscent of Boros' focus on the value of subjectivity, Cox reminds us that the "scientific neutrality argument [may have been taken] to an illogical and irrational extreme." It is the problem itself that drives researchers regardless of the field. We do not reject the quest for cures in medical science, or the understanding and use of nature in physics because they improve human life. These are legitimate pursuits because researchers and society value the ultimate outcome of the results. The researcher's "... earnest commitment to the solution of a problem will make him/her more, rather than less, careful in conducting the research objectively." Sociology must also focus on the human problem and its solution. In short, sociology wins from an applied perspective.

How Effective Are Our Research Methods in Handling Social Change?

What is more fundamental to sociological investigation than survey research? Is it possible that this procedure, so common to all of us, can be viewed as a force for social change? Jim Hougland's article links this valuable research method to public policy formation and change.

Hougland points out that polling has had anything but a dull history! Throughout the twentieth century survey research has been revered as a vehicle for participatory democracy and policy formation on one hand, and the scourge of data-gathering world, on the other hand. As a policy tool, its efficiency is impressive, making national feedback virtually instantaneous. Yet, it is not without its methodological critics. Arguments posed by those opposing its use range from concern over the meaningfulness of respondents' answers to distress over the overuse of survey research. Conflicting results on surveys covering the same issues, conducted at roughly equivalent times, only heighten the opposition and the public's confusion over the validity of this technique. Survey respondents rarely see the benefit to them in answering batteries of questions. While Hougland admits the absence of a polling-perfect world, he cautions that we not be too quick to disregard the benefits of survey research.

Despite limitations, survey results have policy influence. Hougland reminds us that tangible influences on policy makers is limited, often best accepted when conforming "to their preconceived ideas than on results that might be more surprising (and, therefore, from some perspectives, more interesting)." Politicians may find the results useful as soundings to navigate political water. Similarly, surveys get press coverage and polling has been taken under the wing of the newspaper and electronic media.

Turning to applied sociology, public opinion polling is a beneficial vehicle on several fronts.

First, knowledge of the appropriate use of survey research design is a "force multiplier" for sociologists. As a group small in number, sociologists magnify their clout by their conducting this type of research. Second, collection of public opinion data fills a hole in a dwindling federal data collection system. Recordings of the public's views by a reasonably unbiased source is increasingly difficult to find. Third, and of great importance, is the value that sociologists bring to the interpretation and analysis of poll results. Supplying answers to the question: "What does it mean?" has extraordinary value.

Polling is not without its "dark side." Negative usage of polling results, coupled with misinterpretation of results, may have dubious consequences. But, this and other forms of applied sociology produce long-term and short-term value.

8

STRATEGIES FOR CHANGING SOCIETY*

MARVIN E. OLSEN
Michigan State University

Three sets of strategies for intentionally creating social change are examined in this paper. Social Mobilization strategies involve the exertion of influence "downward" by organizational, community, societal or other leaders who are attempting to initiate social change from their positions of power. Social Involvement strategies involve reciprocal influence flows among leaders and citizens who are jointly attempting to change social life. Social Confrontation strategies involve the exercise of influence "upward" by citizens who are dissatisfied with existing conditions and want to change them despite resistance from system leaders. Each of these sets of change strategies is analyzed in terms of its major dynamics, guiding principles, possible courses of action and typical problems. No one set of change strategies is inherently more desirable or effective than the others since they are intended to be used in quite different situations. Each of them is fraught with numerous potential difficulties but each of them can be quite effective in producing intentional social change under particular circumstances.

INTRODUCTION

Social life is never static; it is constantly changing. "The actual world is a process," wrote the philosopher Alfred North Whitehead (1929). Expressed more broadly, "process is reality, and reality is process." Nevertheless, we are often not satisfied with the course of undirected social change, and desire to direct it toward valued goals. How to guide and direct social change is the challenge of applied sociology. Using knowledge acquired through the study of social processes and conditions, applied sociology seeks to give humanity greater control over our collective social life.

* Presidential Address, Sixth Annual Meeting of the Society for Applied Sociology, Chicago, Illinois, October 21-22, 1988. Copyright, Society for Applied Sociology. Reprinted with permission from the **Journal of Applied Sociology,** Volume 6 1989.

In this endeavor, applied sociologists have given particular attention to developing strategies that social activists can use to direct the process of social change and attain desired goals in social life. Three basic sets of strategies for intentionally creating social change are examined in this paper, all of which have proven effective under particular conditions.

One set of change strategies is termed Social Mobilization. These strategies involve the exertion of influence "downward" by organizational, community, societal, or other leaders who are attempting to initiate social change from their positions of power. Their primary concern is to persuade citizens to adopt the intended changes in social life.

A second set of change strategies is termed Social Involvement. These strategies involve reciprocal influence flows among leaders and citizens who are jointly attempting to change social life. The primary concern in this case is to develop procedures for designing changes that are acceptable to all.

The third set of change strategies is termed Social Confrontation. These strategies involve the exercise of influence "upward" by citizens who are dissatisfied with existing conditions and want to change them despite resistance from leaders. The primary goal of these citizens is to overcome that resistance and force leaders to implement the desired changes.

Each of these three sets of change strategies can be analyzed in terms of its major dynamics, guiding principles, possible courses of action, and typical problems.

SOCIAL MOBILIZATION

Major Dynamics

The Social Mobilization approach to creating social change is leader-initiated and downward-oriented. Established system leaders identify an issue that they believe requires attention, formulate a policy concerning it and programs to enact that policy, and then seek to persuade citizens to accept the policy and to participate in the programs. To a highly autocratic system, the leaders might be able to enact their changes by fiat, provided they could exercise enough power to force others to comply. In most situations within modern societies, however, leaders rarely command that kind of absolute power. If their policies and programs are to be successful, they must convince the public that the intended changes will benefit them in some way.

While citizens do not participate directly in policy formation or program development in these situations, they may eventually be able to replace the current leaders if their policies and programs are widely unpopular. More immediately, citizens can express their views toward the proposed changes by either adopting or ignoring them.

Guiding Principles

If the majority of citizens are to be persuaded to adopt the proposed changes, they must feel that they will receive some kind of benefit from their cooperation. Social exchange theory offers several general principles that can facilitate this process. For example, leaders should initially offer some desired services to the public, so that people will feel indebted to them. They should strive to create a climate of trust between themselves and citizens. And they should be as explicit as possible about the kinds of benefits that people will realize through the proposed changes. This process of social exchange need not be strictly equal on both sides--that rarely happens in social life--but people must view the exchanges as fair and worthwhile.

Courses of Action

The possible courses of action constituting this mobilization set can be classified into the three categories of communicative, financial, and regulatory strategies (Olsen and Joerges 1983).

Communicative Strategies

These strategies include providing information, making emotional appeals, and exerting social pressures. With an information strategy, leaders disseminate information about the current problem and the expected benefits of the proposed change. It is very widely used because of its ease and simplicity. Its effectiveness is seriously limited, however, by the fact that most of the information disseminated tends to be received only by people who are already convinced of the desirability of the change. Other people simply ignore the messages.

An Appeals Strategy involves sending messages with strong psychological or emotional appeals concerning the problem and the proposed change. This strategy is often more effective in reaching uncommitted individuals, especially if it touches on their fundamental beliefs and values. Nevertheless, altering individuals' personal attitudes can be very difficult. This approach is most effective when it is aimed at rather specific attitudes pertaining directly to the proposed change. It is much less effective when aimed at very broad attitudes.

A Pressures Strategy seeks to involve people in social situations where they will be influenced by others who already support the change. These situations may be informal neighborhood gatherings, meetings of voluntary associations, or activities of community organizations. Because people tend to be most receptive to new ideas when they are received from individuals they trust or within organizations to which they belong, this strategy is generally the most effective communicative technique. Creating social situations in which the desired pressures will be exerted can be demanding, however.

Financial Strategies

These strategies include price adjustments, financial incentives, and tax disincentives. The Pricing Strategy is entirely passive and unintrusive, which makes it popular with political leaders. They simply allow the price of relevant goods or services to rise or fall in the marketplace according to supply and demand. If an item becomes scarce, its price will rise sharply; whereas, if it becomes overabundant, its price will drop sharply. There are numerous problems with this technique, however, especially when the goods or services are either vital necessities or complete luxuries, and hence display little price elasticity. For this and other reasons, the pricing strategy is very unpopular with the public.

An Incentives Strategy offers financial benefits to people who adopt the proposed change. These incentives may take such forms as grants, loans, tax credits, tax deductions, bonuses, or rebates. Needless to say, this strategy tends to be quite popular with most people. Nevertheless, it is not always successful because the incentives are frequently seen as insufficient to warrant altering established practices, or because people do not trust the offer.

A Disincentives Strategy, which is the converse of the incentives technique, penalizes people who do not adopt the intended change. Disincentives may be applied through taxes, fines, tariffs, or surcharges. Although this strategy does not require trust, it often fails because people find ways of circumventing or avoiding the financial penalty.

Regulatory Strategies

Whereas communicative and financial strategies are aimed at individuals regulatory techniques attempt to manipulate broader social conditions. This may be done by establishing performance standards, allocating goods or services, and restructuring communities or organizations. A Standards Strategy requires a government agency to establish performance or quality standards for goods or services, and to enforce adherence to them by those who produce the goods or offer the services. Because this technique is generally viewed as equitable and is relatively unintrusive, it tends to be rather popular. It does, however have considerable administrative, surveillance, and enforcement costs.

An Allocation Strategy brings a government agency directly into the process through which goods or services are distributed to the public. Tactics can range from simple limits on the amount of items available through complex rationing schemes. This strategy entails all of the administrative, surveillance, and enforcement costs associated with standards, and in addition is normally very unpopular with the public. Consequently, it is usually a last-resort technique.

A Restructuring Strategy is by far the most complex means of promoting social change, and therefore, is generally the least used of all these strategies. Nevertheless, it can be the most effective in the long run. It involves changing the social (and sometimes also the physical) structure of an organization or community, so that it operates in a different way. When the social setting changes people's actions almost invariably change in response to it. But because those action changes are voluntary, people tend to feel that they are in control of their lives and are not being manipulated. The obvious limitation of this strategy is that it can entail considerable planning and implementation costs.

Typical Problems

No matter how strongly leaders may desire to initiate social changes that they believe are necessary and desirable, most of the time they are not likely to be successful unless they can mobilize the public to adopt those changes. This can be a demanding task. Among the countless potential problems that may derail the efforts of system leaders, three are especially noteworthy. First, large numbers of citizens are likely to remain ignorant of the leaders' efforts, be apathetic or indifferent toward them, or flatly reject them. Second, the exchange transaction being proposed by the leaders may appear to be unfair or even exploitative to many people. And third, many of the mobilization strategies described above can be quite costly in terms of time, effort, and resources, without any guarantee of success. Through evaluation studies of these various mobilization strategies, however, we are gradually learning how to use them more effectively.

SOCIAL INVOLVEMENT

Major Dynamics

Because of the many problems inherent in the Social Mobilization approach to promoting social change, a quite different approach has been developed during the last 15 or so years. Instead of taking all the initiative in social change efforts, many leaders have begun to work with citizens rather than on them. The Social Involvement approach is a joint process in which system leaders and citizens work together to create social change. They establish and conduct a cooperative citizen involvement program to resolve a pressing problem, formulate a policy concerning it, and carry out an action program to deal with it.

Although the leaders usually retain final decision-making authority, an effective citizen participation program will involve interested citizens in meaningful ways at every step of the process. Therefore, the recommendations that result from the program are a shared result of collaborative effects. When this occurs, citizens do not need to be persuaded to adopt the proposed change. They do so willingly because they have participated in shaping it.

Guiding Principles

The basis of this approach lies in participatory democratic theory. Very briefly, this theory asserts that all people have a right to participate in making collective decisions which affect them within all spheres of their lives. Formulated during the political upheavals of the 1960s and 1970s, participatory democratic theory goes far beyond the idea of representative democracy as presently practiced in Western societies. Instead of merely selecting leaders to represent them and make decisions for them, all people should take part in actually making collective decisions. Moreover, that mandate is not restricted to the political sphere. It extends to work situations, community affairs, voluntary associations, and even the family. If participatory democracy is actually to occur, however, all decision-making procedures must be organized to facilitate and encourage as widespread and meaningful citizen involvement as possible.

Courses of Action

Most citizen involvement programs conducted thus far have been within communities, and the present discussion is limited to that realm. There is no inherent reason, however, why the process could not be utilized in complex organizations or many other settings.

Initially, many of these programs consisted of little more than one or two public hearings at which citizens expressed their views and feelings toward policies and programs being proposed by community leaders. These hearings were merely a formal ritual, and gave citizens little or no opportunity to make significant inputs to the decision-making process. Gradually, however, citizen involvement programs have been expanded and improved, so that today we know how to design and conduct participation programs which fully involve citizens.

A few years ago, several colleagues and I decided to compile and apply this knowledge. We examined all that was known about such programs, analyzed a considerable number of previous programs to discover their strengths and weaknesses, designed a comprehensive citizen involvement program based on that investigation, and tested it in a community that was struggling with an important policy decision. Since our program is described in detail in a recent book (Howell, Olsen and Olsen 1987), I shall not attempt to go through all its 33 steps here. Several features of our program can be noted, however.

First, it is divided into five phases, beginning at the time when a new policy or action is first being contemplated. It includes laying a foundation for a broad citizen involvement program within the community, organizing that program, conducting the program, reaching a final decision, and implementing the agreed-upon change. At the completion of each phase, the activities conducted thus far are evaluated and the program is modified as necessary to take account of any difficulties that have been encountered.

Second, it is a complex, long-term process. Involving large numbers of citizens in a community decision in a meaningful way cannot be accomplished in a few days or even a few weeks. In our trial community, the entire program lasted for about nine months; although with hindsight, it might have been completed in about six months. This process requires at least one professional leader working more or less full-time to coordinate the program, plus additional part-time staff persons. And it demands a considerable amount of time and effort by numerous citizens if it is to be successful.

Third, the process builds on and operates through the network of organizations presently existing in a community as extensively as possible. This is not intended to be a community organization process. Rather, it uses those existing organizations to ensure that the program is solidly grounded in the social structure of the community. This approach is vital if the program is to be taken seriously by both community leaders and citizens.

Fourth, it employs a number of interlinked techniques to encourage as many people as possible to participate in the program in at least one of several different ways. These techniques include a relatively large Citizen Task Force, a smaller Planning Committee, a Central Steering Committee, numerous Working Groups that focus on specific aspects of the problem, a community survey, a workshop, all kinds of media publicity and information activities, written and telephone inputs from many citizens, and a formal public hearing.

Fifth, this is entirely a voluntary program and consequently tends to attract people who are concerned about and active in community affairs. While the program seeks to involve as many different kinds of people as possible, it is not a public referendum. Therefore, it is not representative of the entire community, but that is not its purpose. Its goal, rather, is to give all interested citizens meaningful opportunities to participate directly in making a community decision, if they so desire.

Sixth, this kind of program can be quite effective. In our trial community, almost everyone who participated in the program expressed strong satisfaction with it in a follow-up survey. More importantly, the process resulted in a final policy recommendation that was acceptable to virtually everyone involved. Although it was quite different from a provisional decision on the issue that had previously been made by the legal authorities, they agreed to adopt and implement the recommended action.

Typical Problems

There are several obvious and some less than obvious problems in conducting a citizen involvement program such as this. Some obvious problems are the time, effort, and resources needed to conduct a meaningful program. In addition, most citizens have little experience in participating in such a program, so that the process must be presented and taught to them in a manner that gains their trust rather than suspicion. Less obvious, but absolutely critical, is the requirement that the legal decision-makers must agree in advance to support and participate in the program, and to give serious consideration to its recommendations. If they make their final decision prior to or outside of the program, it becomes merely a sham exercise to legitimate that decision. If this happens, the public will sooner or later become aware of the situation, and will be unlikely to have any further interest in participating in citizen involvement programs.

SOCIAL CONFRONTATION

Major Dynamics

The Social Involvement approach to creating social change rests on the assumption that both leaders and citizens agree on the necessity of taking action to deal with a social issue or problem, even though they may not initially agree on what actions should be taken. In contrast, the Social Confrontation approach applies to situations in which only a set of citizens define an existing situation as a problem that requires action. In these situations, the relevant system leaders deny the existence of any problem or insist that existing practices are adequate to deal with it. In short, the citizens want change but the leaders do not.

The Social Confrontation approach is therefore a citizen-initiated, upward-oriented process. The concerned citizens must identify the nature of the problem, organize themselves for collective action, bring pressures to bear on leaders to accept a new policy and new programs despite their opposition, and ensure that the change is implemented. This is clearly a challenging process since the citizens are normally operating from a relatively weak power base (at least initially), but nevertheless must overcome the resistance of powerful opponents if they are to be successful. The central dynamics in this process are therefore, power generation and exertion, coupled with negotiation and compromise.

Guiding Principles

The theoretical perspective that is most relevant to this process is social conflict theory. More specifically, the process draws on principles of intentional conflict creation, purposeful power exertion, and conflict resolution. They pertain to the questions of how to create conflict directed toward a specific objective without allowing it to become mass social disruption or rioting. These principles pertain to the matter of how to use social conflict to generate social power and how to focus sufficient power exertion on designated targets to force authorities to consider changing their policies and practices. They also deal with ways of resolving conflicts that are acceptable to all the involved parties.

This last concern is particularly crucial since the process of resolving conflict in a manner that produces desired social change calls for strategies which are quite different from those required to create conflict and exert power. Consequently, this approach demands a basic shift in philosophy and tactics as it progresses, which can be extremely difficult to achieve.

Courses of Action

Throughout human history, relatively powerless citizens have sought to change social conditions despite opposition from powerful system leaders. They have used strategies ranging from passive noncompliance to violent revolution, but a large proportion of those efforts have failed. However, one set of confrontation strategies has proved to be quite effective in such situations. Originating in Henry David Thoreau's concept of "civil disobedience" and demonstrated by Gandhi in his struggle for Indian independence from Great Britain, this approach had been widely used during the twentieth century by labor unions and in the Civil Rights Movement of the 1960s. Analytically, it can be divided into five overlapping stages, each of which involves different kinds of activities.

Organization

In this initial stage, the concerned citizens must create a social movement organization or transform an existing body such as a labor union into such an organization. This involves specifying goals for the movement and developing rhetoric that expresses the problem and those goals in clear and simple language. The movement must find dynamic, charismatic leaders who can attract a core of dedicated and active members and a larger number of less involved supporters. And it must conduct a public relations campaign to gain sympathy with its objectives, attract financial contributions, and legitimize the movement in the eyes of the public.

Conflict

The next step in this stage is to identify key leverage points in the existing system where it and its authorities are especially vulnerable. In the economy, these are likely to be major production activities or consumption practices, while in the political system they may be enforcement of regulations or public images of officials. The movement then carefully designs and carries out actions aimed at those key leverage points that hinder, disrupt, block, or prevent normal activities. Very often this involves strikes, boycotts, sit-ins, demonstrations, or other public protest activities. All such actions must be carefully aimed at specific key targets and not get out of hand. The purpose of these actions is to exert pressures on the system and its authorities that are too costly for them to ignore.

Since the initial reaction of system authorities to the movement's actions is likely to be indifference or repression, the movement must be prepared to continue its conflict activities--often with gradual escalation--until the authorities are willing to negotiate. To gain the sympathy and support of the public in this situation, movement activists must be willing to suffer, without resistance, any punishments or reprisals that may be inflicted on them by the authorities. The moral justice of their cause and their willingness to suffer for it, thus become their primary power resource in the struggle against the existing system. Mass media coverage is quite essential in this effort. In addition, the authorities must be sensitive to public opinion. If their stance is simply to "shoot all demonstrators on sight, and the public be damned," this strategy will obviously fail.

Negotiation

While continuing to exert pressures on the system, the activists must constantly reiterate their desire to negotiate with system authorities. And no matter what kinds of threats or punishments are directed toward them because of their actions, they must not abandon the struggle until the authorities agree to negotiate with them.

When that time comes, the movement must be able to make a crucial transformation. Up to then, its goals will have been lofty and far-reaching, its leaders will have been ideological and charismatic, and its tactics will have been strident and conflictual. Now, however, it is time to sit down at the bargaining table with their enemy and participate in calm, rational bargaining. Some leaders of social movements can make this turnaround in tactics, but many cannot because they are too committed to the revolutionary rhetoric of "Give me liberty or give me death." In that case, they must designate or the movement must select new leaders who can operate more pragmatically.

The members of the movement's negotiating team must be willing to participate in good faith in the bargaining process with system authorities for whatever length of time is needed to reach a settlement. More importantly, they must be able to be flexible and to compromise gradually, letting go on minor points while continuing to stand firm on their most critical demands. In other words, they must be willing to eventually accept partial victory rather than insisting on "everything or nothing." A successful bargaining process must arrive at a compromise that is seen by both sides as a "win-win" resolution of the conflict, so that both feel they have gained some worthwhile outcomes.

Alteration

Once a resolution of the conflict has been agreed upon by both sides, the movement must be willing to cooperate fully with the authorities in developing new programs and practices to implement the intended change. This process is most likely to be effective if the proposed alterations are aimed at the structure of the entire system rather than specific actions of particular individuals, if they emphasize alterations that will have minimal immediate disruptive effects on the system while maximizing long-term beneficial consequences, and if at least some of the system alterations can be implemented immediately so that supporters on both sides of the conflict can see that something is being accomplished. In addition, the movement leaders must insist that the entire process of change be constantly monitored to ensure that the agreed-upon alterations are actually being carried out.

Acceptance

This final stage in the change process calls for movement leaders with a third set of organizational skills. Within the movement, they must be able to convince most of its members and supporters that the agreed-upon plan of action will eventually satisfy the most critical of their desires for change. If the current movement leaders cannot do this, they are likely to be overthrown by ideological radicals who claim that the present leaders have "sold out" to the system. When the radicals are successful in this challenge, the resulting "Thermadorian" reaction usually destroys whatever agreements were reached with system authorities. This throws the movement back to the confrontation stage, and invites severe repression from the authorities.

Outside the movement, its leaders must support the system authorities for their acceptance of the agreed-upon changes so that the authorities no longer feel threatened by the movement. This must be done both privately and in public, so as to encourage public support and legitimacy for the alterations that are being implemented. If these efforts are successful, system authorities who initially opposed all change are very likely to become increasingly accepting of the change as will also the larger public. People's attitudes, values, and beliefs will gradually shift in response to the new conditions. Eventually, the changes will be fully accepted and incorporated into the system so that in the future people may likely wonder, "why was all that controversy necessary?"

Typical Problems

This Social Confrontation approach to creating social change can easily break down at several critical points. The movement organization may not be able to find strong leaders, attract enough members and supporters, or obtain sufficient financial resources. There may be no leverage points where the existing system is vulnerable, or the movement may not be able to identify them or gain access to them. The movement's conflict tactics may not exert sufficient pressures on the system to force its authorities to bargain with the movement, or those authorities may be able to diffuse or squelch the conflict. The movement leaders or the system authorities may be unwilling or unable to negotiate in a spirit of compromise. The negotiations may end in an impasse that neither side can overcome. If agreement is reached on new policies, the more ideologically committed members of the movement may not accept them, or system authorities may fail to implement the programs and practices to which they have agreed. This is indeed a highly problematic way of creating social change. But it can be made to work for the benefit of citizens who are committed to achieving change.

ASSESSMENT

Each of the three sets of strategies for creating social change outlined in this paper--Social Mobilization, Social Involvement, and Social Confrontation---is fraught with numerous potential problems. Nevertheless, each of them can be effective under particular circumstances. No one approach is inherently more desirable or effective than the others, since they are intended to be used in quite different situations.

There are many situations in which system leaders see a need for social change that is not initially accepted by most of the public. A typical example with which I have worked extensively is promoting energy conservation. Beginning in the late 1970s, an increasing number of public officials came to understand that conserving energy can be much more beneficial--both financially and environmentally--than supplying ever-growing amounts of new energy. Yet much of the public was very slow and reluctant to adopt this perspective. Many national and local officials therefore began experimenting with all of the mobilization strategies discussed above, seeking the most effective way of encouraging citizens to conserve energy.

In quite a number of other situations during the past 15 years, especially within local communities, public officials and citizens have agreed that something had to be done to deal with a community problem, but did not initially agree on the best course of action. In several of those communities, citizen involvement programs such as the one described in this paper have enabled them to find a solution to the problem that was generally acceptable to everyone. In our trial community, public officials agreed to abandon their initial plan to build a new dam on a nearby river, and instead to use those funds to weatherize all the houses in the community. As we learn more about designing and conducting such programs, they should become an even more widely used way of achieving desired social change.

Meanwhile, there will undoubtedly continue to be many situations in which citizens seek change but system authorities are indifferent or opposed to their demands. In such situations, the concerned citizens must be able and willing to organize themselves for action if their demands are to be accepted. As we learn more about using confrontation strategies in a purposeful and effective manner, citizens will discover that they are not powerless to change social systems despite strong opposition. The Civil Rights Movement provided dramatic evidence that this approach can be extremely effective when skillfully conducted.

In sum, it is possible to direct the process of social change toward desired goals. To do this effectively, however, we must select a broad approach that is appropriate to the particular situation, and then develop and implement action strategies that will enable us to achieve our goals. Social science-- and especially applied sociology--can provide the knowledge necessary to make these strategic decisions in an informed manner, and thus facilitate the process of intentionally creating social change. Are we willing to undertake this challenge?

REFERENCES

Howell, Robert E., Marvin E. Olsen and Darryll Olsen. 1987. *Designing a Citizen Involvement Program: A Guidebook for Involving Citizens in the Resolution of Environmental Issues.* Corvalis, Oregon: Western Rural Development Center.

Olsen, Marvin E. and Bernward Joerges. 1983. "Consumer Energy Conservation Programs." Pp. 561-591 in *Handbook of Social Intervention,* edited by Edward Seidman. Beverly Hills, California: Sage Publications.

Whitehead, Alfred North. 1929. *Process and Reality.* New York: Macmillan Co.

Marvin E. Olsen*

1936 -1992

Marvin E. Olsen, President of the Society for Applied Sociology in 1987-1988, had a short but remarkably productive career that included faculty appointments at Indiana University (1965-75), Washington State University (1980-84) and Michigan State University (1984-92) where he served as Chair up until 1991. He also served as a Senior Research Scientist at Battelle Human Affairs Research Center in Seattle (1974-79). His contributions to sociology, in general, and applied sociology, in particular, are wide-ranging. His teaching covered the topics of social change, political sociology, environmental sociology, applied sociology, social stratification, urban sociology, social organization, and sociological theory. Over the years he moved from his strong theoretical emphasis to one in which he championed the policy implications of sociological knowledge. He integrated theory with application and sought ways to increase public participation in decision-making. Because of his high standards, Marvin Olsen won the respect of sociologists from all segments of the discipline.

Olsen's success has been described by colleagues as critical in the effort to forge a link between academic and practicing sociologists. Harry Perlstadt states, "I believe that jurisdiction and the divisions within the profession of sociology are central to understanding Marvin Olsen's effort within the Society for Applied Sociology (SAS), the American Sociological Association (ASA), and the Department of Sociology at Michigan State University. His career bridged academia and the world of contract and applied research. He worked very hard to create links between SAS and ASA, to bring together academic and practitioner sociologists, and to expand traditional curriculums to include programs for training practitioners. He had the vision and the drive."

The significant contributions of Marvin Olsen in forging this link include numerous efforts. In 1988 he orchestrated the formation of the Coalition for Utilizing Sociology (CUS), a coalition of the major organizations with a sustained interest in the application of sociology. He served as CUS's coordinator between 1988-1990. At the 1990 meeting of the Society for Applied Sociology, Marv conducted a workshop on "Designing an Undergraduate Applied Program." In collaboration with Jeanne Ballantine, Phillip Obermiller and Theodore Wagenaar, he developed a teaching note which summarized the presentations and subsequent discussion. Perlstadt labeled this *Marv's Manifest* since it marked an important step in creating change through an academic program that would impact both sociology as a teaching-research discipline and an applied practicing profession. At this same time (1990-1992), Marv served as the Chair of the Committee on Sociological Practice Curriculum for the ASA Section on Sociological Practice. He also served on the planning and advisory committee for the development of the Spivack Program in Applied Social Research and Public Policy--a prestigious award granted annually by the American Sociological Association.

Marvin Olsen first came to the Society for Applied Sociology in 1985, when SAS was having its third annual meeting. SAS was struggling with organizational issues (e.g., developing bylaws, creating a governance structure, and institutionalizing a set of administrative procedures) at this stage of its early existence. Marv's decision to become involved when he did was important for SAS in several ways. He was widely respected and, as James Hougland has eloquently stated, "he worked in substantive areas that often differed from those of the early leaders of SAS, his involvement helped to support and validate the work of others in the organization while making it visible to a large number of potential new members...Marv worked with its leadership and succeeded in broadening its membership base, strengthening its ties to other organizations, and increasing the efficiency of its internal procedures." Marv's influence on SAS is also reiterated by Howard Garrison: "Marv helped to lay the foundation for a stronger organization by vigorously supporting the establishment of an executive office, a realistic dues structure, and a prominent newsletter. He was willing to take the risks that were necessary for growth." It is also significant that three of SAS's Presidents were his students during his tenure at Indiana University--Jeanne Ballantine, James Hougland, and Harold Cox. Several other individuals occupying current or recent leadership positions in SAS have worked with Marv on research projects. Marv set an admirable standard for effective mentoring in sociology.

Marvin Olsen's scholarship is considerable. He authored or edited a number of important books, including *The Process of Social Organization, Power in Societies, Handbook of Applied Sociology, Participatory Pluralism, Societal Dynamics, and Viewing the World Ecologically.* He was also the author of over 80 articles, chapters, papers, and reports. Professionally, he integrated theory and practice and served as a mentor in a way that set a high standard for everyone in the discipline.

* This biographical sketch, written posthumously, has been compiled through a number of sources in addition to his vitae:

Hougland, James (1992). Marvin E. Olsen (1936-1992). *The Useful Sociologist,* Vol 13, Fall.

Hougland, James (1993). The Contributions of Marvin Olsen. Presented at the Society for Applied Sociology Annual Meeting, St. Louis, Missouri.

Lodwick, Dora (1995). In Memory of the Works and Life of Marvin Elliot Olsen. *Journal of Applied Sociology,* 12:2, 1-12.

Perlstadt, Harry (1993). Creating Change Through Academic Programs. Presented at the Society for Applied Sociology Annual Meeting, St. Louis, Missouri.

9   The Sociologist As Activist*

HAROLD COX

Indiana State University

Sociology as a discipline originated from a very applied activist orientation. The early sociologists attempted to solve a wide variety of social pathologies including crime, poverty, homelessness, and a multitude of related social ills. More recently, the discipline has moved in the direction of primarily endorsing pure research most often done in a laboratory setting. The article points out a number of advantages for the profession assuming a more activist position; of going beyond the mere description of the social condition to suggesting solutions to current social problems and working systematically to implement them.

INTRODUCTION

The basic premise of this article is that involvement in social movements and efforts to improve social conditions should be recognized as legitimate activities for professional sociologists. I would argue that sociologists as professionals are more skilled and knowledgeable at identifying and suggesting remedies for the injustices of the social system than most other disciplines. Therefore, being an active agent of social change is not something that sociologists should avoid for fear of censorship from the more traditional and conservative branch of the profession, but rather an activity that should be encouraged and cultivated by the profession.

Social activism springs from the social scientists' desire to alter and improve a social condition in such a way as to improve the quality of life. Activists encourage research where the aim is not only to collect information and arrive at a better understanding of a problem but to suggest solutions as well. Social activism completes the circle of professional obligation for the sociologist. It begins with identifying a problem, then investigating the problem with an eye toward its solution, and ends with recommending

* Presidential Address, Tenth Annual Meeting of the Society for Applied, Cleveland, Ohio, October 15-18, 1992. Copyright, Society for Applied Sociology. Reprinted with permission from the **Journal of Applied Sociology,** Volume 10, 1993.

or taking the necessary action to resolve the problem. This is exactly what the medical doctor, psychiatrist and other professionals are rewarded for doing. The medical doctor attempts to identify the cause of health problems, considering possible solutions and recommending courses of action or treatment designed to eliminate the problem. Sociology must follow the same course of action as that of any other profession. Some would argue that sociology and other academic disciplines differ from medicine in that they are research-oriented disciplines, and the creation of knowledge is viewed as a value in itself. However, our traditional role of creating knowledge can be enchanted to the extent that we play an active role as citizens in our communities and societies. Through such involvement, we test the limits of our theory-based understanding and discover unanticipated questions for research. Because our involvement as citizens often leads us to take a particular side on an issue, it may challenge our objectivity. However, sociologists have from the time of Gouldner's (1970) views on the myths of value-free society understood that our objectivity is likely to be limited regardless of our involvement or lack thereof.

In brief, I will argue that social activism is a legitimate activity for sociology and should be encouraged rather than discouraged by the profession. I will also argue that the history of the discipline indicates that it originated with a very applied activist orientation.

SOCIAL ACTIVISM

Sociology originated out of an attempt to solve a wide variety of social pathologies which included crime, poverty, homelessness, and a multitude of related social ills that were associated with the Industrial Revolution and various political revolutions in 19th Century Europe. These were problems of the streets and slums and not of isolated research laboratories.

Many of our founding fathers were social activists. Comte regarded "what you ought to be as more important than what is" (Goode 1984, p. 13). He intended the social laws that he set out to elaborate to form the basis for a new social order. His view of the science of society was a kind of secular religion with sociology as a high priest.

Marx, much like Comte, believed that what "ought to be and what will be" are more or less identical (Goode 1984, p. 14). Marx carefully elaborated his views on what society ought to be and his ideas had a major influence in the development of sociological theory. Durkheim believed that the study and understanding of society would make it a more reasonable and saner place to live. All these earlier thinkers share the view that studying society would represent a step toward improving it (Goode 1984).

As late as the 1950s, the University of Chicago's Sociology Department had a very applied focus in their research endeavors. They conducted numerous studies by going directly to the community to delineate urban patterns and urban problems.

In my opinion the development of the discipline of sociology has moved further and further away from its roots --from action sociology--in the last 40 to 50 years. As our research techniques became more sophisticated, we have tended to idealize and honor pure research carried out in a laboratory setting and to question more critically social research that took place in the streets. In the process, leaders of the profession appeared to want to discourage any activity or presentation of self that would identify us with social reform or social change.

The transformation of sociology from applied to pure science was carried out under the guise of scientific neutrality. The scientific neutrality argument maintains that if we care about what we study, we can't possibly be objective and therefore our research findings are suspect. In my opinion we have carried the scientific neutrality argument to an illogical and irrational extreme. Medical researchers genuinely want to find a cure for cancer, AIDS, diabetes, and a host of other infirmities. We do not automatically assume because the medical researcher wants to find a cure for cancer, generally cares about the future welfare of a large number of sick people, that she/he can't possibly be objective in carrying out the research. One could make the exact opposite argument. It is precisely because the researcher does care about the welfare of a large number of affected persons and thus seeks a cure for a life threatening disease that he/she will be even more careful to develop a research design that is more objective and free of any possible subjective error. His/her earnest commitment to the solution of a problem will make him/her more, rather than less, careful in conducting the research objectively.

Similarly, we in sociology should not automatically assume that a value commitment to improving the social system on the part of the researcher is necessarily going to make him/her any less objective. These very values could make us more careful in developing our research designs because we do genuinely want to find intervention strategies that work best in solving basic social problems. We do not assume that black sociologists could not possibly do research on civil rights because they care and could not therefore be objective. We do not assume that women could not write scientifically about feminism and the feminist movement because they have a stake in the outcome and therefore could not possibly be objective. Given current research methods and techniques, there is no necessary reason that any scientist could not conduct research on any topic in which he or she might be subjectively involved and at the same time control his/her personal bias. Having a genuine concern for the subject matter which you are investigating can make you a more dedicated and productive scientist rather than a subjectively biased and unreliable one.

Social Activism and the Utility of Knowledge

In 1917, Lenin broke off working on The State and Revolution, explaining that it was more pleasant and useful to go through the experience of a revolution than to write about it (Oppenheimer 1966). I know that not everyone would agree with Lenin's statement that it is more fun to be involved in a revolution than to write about it. I would argue, however, that involvement in social change activities brings to the sociologist greater knowledge, sensitivity and skill in dealing with the subject matter being investigated. This is true whether he/she is researching, writing, or advocating in favor of change.

Unger (1983) notes how sterile scientific research can become when conducted in a purely laboratory setting when she states:

> Context stripping is the term used by critics of a pure ex-
> perimental approach to psychological research to refer to

(1) the idea that science develops without influence from the surrounding cultural environment and (2) the tendency of laboratory experiments to become sterile, because the control of the extraneous variables leaves little room for insight into how things operate in the natural environment (p. 215).

Unger's (1986) criticism of carefully controlled laboratory experiments of individual and social phenomena is that they result in pure truth which may well be of little use since it is so void of critical variables operating in a more natural environment. The implication is that the carefully controlled laboratory experiments give us pure truth but it is of little use.

While I have argued that the researchers' subjective involvement in her/his subject matter need not destroy her/his objectivity, others have gone much further asserting that these researchers raise the most critical questions. Samuelson (1978) believes scientists doing research on topics that they are subjectively involved in and care about results in different and more crucial questions being raised by the researchers. Samuelson continues that social psychologists after World War II were much more likely in their research to focus on racial prejudice (the perception of differences) within the dominant population rather than racial difference, per se (assuming the source of the difference lies within the groups) which had been the focus of scientists prior to World War II. Samuelson also notes that this shift parallels the entry into the profession of a large number of social psychologists with diverse ethnic origins. Similarly, Unger (1986) notes that a shift from the study of sex differences to the study of sexism took place as an increasing number of active female researchers entered the field.

Other researchers have noted the numerous advantages of the sociologist being actively involved in community intervention and social change. In the Topeka, Kansas project, Key (1965) and other scientists were placed in an urban community where residents were being forced to relocate in order to assist with a crisis. Key believed that as a scientist he learned more about the plight and problems of lower class Americans than he might ever have learned had he not lived with them in their community. He states:

> Personally my greatest satisfaction has come in develop-
> ing a situation where research and clinical work are func-
> tionally integrated, where clinicians are concerned about
> research issues and researchers are sensitive to clinical
> issues and neither demands sacrifices in the quality of the
> other (p. 115).

The point made is that being actively involved in community intervention projects, in social movements and social change activities sharpens our insights and enriches our understanding of the human condition. If pure laboratory work strips concepts as Unger (1986) suggests, then research and activist projects that take place on the streets should enrich them. As Unger (1986) observed, many sociologists of an earlier time were more committed to applied investigations than their successors and were, therefore, less likely to lose sight of the importance of the relationship between the individual and society.

The value of social activism to the scientist and the scientific community in building knowledge and addressing real social problems is perhaps best noted by Kirk, quoted by Oppenheimer et al. (1966) when he stated:

> Within the last five years a relatively small group of social
> scientists (historians such as Staughton Lynd, Howard Zinn
> and Auguste Meier; psychiatrists such as Robert Coles;
> and a few sociologists from the more traditional "race rela-
> tions" field) have become involved in the movement not
> only as a citizen but also as scientists bringing with them
> their special know-how. Those of us involved have not lim-
> ited ourselves to demonstrating and picketing nor have we
> been content with research divorced from the immediate
> problems of the movement. We have gone further to act as
> consultants to the movement, negotiators and interpreters
> for it, teachers and trainers within it, and we have in other
> ways applied our specialties to its day-to-day problems.
> Hence the term "sociologist-activist" (p. 136).

Being a sociologist activist is not only a legitimate professional role which facilitates our knowledge and understanding of our subject matter; it also opens up a great variety of applied community roles which our colleagues and students are well qualified to fill.

Professionalization and Social Activism

A number of past studies have indicated that the more professionally-oriented members of a profession are the most likely to be involved in social activism. Reeser and Epstein (1990) observed that social workers work endless hours helping the poor adjust to their environment. Ultimately the more professionally-oriented realize that the way they can be most helpful to their clients is to attack the causes of poverty and to try to change the conditions in society that produce a deprived class. They argue that activism does not disappear with professionalization; instead it is expected to increase.

Coles (1969), Corwin (1970) and Cox (1980) found that the more professionally-oriented public school teachers were most likely to be active and militant in their attempts to improve their working conditions These studies contended that increasing alienation among teachers often results from the greater professionalization of teaching and the concomitant rigidity of the organizational structure of most school systems. Throughout the United States the long range trend has moved toward upgrading teacher training programs. Teachers are experiencing longer and more strengthened educational programs in both subject matter and pedagogical technique. Thus, teachers are becoming more capable of exercising a domain of professional expertise and are demanding a new role for themselves which includes greater professional autonomy and a larger voice in the school system decision making process. When the more professionally-oriented teachers find school boards unwilling to grant them what they believe to be their legitimate role in education, then they are willing to back up their demands with militant action if necessary.

In terms of the individual characteristics of professional activism Tygart (1984), in a study of college professors, found that activist subjects almost always exhibited a world view that was 1) low in authoritarianism, 2) low in dogmatism, 3) highly efficacious, 4) low in traditional religiosity, 5) high in moral autonomy, and 6) politically liberal. Moral autonomy showed the greatest multivariate effect for activism. Moral autonomy is the strongest predictor of activism because, in addition to measuring whether social change is perceived to be possible, it measures whether the individual believes that it is morally incumbent on her/him to attempt to bring about social change.

The conclusion of all these studies is that there is nothing inconsistent or incongruent in professionals becoming actively involved in efforts to bring about social change. On the contrary, the greater the professional orientation the greater the likelihood of being actively involved in movements aimed at changing and improving society in some way.

AUTOBIOGRAPHICAL EXAMPLES OF ACTIVISM

Summary of the Struggle Between Teachers Union and School Administration

In 1963, I was teaching in the public schools in Danville, Illinois, and working evenings and summers on a master's degree in sociology at Indiana State University. In November of 1963, the Danville school board floated a bond issue before the voters to raise money to continue to operate the schools as they had been in the past. The board claimed they were operating at a deficit and simply had to have more money. The voters turned down the bond issue. I don't think the voters were dissatisfied with the schools. In my opinion, the voters were making a statement about taxes, more than they were about public education *per se*. Regardless of the reason, the bond issue was rejected, the school board had to begin to look for places to cut spending.

In February, the board announced their plan to cut the budget. They were planning to eliminate all extra curricular activities. The schools doors were to be closed at 3:15. There was to be no football, basketball, track, or baseball. No dramatic club plays, no orchestra, or band presentations after 3:15 in the afternoon. No coaching salaries, no expensive football equipment, etc. By cutting the extra curricular activities, the board believed that they could live within their budget. This plan of action, which had been voted on and approved by the board, lasted about two weeks. The community and its leaders objected vehemently to this plan. From the Chamber of Commerce to the parents there was a public outcry against this plan of belt tightening. Two weeks later, at their March board meeting, they rescinded the budget cutting plan and announced at that time the only way they could live within their budget was to cut teachers' salaries. Since contracts had already gone out for the next school year, the board began to prepare to cut teachers' salaries for the following year.

At that time I was earning $4,700 a year as a teacher, going to graduate school at night, and working part time in a gas station to make ends meet. I had been for sometime a loyal member of the National Education Association. I went to the next Danville Teachers Association meeting (the local branch of the NEA) and asked them what course of action they planned to take to stop the board from cutting teachers' salaries. The leaders shrugged their shoulders and said we have talked to the board but they are adamant and we don't know what to do.

Realizing that the local teacher's association was going to do nothing about the proposed salary cuts, approximately a dozen of the teachers, of which I was one, began to meet and discuss what different courses of action we might take to prevent this from happening. In May of 1963, we formed a local branch of the American Federation of Teachers. By September, we had over 150 members in a school system which employed 400 people including teachers and administrators. We engaged in a variety of activities designed primarily to stop the board from reducing the salaries of, in our opinion, an already underpaid teaching staff.

As a young sociology student working on a master's degree at Indiana State University, I was taking classes from Dr. Conyers in Social Stratification and Social Change. I was being introduced to the concepts of social power, social classes, elites, functionalism, conflict theory, and a host of related ideas. While I was learning about these concepts from an academic perspective, the teacher's struggle certainly reinforced and embellished these terms in my mind. They had considerably greater meaning for me after I understood how they operated in the real world than I would have ever had from just reading them in a textbook. Moreover, I believe that my sociological education made me more aware of how the teacher struggle was affecting the power balance between diverse groups in the community. Sociologists are taught to evaluate and critique social class and power relationships in the community and society. In my opinion, this background and perspective allowed me to assist the teachers' union in making decisions that would ultimately prove most effective in protecting the interests of the teachers.

The struggle between the school administration and the teachers' union lasted for two years. During that time, the administration attempted several times to intimidate the teachers' union but failed to do so. A few of these attempts at intimidation included: transferring a high school teacher to a third grade position as a means of punishment; threatening to fire teachers on trumped up charges; doing away with a junior high music program in order to get rid of a teacher; and visiting teachers' classes for two and three weeks at a time in an attempt to find an excuse to dismiss them. Doing away with the music program in order to fire a teacher was the only one of these tactics that succeeded. At the end of a two year struggle the teachers, instead of receiving a pay cut, got an $800 raise. The superintendent and assistant superintendent of schools left the district and took other jobs.

I would argue that my involvement as an activist attempting to bring about change made me a better sociologist than I would have been otherwise. I certainly had a better understanding of social power and conflict than I would have gained from just the classroom. From that experience, I ultimately went on to write a dissertation and publish several articles on teacher militancy. In reflecting on the experience the only question I have is--do all learning experiences have to be so painful? (For a detailed description of the teachers struggle, see appendix A.)

Summary of an Environmental Fight

Casually reading a newspaper in the summer of 1988, I was inadvertently lead to being involved in another activist movement. From January of 1988, I had been reading about a major chemical company's plans to build a paint factory in Terre Haute. Because of the promise of 300 jobs, practically every citizen and community leader seemed to be welcoming the new venture. In August of 1988, the representative of the chemical company who had been selling the public on a paint factory announced: "Oh, by the way, we also plan to build a toxic waste incinerator and toxic waste landfill and to haul in waste from our plants across the U.S. for disposal." Shortly thereafter, I ran across an article in the *Evansville Courier* (September 18, 1988) that indicated that the residents of Evansville, Indiana had asked the company not to locate in their community because they considered the proposed toxic waste facility to be a threat to the health of the community. Basically, I was having trouble understanding why Terre Haute political leaders were welcoming a company their neighboring community was rejecting. Being curious, I called the *Evansville Courier* and asked for the name of the leader who had opposed the paint factory and toxic waste facility. I was given the name of John Blair. I called Blair and asked why the residents of Evansville were opposed to the proposed facility. He pointed out a series of past actions taken by the company that convinced them that they had an extremely bad environmental and labor track record and should not be allowed to locate in their community. Moreover, they believed the proposed incinerator and landfill would be bad for the health of the community. (For a detailed description of a few of the past events regarding the chemical company's environmental and labor record, see Appendix C.)

After some discussion among neighbors during August of 1988, a small neighborhood meeting was planned to determine if we would or would not oppose a paint factory and toxic waste facility being located in our neighborhood. We were to meet at the Pimento Firehouse at 7:00 p.m. on September 15. An hour before the meeting the mayor, the county commissioners, and a public relations representative of the chemical company showed up and stood outside the doorway of the firehouse. If the mayor's intent was to intimidate the citizens, it failed. The citizens filed past the politicians and into the meeting room. Mr. Wilson, a resident from Evansville, spoke on why their community had asked the chemical company not to locate there. A heated debate between the citizens of the community and the political leaders on the advantages and disadvantages of the proposed facility ensued. The debate polarized the two sides and convinced citizens living in the community that the proposed facility would be bad for the community.

News of the firehouse debate spread rapidly throughout the community. A group titled Citizens for a Clean County (CCC) was organized against the proposed facility and within weeks had grown to a membership of over 500 persons.

The strategy of the CCC in conducting the campaign against the toxic waste facility was initially an educational and public information one. A number of experts on toxic waste facilities from across the country were brought in to give the community their assessment and opinion of what the advantages and disadvantages were of locating such a facility in the community. Public meetings were held allowing any interested citizen to hear the views of the scientists. The two speakers that were the most knowledgeable and articulate on this subject were Hugh Kaufman, of the Environmental Protection Agency, and Paul Connett, a chemist from St. Lawrence University, who is also on the advisory board for environmental matters to the U.S. Congress. Both Kaufman and Connett advised the citizens not to let a toxic waste facility be built in their community. It would be an environmental catastrophe that definitely would not be good for the community and the health of its people. They both pointed out that all landfills, no matter how thick the liners, will eventually leak and pollute the underground water. Similarly, no matter how carefully engineered, all incinerators emit a variety of toxic emissions, pollutants, and gasses. Moreover, metals are never fully destroyed by the incinerator. They accumulate over time on the surrounding foliage for miles around and ultimately make it into the food chain threatening the health of the people who eat the food. As a result of Kaufman, Connett, and a variety of the local scientists' warnings, the public began to be concerned and restless about allowing the toxic waste facility to be built. At one point a poll indicated that 67 percent of the public was opposed to the plan to build the toxic waste facility. The political leaders were undaunted, however, and moved ahead in their plans to sell land in the industrial park to the chemical company for whatever use.

In December of 1988, as required by law, the Economic Development Commission held a public hearing to discuss the sale of the land in the industrial park to the chemical company. The Economic Development Commission had been established by the Vigo County political leaders as the group responsible for selling land in the Industrial park. The hearing began at 7:30 p.m. Moreover, the chemical company was so confident of winning the debate, that they paid to have the hearing aired live on a local television station. Proponents of selling the land to the chemical company were allowed to speak first. They talked for three hours (assuming perhaps that most of the opponents to the sale would give up and go home before their time to speak came). The opponents took the floor at approximately 10:30 p.m. that evening and spoke against the plan until 5:00 a.m. the following morning. The meeting had to be reconvened on two other evenings. Ultimately, the opponents gave over thirty hours of testimony against selling the land in the industrial park for the purpose of building a toxic waste facility.

Regardless of the arguments presented at the public hearing, the Economic Development Commission announced at the closing of the hearing their intentions to sell the land to the chemical company for the building of the toxic waste facility.

During the next two years, there were two lawsuits filed by citizens' groups opposed to the construction of the toxic waste facility. Both of these suits were intended to prevent the county from selling land in the industrial park to the chemical company.

The first lawsuit was filed by CCC in March of 1989. The suit challenged the neutrality of the Economic Development Commission. In April of 1989, Judge Nardi found in favor of the CCC suit pointing out that three of the five Economic Development Commissioners would gain financially if land in the industrial park was sold to the chemical company.

In July of 1989, the Vigo County Commissioners announced their intention not to create a new and truly neutral Economic Development Commission which Judge Nardi had recommended in his ruling. Instead, they declared the land in the industrial park surplus and put it up for public bid planning to sell the land directly to the chemical company.

In September of 1989, CCC merged with three other citizens' groups to form The Environmental Rights Coalition (TERC).

Originally the land in the industrial park had been purchased by the Vigo County Commissioners from the federal government. In April of 1990, TERC filed a second lawsuit attempting to void the Government Services

Administration's (GSA) initial sale of the land to Vigo County. The TERC lawyer claimed the land was sold without public bid which is required by law and without an environmental impact study, which is required if there is a floodplain or wetlands on the property (both of these conditions were present on the land). Moreover, the citizen's lawsuit claimed that the federal government and the chemical company had formed a partnership in the land sale and that the county was merely a conduit.

Confronted with another lawsuit challenging the sale of land in the industrial park and perhaps months in court, the chemical company announced that they were no longer interested in a midwest location. At this point the citizens' efforts to block the construction of the toxic waste facility was complete. The citizens had won their battle against the political and business leaders of the community. Fifteen months later in December 1991, Judge Tinder refused to void the GSA sale of federal land to Vigo County. Since the chemical company was no longer interested in purchasing property in the industrial park, the loss of this lawsuit was anticlimactic.

The Vigo County political leaders' attempts to intimidate the leaders of the citizens groups opposed to the construction of the toxic waste facility was one of the most significant events of the struggle. George Pring and Penelope Canan (1992) have carefully outlined and described what they have defined as "Strategic Lawsuits Against Public Participation" (SLAPP suits). The strategy of business and political leaders in filing SLAPP suits is to scare the leaders of citizens groups from challenging any new development or construction projects. It makes no difference whether the citizens are challenging these projects because of environmental, financial and other reasons. The goal is to frighten them from questioning any proposed course of action or project. The threat to the citizen is that they will be tied up in court for months and perhaps years at great expense to themselves even if they win in court. Should they lose in court they may have to sacrifice all their assets and properties to pay the damages the lawsuits against them have charged.

In June of 1990, the Vigo County Commissioners filed a lawsuit against Peggy Berry as President of TERC and Harold Cox as Vice President of TERC asking for legal fees and lost revenues of several hundred thousand dollars. This lawsuit was an attempt to frighten Berry and Cox as leaders of TERC into dropping the second lawsuit the citizens had filed against the GSA.

In June of 1992 (eighteen months after the TERC lawsuit against the GSA had been decided in court and one day before TERC lawyers planned to file their formal civil rights suit against the Vigo County Commissioners in behalf of Berry and Cox), the commissioners dropped their SLAPP suit against Berry and Cox. (For a detailed description of the environmental struggle, see Appendix C.)

Clark and Wilson (1961) argue that there are basically three incentives that any organization can offer to attract and hold the support of its members. These are material incentives such as money, dividends, and goods; solidary incentives such as prestige, status, respect, and a sense of belonging; and purposive incentives such as the ability to bring about what members perceive to be needed changes in the social system. While any organization offers a multiplicity of incentives to its members organizations may be categorized as material, solidary, or purposive according to the principal incentive offered to its members.

Clark and Wilson (1961) argue that executives will usually avoid heavy reliance on purposive incentives because they produce less stable and less flexible organizations:

> It is difficult to maintain consistent efforts, for, to be effective, purposes must be popularized and made widely known to contributors. But this very popularization makes failure to achieve purposes more obvious to contributors, which in turn produces restlessness and dissatisfaction (p. 150).

Nonetheless, Clark and Wilson (1961) maintain that there are circumstances under which organizations may be expected to rely heavily upon purposive incentives. These include: 1) in their formative stages most organizations necessarily rely on purposive incentives since they have few material and solidary incentives to offer; and 2) any organization may rely on purposes when coping with crises, i.e., interruption in the expected normal flow of incentives and rewards for belonging. Wilson (1973) contends that commitment to purpose is especially salient among groups lacking more tangible resources and material incentives. Freeman (1983) developed a model for analyzing social movement organizations based upon an understanding of the resources available at a given time, the limits of those resources and the way in which the resources are deployed.

As a result of my involvement in the environmental struggle that took place in my community, I have a much better understanding of problems involved in holding purposive groups together. Members of purposive groups are predicted to become restless when they feel the group is not achieving its goals. As president of CCC and vice president of TERC, I spent considerably greater amounts of time, energy and effort stamping out fights and quarrels among our own membership than I ever did fighting with the opposition political leaders. As long as we were picketing, debating the other side, holding public hearings, or in court the followers were involved and happy. However, this fight took place over four years and inevitably, there were weeks and sometimes months when we weren't in court and not much was actually taking place. During these lulls in the fight, people were frustrated--they had pent up hostility and anger about our inability to change the politicians' minds about this project. When they couldn't attack their political leaders, they attacked their own leaders for not doing enough to win the battle. I would not have the understanding and appreciation of the in-fighting and how difficult it is to hold purposive groups together had I not been involved in this struggle. Similarly, I have a much better understanding of the meaning of "community" than I would have ever had by merely reading the concept in a textbook. I saw large numbers of people expend enormous amounts of time, energy, effort, and money protecting their community from what they considered to be an environmental catastrophe. They spoke out at public hearings on the matter, they got over 5,000 signatures on petitions against the project, they picketed the court house on several occasions, raised over $200,000 primarily used for advertising and legal fees, and they went to court twice over the matter. They made a supreme effort to protect themselves and their community from what they considered to be an outside invasion. They were in my opinion dedicated people.

CONCLUSION

Accepting sociological activism as a legitimate professional role brings a number of benefits to our discipline. Inevitably, going to the streets, neighborhoods and communities to address social problems will increase our understanding of the problems and the critical variables related to them. Rather than concept stripping, as Unger (1986) identifies occurring in pure laboratory experiments, we will have concept enrichment in which we have a more complete understanding of the critical variables and their contribution to the problem. Inevitably, we will become aware of additional contributing factors to the problem that our current paradigms fail to include. We will have an entire picture of the issue rather than a narrow, partial, and often overly categorized one. In all probability, we will have a better understanding of how the critical variables interact. Finally, we would be in a position of completing the cycle of professional commitment which goes beyond the mere description of the problem and requires us to both recommend solutions to basic human problems and to work systematically to see that these solutions are implemented.

We would move away from the current elitist position that the only thing we train our students for is pure research in a laboratory setting. While pure research is a legitimate sociological role, there are numerous other ones that are equally valuable and would broaden the opportunities for members of the profession as well as enrich and enliven the discipline.

REFERENCES

Clark, Peter B. and James Q. Wilson. 1961. "Incentive Systems: A Theory of Organizations." *Administrative Sciences Quarterly* 2 (September): 129-150.

Cole, Stephen. 1969. *The Unionization of Teachers: A Case Study of the UFT.* New York: Praeger Publishers.

Corwin, Ronald. 1970. *Militant Professionalization.* New York: Appleton Century Crofts.

Cox, Harold. 1980. "Professional Orientation, Associational Membership and Teacher Militancy." *Sociological Inquiry* 50(1):57-64.

Evansville Courier (Evansville, Indiana), 18 September 1988.

Freeman, Jo. 1983. *Social Movements of the Sixties and Seventies*. New York: Longman.

Goode, Erich. 1984. *Sociology*. Englewood Cliffs, NJ: Prentice Hall.

Gouldner, Alvin. 1970. *The Coming Crisis in Sociology*. Basic Books.

Key, William. 1965. "Controlled Intervention and Directed Social Change." In *Sociology in Action*, 115-123. Edited by Arthur Shostak. 1965. Homewood, IL: Dorsey Press.

Morning Advocate (Baton Rouge), 11 September 1984.

Oppenheimer, Martin, Jonathan Freedman, Kurt Lang, and Jerome Kirk. 1966. In *Sociology in Action*, 135-141. Edited by Arthur Shostak. Homewood IL: Dorsey Press.

Pring, George W. and Penelope Canan. 1992. "Strategic Lawsuits Against Public Participation (SLAPPs): An Introduction for Bend, Bar, and By-standers." *University of Bridgeport Law Review* 12(4):937-962.

Reeser, Linda Cherrey and Erwin Epstein. 1990. *Professionalization and Activism in Social Work: The Sixties, The Eighties and the Future*. New York: Columbia University.

Samuelson, F. 1978. From "Race Psychology to the Studies in Prejudice: Some Observations on the Thematic Reversals in Social Psychology." *Journal of the History of the Behavioral Sciences* 14:265-278.

Tygart, C.E. 1984. "Moral Autonomy and Social-Political Activism Among the Faculty and Staff of a West Coast University." *Sociological Inquiry* 54:16-25.

Unger, Rhoda K. 1986. "Looking Toward the Future by Looking at the Past: Social Activism and Social History." *The Society for the Psychological Study of Social Issues.*

_____. 1983. "Through the Looking Glass: No Wonderland Yet! (The Reciprocal Relationship Between Methodology and Models of Reality)." *Psychology of Women Quarterly* 8:9-32.

Wilson, James Q. 1973. *Political Organization.* New York: Basic Books.

APPENDIX A

The following are just a few of the events I witnessed in the struggle between the teachers union and the administration of the Danville public schools.

1. A high school home economics teacher was transferred to a third grade classroom for asking the superintendent a question at a public meeting. The Teacher's Union filed a grievance in behalf of the teacher which six months later, after all other channels were exhausted, reached the school board. The board voted unanimously to uphold the superintendent's decision.

2. Late one Friday afternoon, an AFT member was called in by the assistant superintendent of schools and was told that the administration had found out that he had been arrested for a Halloween prank when he was a kid. He was told that if he didn't resign his job by Monday morning, he would be fired. After consulting an attorney, who found the superintendent's charges groundless, the teacher returned to work Monday morning and resumed his duties.

3. The superintendent of schools did away with the junior high music program so that he could fire a tenured music teacher that was raising too many questions about the superintendent's actions.

4. The assistant superintendent of schools came to visit some of the teachers union members' classrooms and would stay as long as two weeks straight trying to find some excuse to fire them. (They never succeeded in getting one teacher fired for being incompetent.) They did get the junior high music

teacher dismissed by doing away with the program.

5. Two school board members who had been elected with the assistance of the local labor unions consistently voted for the superintendent's policies and, thereby, against the teacher's union. They were not reelected the next time they ran.

APPENDIX B

A few of the past events regarding the chemical company's environmental and labor record included the following.

1. A fine of $66,700 in 1986 by the Louisiana Department of Environmental Quality for the unauthorized release of 16,000 pounds of Toluene into the atmosphere. The Department of Environmental Quality charged that more than 55 hours elapsed from the time the company discovered the leak until they shut down and repaired the faulty equipment.

2. In 1988, the company was fined $ 1.3 million by the Environmental Protection Agency for illegally importing and processing restricted chemical substances.

3. In 1984, Louisiana's *Morning Advocate* (September 11, 1984) reported the company's release of large amounts of hydrochloric acid into the ground had contaminated the ground water at 16 of the company's sites.

4. Labor problems: For a number of years, the workers at one of the company's facilities had been locked out of the plant as a means of ending the labor contract negotiations. As a result of this lockout, in 1985 the company was labeled by the national AFL-CIO as one of the top ten anti-worker companies in the United States.

APPENDIX C

The following is a list of just a few of the activities that occurred in the fight over the proposed toxic waste facility in the next four years:

1. In 1986, Vigo County (Indiana) bought 1,476 acres of land from the federal government at approximately $100 per acre (extremely low agricultural land value).

2. In 1986, Vigo County declared the land to be an industrial park and sought buyers. Established an Economic Development Commission of 5 members to sell the land in the industrial park.

3. In March of 1988, a representative of a German chemical company came to town proposing to buy the entire industrial park to build a paint factory. He spoke to any interested local group for the next five or six months promising industrial development and 300 jobs initially with more to come later.

4. In August of 1988, after 5 months of promising a paint factory and 300 jobs, the chemical company spokesman announced that they also plan to build a toxic waste incinerator, create a landfill and haul in toxic waste from their factories all over the United States for disposal.

5. Upon hearing of the proposed toxic waste facility, local land owners became concerned. In September of 1988, Citizens for a Clean County (CCC) was formed, with Harold Cox as president. CCC invited representatives of the scientific community to advise them of advantages and disadvantages of a major toxic waste facility being located in their community.

> A. In October of 1988, Hugh Kaufman of the Environmental Protection Agency warned the community of the health hazards and environmental problems that such a toxic waste facility creates wherever they are located.

> B. In November 1988, Paul Connett, a chemist who is on the advisory board for environmental matters for U.S. Congress, warned the community of the imminent health risks for the community of such a venture.

> C. Both Kaufman and Connett advised the citizens: "Do not let them build a toxic waste facility in your community. It will be an

environmental catastrophe for the community."

D. Several local scientists from Indiana State University shared this prognosis.

6. In December of 1988, as required by law, the Vigo County Economic Development Commission held a public hearing to discuss the sale of the land to the chemical company.

A. Proponents of sale of the land went first and talked for 3 hours. (Assuming, perhaps that most of the opponents will give up and go home before their turn to speak comes.)

B. The meeting began at 7:30 p.m. one evening and lasted until 5 a.m. the following morning.

C. Had to be continued two other times.

D. Ultimately the opponents gave over 30 hours of testimony against the proposed facility.

E. Regardless of the overwhelming community opposition, the Economic Development Commission at the conclusion of the hearings announced their intention to sell the land to the chemical company for the proposed paint factory and toxic waste facility.

7. In March of 1989, CCC filed a suit against the Economic Development Commission claiming that they are not a neutral body.

8. In April of 1989, after a court hearing, Judge Nardi abolishes the Economic Development Commission ruling that 3 of the 5 Commissioners stood to gain financially if the land in the industrial park was sold to the chemical company.

9. In July of 1989, the County Commissioners declined Judge Nardi's recommendation to create a truly neutral Economic Development Commission. Instead they declared the land surplus and put it up for public bid. The

intent of this was to allow the chemical company to purchase the land directly from the county without going through an Economic Development Commission.

10. In September of 1989, Citizens for a Clean County, The East-siders, Mothers Against Toxic Chemical Hazards, and Majority of One merge to form The Environmental Rights Coalition (TERC). Peggy Berry was elected President and Harold Cox was elected Vice President.

11. In April of 1990, TERC filed a suit against the Government Services Administration for not following its own rules when they originally sold land in the industrial park to the County. The rules violations cited include:

> A. The land was sold without a public bid which is required by law.

> B. Although both a floodplain and wetlands are located on the land and the potential for hazardous waste to be located there, the G.S.A. did not conduct an environmental impact study as required by their own rules. The G.S.A. maintained that a "FONSI" (a statement they perceived no significant environmental impact was enough) and that no environmental impact study was necessary.

12. TERC lawsuit also claimed the Federal Government and the chemical company had formed a partnership in the land sale and the county was merely used as a conduit. Claimed misuse of HUD and Department of Labor funds were involved. Judge refused to allow the attorney to present arguments of a partnership between federal government and the chemical company. Judge allowed only arguments over procedural violations.

13. In May 1990, Vigo County Commissioners filed a brief asking for a dismissal of TERC case against the G.S.A.

14. In June 1990, Vigo County filed a lawsuit against Peggy Berry and Harold Cox claiming that they maliciously interfered in county business, asking for legal fees and lost revenues of several hundred thousand dollars to be paid by Berry and Cox.

15. In September of 1990, Judge Tinder denies Vigo County's motion to dismiss TERC's case against G.S.A. and agreed to hear the case.

16. One week later the chemical company announced that it is no longer interested in locating in the midwest. An irate Mayor Pete Chalos suggested on evening television that jobless people "go after these environmentalists." Richard Wangelin, a local M.D., and Harold Cox, who have been identified as the leaders of the environmentalists, received life-threatening phone calls. Cox experienced vandalism as a window is broken out of his truck. A 38- year old unemployed white male was arrested by the state police and charges were filed related to the threats on Wangelin and Cox. The defendant pleaded guilty, was sentenced to jail and almost immediately released on parole for "jail shock." He is currently on probation.

17. In December of 1990, Berry and Cox filed a Tort Claim in Federal Court which tells the Vigo County Commissioners that they will be filing a civil rights suit against them claiming the commissioners were trying to stifle free speech of its citizens as well as the citizens' right to petition their government.

18. In December of 1991, the court ruled against TERC's suit against the G.S.A. and refused to void the sale of land to Vigo County.

19. In June of 1992, the Vigo County Commissioners dropped their suit against Berry and Cox with the understanding that Berry and Cox would not file a Civil Rights Suit against the County Commissioners.

Harold G. Cox

1935 -

Harold Cox, President of the Society for Applied
Sociology 1992-93 was born and reared in Danville,
Illinois. Received a bachelor's degree in history at
Eastern Illinois University in 1960. Received a
master' degree in sociology from Indiana State Uni-
versity in 1964. After receiving a master's degree in sociology, was asked
to join the faculty at Indiana State. While a faculty member at ISU, he
began working on a Ph.D. at Indiana University, which he received in 1972.

Harold has taught courses in introductory sociology, the family, statistics,
occupations and professions, and social gerontology. His research has focused primarily in the areas of occupations and professions and gerontology. His Ph.D. dissertation addressed the widespread teacher strikes and
teacher militancy of the 1960s and was titled "Bureaucracy, Alienation and
Teachers Organizations." Following the completion of the dissertation, he
later did a study of retirement adjustment and thereafter began to focus
most of his research in the area of gerontology. He has written and published widely in both his areas of interest. He is the editor of a book title
Aging, which is published by Duskin Publishing Group and is in its 11th
edition. He is also author of a textbook titled *Later Life: The Realties of
Aging* published by Prentice Hall which came out in the 4th edition in 1996.

Much of the teaching, writing and research that Cox has done has been in
the field of aging. Gerontology is a multi-disciplinary and very applied field.
From medicine to psychiatry to social gerontology, the emphasis in research
on aging has always had an applied thrust. The government policy makers
and planners from the 1960s on were confronted with an ever growing
number of older Americans needing and demanding government services.
Governmental agencies and funding institutions wanted answers to how to
successfully serve the needs of older Americans. They wanted research
that was applied in orientation and gave answers to what policies and programs would best serve older Americans. Gerontologists have focused the

bulk of their research on the applied practical and policy making implications of their work as they addressed the issues confronting an ever increasing population of older Americans.

Harold Cox, Al Bhak, Alex Boros, and Gurmeet Sekhon, in the late 1970s, were sharing a meal at a meeting in Cleveland, Ohio of the North Central Sociological Association. The four friends were complaining about the fact that the applied sections of the NCSA were always on the last day when most of the audience had departed for home. This led to the formation of the Society for Applied Sociology. Alex Boros took the lead in organizing the Society for Applied Sociology and was joined by Mark and Joyce Iutcovich, James Hougland, Harold Cox and others who served on the board of directors during the early years of the organization's development. In 1983, Joyce Iutcovich and Harold became co-editors of *The Journal of Applied Sociology* and remained in that capacity until 1990. Under Harold's direction, Indiana State University hosted the 1986 meeting of the Society for Applied Sociology. In 1992/93, Harold Cox was President of the SAS. He is currently serving as Publications Chair for the organization.

A part of Harold's applied work includes working as a consultant to governmental and social service agencies. During the summers of 1974 and 1975, he served as a consultant to the Indiana Commission on Aging and Aged to assist in the development of their Grants Management and Service Delivery System. From 1976-80, he served as a consultant to Indiana Commission of Aging and Aged to assist in the development of educational training programs throughout the state. Harold served on the Advisory Council of the Indiana Commission of Aging and Aged from 1976-1991. He has also served as President of the Vigo County Council on Aging from 1978 to the present and on the Area Agency on Aging Advisory Board from 1986 to 1996. In 1976 Harold initiated the Master's Program in Social Gerontology at Indiana State University. In addition to these activities, Cox was one of the leaders in his community from 1988-92 of an environmental fight to stop a major chemical company from locating a toxic waste incinerator in his community. This led to his presidential address on the responsibility of applied sociologists to include social activism in pursuit of change as a legitimate activity for the sociology profession.

10

Giving Voice To the Public: Survey Research, Applied Sociology, and Public Policy*

JAMES G. HOUGLAND, JR.
University of Kentucky

Throughout the history of survey research, disagreement has existed as to its value for public policy. Those who work with social surveys are aware of limitations involving question wording and other technical points as well as possible distortions in result interpretation. Despite these problems, it is argued that survey research--when carefully executed and presented--can become an effective voice (although only one of several voices) as decisions are being made. For these positive results to occur, sociologists must be committed to talking to a variety of interested parties as studies are being designed and as results become available, to insuring that results are stated in terms that can be understood by nonsociologists, and to identifying important topics for research even if they happen to be unfashionable.

Survey researchers and other sociologists who rely on the cooperation of members of the general public for their data often confront reluctant and even hostile respondents. Because it is not obvious to some of our chosen respondents that their participation in our research will lead to benefits that justify their investment of time, it is useful to reflect on the importance of survey research and, by extension, applied social research in all its forms.

While I attempt to develop a case for the importance of applied social research, I do not mean to imply that respondents or other research subjects should be forced to subordinate their well-being to the convenience of an applied sociology juggernaut. One need only recall the Tuskegee medical research team who wanted to observe the various stages of disease and withheld penicillin from a group of black men with syphilis--without their informed consent--to realize that scientists are capable of trampling over

* *Presidential Address, Seventh Annual Meeting of the Society for Applied Sociology, Denver, Colorado, October 20-22, 1989. Copyright, Society for Applied Sociology. Reprinted with permission from the **Journal of Applied Sociology**, Volume 7, 1990.*

the rights of their subjects. However, I do mean to imply that inappropriate attempts to discourage social research can have unfortunate and damaging effects on the larger social order.

Because I am most heavily involved in survey research, I will use that "industry" as the source for most of my examples, but I will make some attempt to generalize to other forms of research.

Classic Positions on the Usefulness of Survey Research

As a starting point, we might consider the early thinking of Archibald Crossley, who said in 1937:

> Scientific polling makes it possible within two or three days at moderate expense for the entire nation to work hand in hand with its legislative representatives, on laws which affect our daily lives. Here is the long-sought key to "Government by the people" (quoted in J. Converse 1987, p.122).

Crossley's optimistic view was shared by George Gallup, but it has never had everyone's agreement. In 1926, the 23rd Annual Meeting Of Experimental Psychologists passed a resolution stating:

> Resolved, that this meeting deplores the increasing practice of collecting administrative or supposedly scientific data by way of questionnaires; and that the meeting deplores especially the practice under which graduate students undertake research by sending questionnaires to professional psychologists (quoted in Ruckmick 1930, p.34).

Writing in the 1930 volume of Journal of Applied Psychology, Ruckmick expressed concern with "the promiscuous use of this form of inquiry" (1930, p.33-34) and noted that:

> At present the questionnaire seems to have considerable vogue in some disciplines, like education, sociology, and religious education which appear to be still on the

prescientific level. It may be that as experimental procedures develop the questionnaire type of investigation is
gradually cast off for better methods and that the maturity
of a science can be measured inversely by the number of
questionnaires which it sponsors (1930, p.41).

More recently, American Sociological Association President Herbert Gans
declared:

Mindlessness is grounding the analysis of a complicated
phenomenon on survey questions without any idea how
respondents understood the question (1989, p.10).

(He expressed concern about inappropriate uses of other methodologies as
well.)

Limitations of Survey Research

In view of these attacks from the outside, I regret to say that few if any
serious survey researchers would accept Crossley's statement without qualification. Those of us who try to develop questions to which respondents can
provide unbiased answers are well aware of the difficulties of doing so. For
example, a variety of polls conducted over the past decade have found
considerable support for restriction of smoking in public places. Perlstadt
and Holmes (1987), however, have shown how two surveys commissioned
by the public relations firm representing the Tobacco Institute produced
very different results by beginning the surveys by asking respondents to
agree or disagree with two statements:

"There is too much government in people's lives."

"Government should not be in the business of regulating private, personal
behavior."

and then by violating common standards involving balanced response
options and item rotation.

Even if no problems are caused by question wording, order effects, or other matters under the survey researcher's control, public opinion may have been manipulated by officeholders or others. Consider responses to the following three items, all of which were included on general population telephone surveys conducted by the Survey Research Center of the University of Kentucky:

1. From a statewide Kentucky survey conducted December 1988:

> There has...been a lot of talk about whether holiday decorations on government property should include a Nativity scene. Some say that Nativity scenes should not be on government property because this violates the separation of church and state. Others say that it is all right for Nativity scenes to be on government property because they are part of the historical celebration of Christmas. What is your view? Should Nativity scenes be on government property, or not?

Yes, should be	82%
No, should not be	11%
Don't know	7%

2. From a Lexington-Fayette County survey conducted July 1989:

> President Bush has suggested an amendment to the United States Constitution that would make it punishable by law to burn or otherwise desecrate an American flag as a means of political expression. Do you strongly favor, somewhat favor, somewhat oppose, or strongly oppose such an amendment to the constitution?

Strongly favor	48%
Somewhat favor	13%
Somewhat oppose	11%
Strongly oppose	23%
Don't know	5%

3. From a Lexington-Fayette County survey conducted February 1989:

Adults have the right to buy and see magazines, movies, and videocassettes that have sexually explicit content if they choose.

Strongly agree	46%
Somewhat agree	36%
Somewhat disagree	7%
Strongly disagree	11%
Don't know	1%

Concentrating only on answers to the first two of these questions could lead one to believe that the public is ready to support the state's endorsement of some types of religious expression over others or to penalize certain forms of expression that currently enjoy protection under the First Amendment, but responses to the third question provide a very different view of the public's commitment to the First Amendment. The results therefore show that the degree of attachment to abstract principles can be very issue-specific.

At least one difference between the first two questions and the third one is that powerful officials (Kentucky Governor Wallace Wilkinson and President George Bush) had taken strong public stands that may have had the effect of mobilizing public opinion. No office holder has had comparable influence over Lexington residents on the subject of sexually explicit materials. Nothing in our methodology can determine whether respondents to these questions were reacting to the specific issue, to a more abstract set of constitutionally based ideas, or to strong stands taken by public officials. Because of the difficulties of relating survey questions to a specific social context, the conceptualization of survey results as something analogous to a referendum is claiming more than many survey researchers would want to have to deliver.

Because the ability to provide a "true" measure of public opinion is limited, it may almost be a source of comfort to note that the ability to convert survey results into tangible influences on policymakers is limited as well. At first glance, this statement is paradoxical. After all, surveys are often commissioned by policymakers or their professional staffs. In my experience, those who commission surveys work hard at formulating questions and pay careful attention to results, often requesting additional analysis. However, it does not take many experiences presenting results or delivering testimony to recognize that many (though not all) policymakers tend to focus more closely on results that conform to their preconceived ideas than on results that might be more surprising (and, therefore, from some perspectives, more interesting). I will argue shortly that such presentations do provide a meaningful form of influence, but one must be careful to understand the potential limits on the influence of social scientists in such arenas.

A similar point can be made regarding press coverage. Surveys typically receive a good press. Gallup, for example, built a reputation by selling presidential preference polls to newspapers and urging editors to run his predictions alongside predictions from the ill-fated *Literary Digest* (J. Converse 1987, p.118). It is not unusual for newspapers and the electronic media both to run their own polls and to give ample coverage to results generated by other organizations. Many reporters and editors have considerable knowledge of survey methodology. If nothing else, margin of error will be reported as an obligatory ceremonial gesture. However, those releasing survey results often find that they have been made to fit a certain "handle" on their way to the press. The process may never involve deliberate distortion. Rather, emphases are changed to improve an article's interest level.

For example, a recent release from the University of Kentucky's Survey Research Center led with an unexpected and potentially important set of findings--satisfaction with many government services in Kentucky had reached their lowest level since this set of questions was introduced ten years ago, and expressed willingness to increase spending and (according to one question) taxation for government services was on the increase. To show that Kentuckians were not condemning everything, the release also noted in less detail that performance ratings for the Governor had improved over the past year and that perceived benefits of a major manufacturer (Toyota) had reached their highest levels since the weeks shortly after Toyota's 1985 announcement that it would locate in Kentucky. We felt that the combination of institutional optimism and specific dissatisfactions posed some unique opportunities for the state's leadership, so we were interested to see what kind of press coverage would result.

The resulting press coverage was revealing. With the exception of a public radio station, the release was largely ignored by the broadcast media. It received more extensive newspaper coverage, but the state's two major newspapers (both of which tend to support moderate to liberal views on their editorial pages) approached the story in very different ways. While both newspapers failed to mention the Governor's approval rating, one of them reported the story essentially in the way we had hoped. The other, which has devoted considerable space to Toyota since its decision to locate in Kentucky, treated the Toyota item in the lead paragraph (and several subsequent paragraphs). A synopsis of the service rating and taxation findings was provided in a final brief paragraph. Both articles were free of distortion and misrepresentation, but readers of the latter are likely not to have received the message we considered most important.

Conditions for the Effective Utilization of Applied Social Research

So far, I have argued that applied social research in general and survey research in particular are very important, but I have spent most of my time discussing limitations of their impact. I intend the remainder of my remarks to be more optimistic in tone, but I do not consider unjustified and naive optimism to be an effective stance for answering critics and skeptics. What I want to argue, instead, is that applied social research--when carefully executed and well presented--can become an effective voice (although only one of several voices) as decisions are being made. As Herbert Gans has reminded us, "we are...only 20,000 in a country of 230 million" (1989, p.3). I would quickly add, however, that we have inherited a perspective sufficiently powerful to give us a voice that is more influential than our numbers would indicate. While all social science disciplines have something to contribute to policy decisions, sociology's emphasis on social structure, its efforts through social psychology to understand individuals and groups in their social context, and the efforts of social demographers to understand changing population trends can provide broad, societally based insights that are unlikely to come from other disciplines.

Applied social research is needed in part for the insights it can provide. Unfortunately, it is also needed because many important research programs are not being performed by anyone else. Although demands to generate information necessary for coping with a complex world have increased, appropriations for federal agencies that produce statistics declined--often precipitously--during the 1980's. As Katherine Wallman (1988, p.6) notes, federal agencies have had to respond by (1) collecting information less frequently; (2) reducing the sample size, content and/or geographic coverage of particular surveys; (3) extending the time between data collection and publication; and (4) eliminating or reducing the frequency, scope, and distribution of publications and other products. To cite an example of specific sociological relevance, "Social Indicators" reports--statistical compendia combining data on a variety of topics--were published in 1974, 1977, and 1980.

> Since 1980, however, there has been no formal mechanism within the statistical system to publish indicators of status and change in areas such as family composition; health and nutrition; housing; transportation; public safety; education; social security and welfare; income and productivity; social participation; and use of time (Wallman 1988, p.7).

Funding cutbacks, combined with the increased difficulty (under the provisions of the Paperwork Reduction Act of 1980) of securing approval for federal data collection efforts, mean that policy decisions are more likely to be made with inadequate information. Even in a "kinder and gentler" nation, it is doubtful the federal statistical system will be restored to its pre-1980 level. As a result, the responsibility for social scientists working at the local and state levels to develop plans and to find funding for innovative policy-related research will probably increase.

The weakening of the federal statistical system has a number of serious consequences, but if it also has the effect of inspiring sociologists and other social scientists to find more innovative ways to fund research projects and to deliver their results to the appropriate decision makers, some benefits will have occurred. Even at their peak, federally generated statistics could tell

us relatively little about how the social and economic trends they documented were being *perceived* and *experienced* by people. An adequately
funded and administered system of federal statistics is a *necessary* part of
an information system, but it has never been *sufficient*. Sociologists working at various levels have had an important role to play, and they have
shown themselves more than equal to the task. Many worthwhile studies
are done, often on very small budgets, and methodological improvements
are occurring on a regular basis. To cite a few examples from survey research, sample designs have improved, increased attention has been
devoted to specialized segments of the public, trends in public opinion are
being charted, and numerous question styles are being tested (Crespi 1987,
p.S177). Despite occasional well-publicized travesties (e.g., phone-ins to
900 numbers, surveys on sexual practices with respondents drawn from
singles bars or the readers of newspaper advice columns), few if any serious users of survey results would make the mistake today of favoring a
large sample over a representative one (Sheatsley 1987, p.S186).

One can always hope that larger proportions of sociologists will equip themselves to participate on the cutting edge of methodology (Blalock 1989), but
my sense is that most studies are being competently executed and that
sociologists are increasingly sensitive to possible limitations in their methods. (For a useful meta-analysis of surveys on satisfaction with community
services, see Miller 1987).

Assuming a study is appropriately conceptualized and competently executed,
a larger concern is whether it will have the impact it deserves. I may have
sounded pessimistic on this point earlier, but, if we conceptualize "impact"
appropriately, I think we can expect to be very pleased with the kind of
impact that is possible. A continuum of "influence" has been provided by
Philip Converse (1987, p.S21-2):

> If we restrict our definition of influence to instances in which
> a political representative is a blank slate until s/he learns
> what public opinion is on an issue and then runs like an
> automaton to implement the public will, then there is prob-
> ably little influence which occurs. If, on the other hand,
> any deflection whatever of behavior by the representative

> which arises as a result of some exposure to poll data,
> even the most vague "taking account of it," classifies as an
> instance of actual influence, then of course public opinion
> in poll form must be said to have a great deal of influence.

In an interesting analogy, Converse says that politicians consult poll data for much the same reason that a riverboat captain would consult the latest mapping of sandbar configurations--not so much to find out where to go as to find out where *not* to go:

> Few politicians consult poll data to find out what they should
> be thinking on the issues...But they have little interest in
> flouting the will of their constituency in any tendentious,
> head-on way (p.S22).

This kind of "negative" usage of specific poll results certainly occurs, but applied social research (if not any particular poll or short-term study) can have more important long-term impacts as well. The thinking of Carol Weiss and Lee Cronbach and associates is helpful in understanding this point.

As Weiss (1980) has observed, few social scientists are likely to witness the "direct and immediate application of their results to a specific situation." Lee Cronbach and associates (1980) provide a partial explanation for this phenomenon when they note that policymakers, who are part of ongoing political processes, are exposed to information from a variety of sources. Legislators, for example, are exposed to pressure from constituents, lobbyists, and party leaders, among others. If they are exposed to research results, these will be added to mix of information, but in the short run, "Information from research does not normally carry greater weight than other kinds of information" (Cronbach et al. 1980, p.121). Assuming that research results are effectively presented and motivated by an interest that is more sustained than shifting political currents, however, the cumulative impact of social science research can be very important indeed. Impacts occur both with stakeholders and decision makers. If properly disseminated, research results can "help those with a legitimate interest in a given issue to recognize what is at stake for them" (Cronbach et al. 1980, p.105). Looking more specifically at effects on decision makers, Weiss notes that:

> Social science research can affect the premises of policy
> argument. It can provide concepts, sensitivities, models,
> paradigms, theories. Such conceptual derivatives from re-
> search can influence which issues are placed on the policy
> agenda and which kinds of policy options are considered.
> They can enter into decision makers' orientation toward
> priorities, the manner in which they formulate problems,
> the range of solutions they canvas, the criteria of choice
> they apply (1980, p.12).

Even these long-term results do not come easily. They require a willingness
to talk to a variety of interested parties as studies are being designed and as
results become available, to insure that results are stated in terms that can
be understood by nonsociologists, and to identify important topics for research even if they happen to be unfashionable. If we attend carefully to
these matters, our efforts may continue to be sufficiently important to justify the time and effort that we ask our fellow citizens to devote to our
research.

REFERENCES

Blalock, Hubert M., Jr. 1989. "The Real and Unrealized Contributions of
Quantitative Sociology." *American Sociological Review* 5f4 (June):447-
460.

Converse, Jean M. 1987. *Survey Research in the United States: Roots
and Emergence 1890-1960.* Berkely: University of California Press.

Converse, Philip E. 1987. "Changing Conceptions of Public Opinion in the
Political Process." *Public Opinion Quarterly* 51 (Winter):S12-S24.

Crespi, Irving. 1987. Untitled remarks in "The Future Study of Public Opinion: A Symposium," edited by Leo Bogart. *Public Opinion Quarterly*
51 (Winter):S177-S178.

Cronbach, Lee J., Sueann Robinson Ambron, Sanford M. Dornbusch, Robert D. Hess, Robert C. Hornik, D.C. Phillips, Decker F. Walker, and Stephen S. Weiner. 1980. *Toward Reform of Program Evaluation: Aims, Methods, and Institutional Arrangements.* San Francisco: Jossey-Bass.

Gans, Herbert J. 1989. "Sociology in America: The Discipline and the Public." *American Sociological Review* 54 (February):1-16.

Miller, Thomas I. 1987. "The Nine Circles of Citizen Survey Hell." *Management Science and Policy Analysis* 4 (Spring):26-32.

Perlstadt, Harry, and Russell E. Holmes. 1987. "The Role of Public Opinion Polling in Health Legislation." *American Journal of Public Health* 77 (May):612-614.

Ruckmick, Christian A. 1930. "The Uses and Abuses of the Questionnaire Procedure." *Journal of Applied Psychology* 14:32-41.

Sheatsley, Paul B. 1987. Untitled remarks in "The Future Study of Public Opinion: A Symposium." edited by Leo Bogart. *Public Opinion Quarterly* 51 (Winter):S177-S178.

Wallman, Katherine K. 1988. *Losing Count: The Federal Statistical System.* Washington, D.C.: Population Reference Bureau.

Weiss, Carol. 1980. *Social Science Research and Decision Making.* New York: Columbia University Press.

James G. Hougland, Jr.

1945 -

James G. Hougland, Jr., President of the Society for Applied Sociology in 1988-89, attended the inaugural meeting of SAS at Kent State University in 1983 and quickly became involved in its governance. He served as Vice President from 1984 through 1986. In that capacity, he worked with Mark Iutcovich and others to organize the 1985 SAS meeting held at Edinboro State University and with Harold Cox and colleagues to organize the 1986 SAS meeting held at Indiana State University. In 1987, he served as co-organizer (with Jeanne Ballantine) and co-chair of the Local Arrangements Committee (with Lenora Finn Paradis) of the SAS meetings held in Lexington, KY. Although the 1987 meeting was hosted by the University of Kentucky, it was the first SAS meeting to be held entirely in a hotel. The Lexington meeting also was the site of the decision to hold the 1989 meeting in Denver, representing SAS's first venture into the Western United States. The Denver meetings, where Jim delivered his Presidential Address on "Giving Voice to the Public: Survey Research, Applied Sociology, and Public Policy," was characterized by high attendance, lively discussion, and interesting cultural activities. Jim worked closely with the Program Committee (chaired by Penelope Canan) and the Local Arrangements Committee (chaired by Dora Lodwick) in planning the 1989 meeting and credits these energetic and effective committees with the meeting's success.

During Jim's tenure as President, the SAS Council approved the initiation of a search for a paid Administrative Officer. This decision reflected Jim's view that, as SAS increased in membership size and professional visibility, it needed to provide an increased range of member services and to routinize such activities as maintenance of membership records and mailing lists, freeing elected officers and committee chairs for more creative activities. In addition, Jim encouraged serious discussions about the future of SAS publications by appointing an ad hoc committee, developing a membership questionnaire, and calling an open meeting on publications in Denver. These efforts served to give the newly selected editors of SAS publications an increasingly clear idea of members' preferences regarding publications.

Since earning his Ph.D. at Indiana University in 1976, Jim has been a faculty member in the Department of Sociology at the University of Kentucky. He was promoted to Professor in 1987 and appointed Chair of the department in 1990. Prior to becoming department Chair, he served as Acting Director of two multidisciplinary centers at the University and as Director of the Survey Research Center of the University of Kentucky. In these positions, he drew on his sociological expertise to assist a variety of academics, government officials, and others with program development and evaluation, questionnaire development, and interpretation of survey results. During his five-year tenure as Director of the Survey Research Center, its annual revenues increased by more than 300 percent. Although Jim has returned to a more academic position, he continues to be involved in program evaluations, and he frequently works with students who are planning careers in applied social research.

Jim's research focuses on the evaluation of social programs, the impact of new industry on communities, the effects of experiences in organizations on individuals, and methodological issues in survey research. He is the author of 40 refereed journal articles as well as numerous research reports and book chapters. In addition to SAS, he is an active member of the American Sociological Association, where he currently is a member of the Graduate Education Committee, as well as other professional organizations.

PART FOUR:

A Vision for Applied Sociology

INTRODUCTION

Where do we go from here? Both Irwin Deutscher and Joyce Iutcovich lay out their respective road maps for applied sociology. But to put these in perspective we need to return to the founding address by Boros, *Sociology: A Workable Myth*. Boros provided fifteen challenges facing applied sociology, as such, he also addressed the future of applied sociology. How far have we progressed? What are our continuing challenges? To address these questions, we need to reexamine the challenges posed by Boros and the views of the future identified by Deutscher and Iutcovich. Their views of what lies ahead are briefly summarized.

Bridging the Gap Between Basic and Applied Sociology

Iutcovich, Boros, and Deutscher all question what the future will hold for the relationship between basic and applied sociology. The nature of our collective identity is a major concern. Establishing a seamless connection whereby sociology's two sides complement one another is of critical importance if sociology is to prosper. Getting to this point will not be easy.

Public Understanding and Viability of Sociology

The dissemination of sociology and its public understanding is a significant issue. Deutscher reminds us that while there is evidence that the public may be more sensitive to our views, we still may "come up short on answers" to important social questions. Iutcovich identifies a dilemma here. On one hand, sociology needs to establish its legitimacy as specifying a body of knowledge and methods to which it can lay claim. Yet, by doing so, we lose our flexibility in the marketplace. At the current time, since the public does not know who we are or what we do, we are not viewed by the public as a useful discipline. Given this, how are we to avoid being locked out of jobs that are within the expertise of sociologists? In this light, what is the viability of sociology? Are we to be like Deutscher's summary of the Abbot and Costello shtick in which sociology turns out to be "boss over nothing."

Our Collective Identity

What will we collectively become? Deutscher recommends a "weak disciplinary chauvinism." Here, similar to Boros' and Iutcovich's view, he maintains the centrality of sociology in our professional identity. Boros and Iutcovich suggest that creating this identity will include the certification of practitioners and the accreditation of applied sociology programs. Boros further argues for a literature on application *experiences* and *theories* of application. Furthermore, Deutscher would "mine the discipline" for meaningful concepts to get a job done. What this collective identity will specifically become is unclear.

Interdisciplinary Collaboration

Applied sociology is real-world problem centered. As such, it demands collaboration with those from other disciplines. Working in a team is the nature of the applied experience, we rarely have all the answers. Iutcovich argues we must learn to effectively work with others; we must bring important skills and a clear identity to the interdisciplinary problem-solving table.

Applied Training, Programs and Students

Boros reminds us that we have great wealth in the students who seek career venues in social action. The energy and "interventionist spirit of students" are resources in the shaping of applied sociology. Our challenge is "to continue developing effective applied training programs" while fostering "teachable practice applications." Both Boros and Iutcovich call for the development of an accreditation process and set of standards for applied sociology programs.

Professional Status

Iutcovich encourages us to reflect on sociology as a profession, noting that we still lack some of the essential characteristics of a professional occupation. Boros would suggest that the challenges here include developing rules to live by, a code of ethics for applied work, suitable rewards for applied work inside and outside academia, and reasonable means to be "professionally accountable."

Gaining Prestige for Applied Sociology

Are we to be "a friendly club" or a social movement? Deutscher indicates that we are not at a loss for successful social movement models within the field of sociology. Both the womens' movement, which has successfully gained status and power in the American Sociological Association, and the teaching movement, which has over two decades enhanced the position of teaching in the discipline, are indicative of paths we could follow. Concerted and organized effort is required, however. Consciousness raising and collective social action are central. If we are to move in this direction it will require "deliberate" action.

In conclusion, we recognize that the future offers extraordinary challenges.

11   Sociological Practice: The Politics of Identities and Futures*

IRWIN DEUTSCHER
The University of Akron

Taking their cue from the success of both the women's movement and the teaching movement in sociology, applied and practicing sociologists need to unify as a social movement if they hope to control their collective future. Collectively we can choose that future; perhaps full integration and acceptance into the larger sociological community or perhaps complete independence from that community. The costs and benefits of creating such a movement are considered here along with the nature of our collective identity as practitioners and the importance of the sociological perspective in our work. It is argued that the dour forecasts for the discipline by many leading sociologists are wrong. To the contrary, there is evidence suggesting a bright and prosperous future for sociology--especially for those who choose to engage in applied and practice work. This article observes that "the temper of the times is right and the outlook is rosy."

The theme of a meeting I attended earlier this year, was "contested boundaries and shifting solidarities." Sitting in a stuffy room and unable to avoid the droning monotony of a voice buried in what looked like a very long paper, I reflected on the two usual means of escape: doodling and dozing. Thanks, however, to the theme of those meetings, I found a more constructive escape. I began thinking about contested boundaries and shifting solidarities as they relate to the practice of sociology. I confess that, although most of my career has been spent doing applied sociology, I never paid serious attention to any boundaries between applied and basic sociology,

* *Presidential Address, Twelfth Annual Meeting of the Society for Applied Sociology, Detroit, Michigan, October 14-23, 1994. Copyright, Society for Applied Sociology. Reprinted with permission from the **Journal of Applied Sociology,** Volume 12, 1995. After finishing this paper it occurred to me that if a presidential address could be dedicated to someone, I would dedicate this to Arnold M. Rose, my friend and mentor who I noticed (after the fact) is a usually unacknowledged co-author of both **An American Dilemma** and **The American Soldier in World War II: Vol. 2, Social Psychology**. Both of those volumes figure prominently in this paper.*

nor did I ever feel any particular solidarity with colleagues because they happened to be doing applied work.

All of that changed quite suddenly in the late 1970s for reasons I will mention later in this article.

This little pep talk was constructed from the free association reflected in the notes I scribbled at that boring session. I intend to say a few things about the women's movement and the teaching movement in sociology. I will highlight some of the qualities they share and will eventually suggest what they could have in common with us. The nature of our collective identity is perhaps the central theme of this article and along the way I will insist that sociological practice must be sociological if it is to be anything at all. I will maintain the importance of sociological concepts in facilitating our understanding of where we are and where we might be going. Finally, I will advise you that there are choices to be made in shaping our future and those choices are yours.

Contested Boundaries and Shifting Solidarities

Gender was one of the emerging boundaries and solidarities that received attention at the meeting where I chose to neither doze nor doodle. The women's movement has had a profound impact on the contemporary world. I don't know who now reads C. Wright Mills (1959), but the women's movement was a deliberate consciousness-raising effort--an attempt to convert private troubles into public issues. It transformed in-group self-hatred ("Why am I and others like me so inferior in the ways men tell me we are?") into a collective consciousness ("We are all in this together and they are wrong about us"). There may be a few sociologists who now study social movements even though it is not a fashionable field. Yet there is no better conceptual framework for fathoming social change in the contemporary world. Who now studies the "funny words" Everett Hughes insisted were at the heart of understanding any social entity? The women's movement converted the grammatical term "gender" into the accepted core of their enterprise and they relegated to obscurity the epithet "women's libber," substituting the more dignified "feminist" to describe themselves and their enterprise. Finally, like all social movements they launched a successful search for heroic ancestors.

What has all this to do with the politics of sociological practice? For the moment I will give you a clue. The old boy system which governed the American Sociological Association as well as the regional professional societies well into the 1980s met its final demise with the 1994 ASA election; no male was nominated for President, Vice President or Secretary--the three most important elected offices in the society. Things do change, but not of their own volition. On a smaller scale, but equally close to home, consider another movement. In the late 1970s I served as evaluator of the ASA teaching projects which were perceived by the still entrenched elite as a harmless device for keeping the natives from getting restless.

Under the leadership of Hans Mauksch, an addicted user of sociology in any of his ventures, those teaching projects became instead a device for illuminating and publicizing the private troubles of the alienated and unknown teachers of sociology. No matter how magnificently they performed in the classroom, they would never gain the prominence enjoyed in the discipline by their vain colleagues who fancy seeing their names in print. Mauksch made a deliberate effort to create a social movement, and in doing so converted into public issues the private troubles of faculty in institutions ranging from obscure community colleges to elite four year institutions. Hundreds of these teaching sociologists were organized and learned, among other things, the power of the ballot by successfully electing some of their own candidates to the council of the ASA.

Their success is witnessed not only by the establishment of an ASA teaching section, but by the creation of an enduring and extensively used teaching resource center within the ASA executive office and the widening recognition of teaching as an honorable and legitimate activity for a scholar. Like the women's movement, the temper of the times played no little part in enabling the teaching movement to succeed to the degree that it did. But the temper of the times concerns the sociology of knowledge and that is another story, although I will return to it briefly. What has all this got to do with the politics of sociological practice? Patience! I will return to the topic of social movements, but first let us consider who we would like to be. What choices do we have in forming a collective identity?

Our Identity

What does it mean to say we are "practicing sociologists?" Are we like practicing anthropologists, truly proud of our professional identity? If so we must, like them, be compassionate for our colleagues whose lives are stuck in the stale mud of universities and colleges where they do research no one cares about and bore large classes of disinterested students while entertaining themselves with the petty politics of academia. These great power struggles are best captured by the Abbot and Costello shtick in which the big guy says to the little guy, "Remember this, I am the boss!" To which, the little guy meekly asks, "And what am I?" "You," says the big guy, "are nothing." The last word is the little guy's: "So, that makes you boss over nothing. " So it is with the great power politics of academic departments.

An alternative to this sense of superiority is a whining sense of inferiority. Do we perceive ourselves as inferiors who, in failing to get a "good job" (with tenure) are now forever doomed to perform the dirty work of the discipline? My sinister musings about sociological practice as dirty work are the subject of an ancient keynote address to this organization (Deutscher 1984). It seems to me, however, that there is little to be gained from either a collective smugness or a collective self pity. In both instances we are defining ourselves in comparison to other sociologists, rather than by our own standards.

It should be understood that we are above all, sociologists. We differ from some of our colleagues, solely because our work directly impinges on the empirical world. It may or may not change anything and it may change some part of that world for better or for worse, but the fact is that it is our intention to do work which alters existing social arrangements in large or small ways. It should be said that an undergraduate sociology major does not a sociologist make any more than an undergraduate major makes a philosopher, historian, or chemist. It is possible that, equipped with the proper tools, a technician can ply a research trade with pride. Such a person may be a craftsperson, but is not a practicing sociologist.

It is a weak version of disciplinary chauvinism that I recommend--weak because there is no implication that sociology is any better than any other discipline. It is, however, different. It is because of that difference that it is important to maintain the identity of a sociologist. That identity is what provides us with the option of contributing something which others do not. Without a sociological perspective, the picture is incomplete and fragmentary. Medical practitioners view people as sick or healthy or somewhere in between; psychologists view people as sane or crazy or somewhere in between, but that is not our language nor is it the way we perceive the empirical world. Medical practitioners are better equipped to practice medicine than us; psychologists usually do better psychology than us; even economists sometimes do better economics than us.

We may not be aware of how much the world has caught up with us in recent years. My home town newspaper, *The Washington Post*, regularly cites the authority of sociologists on issues of religion, race, politics, crime, the military, the family, and urban problems. A personal anecdote illustrates the extent to which the sociological perspective is penetrating the American consciousness. I was engaged in a cocktail party conversation with a recently retired air force colonel. He was intrigued by the fact that he had met a real sociologist and immediately began interrogating me about the frequency of black on black shootings. Let me paraphrase the conversation: "What do you sociologists suggest be done about this?" he inquired. "I know," he continued, "that these kids are not sick and they are not crazy. I understand that they are acting under some sort of social rules and cultural values which make sense to them in their world." Having succinctly stated this sociological perspective much to my satisfaction, the old soldier then repeated his demand: "What do you sociologists suggest be done about this?" Much to my regret, I stuttered, stammered, wheezed, and made some sort of half-hearted comment about the need to restructure the social world in which these young people found themselves. The point of the anecdote is not my inarticulate solution, but his lay person's articulate sociological statement of the problem. The sociological perspective is increasingly understood by the ordinary citizen. That bodes well for our future.

Applied work in the empirical world is, of course, often interdisciplinary. People working together approach issues from a variety of perspectives which hopefully can provide a more complete picture of problems and solutions. When a practitioner is part of a team because of his or her disciplinary perspective, then it is an abandonment of responsibility to ignore that perspective or to mimic another one.

Perspectives and Concepts

In discussing our perspective, I have avoided the word "theory" because there is no single coherent theory in sociology which is fit to guide our practice. But we do have perspectives and we do have concepts which are useful. I have mentioned C. Wright Mills' (1959) conceptual distinction between private troubles and public issues, the notion of social movements, and E.C. Hughes's concepts of "dirty work" and "funny words." Hans Mauksch was explicit in his use of Gunnar Myrdal's *An American Dilemma* (1944) as the conceptual foundation for his efforts to organize teaching sociologists into an influential social movement. *The halyard of quality sociological practice is the ability to mine the discipline for concepts appropriate to the job on hand.*

Useful concepts can range from the grand to the tiny. Richard Cloward and Lloyd Ohlin (1960), borrowing from R.K. Merton, planted their "Opportunity Theory" on Lyndon Johnson's lap, and the so called "War on Poverty" was born. At the other extreme, we find Sam Strong of Carlton College spending his weekends in the 1950s at the state mental hospital in Minnesota. Strong played chess with schizophrenic catatonics. To the amazement of the psychiatric staff, he was able to engage some of these extremely withdrawn patients into human interaction. He was a student of Herbert Blumer and assumed that in order to play chess effectively, one had to take the role of the other--to step into the other person's shoes and anticipate how that person would respond to a chess move.[1] I suppose Sam Strong was one of the first clinical sociologists, although that term was not then fashionable.

The concepts and perspectives which I have found useful in this article are not necessarily those that are currently fashionable. Such tools may or may not derive from obscure sources. The criterion for selecting them is their usefulness in illuminating the issue, not their popularity. The idea of "relative deprivation," for example, is rarely cited in contemporary sociology--applied or otherwise. This notion was developed by a team of sociologists during the second world war. It was their job to help the military deal with some of the anomalies in morale among American soldiers. Relative deprivation can illuminate many organizational paradoxes especially in conjunction with the concept Merton derived from it. His little theory, tagged "reference group" may be one of the least used and most useful in American sociology.

The sociologist-practitioner must rake through the useless chaff which is usually taught in "theory" courses, in order to discover the occasional grain. Note, however, that reference group theory did not blossom from the musings of a professor in an ivy covered tower. The origins of that useful little theory lie in the practical efforts of a team of sociological draftees doing their job for the army. This article is not the proper place to provide an encyclopedia of good sociological practice. In fact, it may be a rather thin volume when it is produced, not because of the quality of practice, but because of the quality of sociology. Nor will I dwell upon the history of sociological practice. People like Jan Fritz and John Glass (1982) and Calvin Larson (1993) have already recorded much of that for us. What I will do is return to the women's movement and the teaching movement and offer one final option.

Choose The Future: A Social Movement or A Friendly Club?

There is another choice that is ours. The options are both good but they are very different. One future we can pursue is the path we are now on. We have our lovely little clubs where we meet once a year, exchange gossip, get updated on what is happening in the field, grumble about the elite establishment in the universities and in the ASA, have a good time with old friends and go home to work until the following year. I enjoy all of that immensely. It is what our meetings and those of our fellow practitioner organizations are all about. Some practitioners would, however, choose a different kind of organizational future.

Suppose one would prefer to have sociological practice become an integral part of the discipline and to gain the kind of collective *influence* and *respect* that SWS achieved for women in sociology and which the teaching projects achieved for teachers of sociology? It then becomes necessary to create the kind of social movement they created. I referred earlier to the temper of the times. I suspect that the temper of the times is unlikely to ever again provide a more hospitable milieu for such a movement. This is even more true today for sociological practice than it was for the teaching movement a decade ago. At the start of this article I claimed that I had never paid serious attention to the boundaries between basic and applied sociology. I also claimed that I never felt any particular solidarity with colleagues because they happened to be doing applied work. I also confessed that all of that changed quite suddenly in the late 1970s.

At about that time, a sea of change began to occur in institutions of higher education. That change, viewed as so terrifying to academics, provided the milieu within which the teaching projects were able to succeed. With some of the recent shifts I have mentioned in this article, it is even more possible today for a sociological practice movement to succeed. I am speaking of times characterized by the imposition of severe budget restrictions in general, the demands for accountability in particular, student preoccupation with the job potential of their education, the desperate need of ASA to expand its membership, and increasing public recognition of the importance of sociology followed by an inevitable increase in demand for practicing sociologists--all of these and other ingredients of the temper of the times result in a climate that is hospitable to such a movement. The little lapel button proclaiming "Sociology, Use it or Lose it!" has more serious implications than its wearers may intend.

I beg you to take no pleasure in the problems such a milieu presents to our academic colleagues. Perhaps more than anything else, a healthy discipline needs to provide opportunities for curious people to pursue research out of no better motive than the curiosity itself. Nevertheless, what appears to be happening, although regrettable, is clearly to the benefit of those engaged in practical problem solving activities.[2]

As for the more dismal forecasters in the discipline, I simply disagree. A recent issue of *Sociological Forum* was dedicated to the (loaded) question "What's Wrong With Sociology?" Although the editor reminds readers that one of the problems dealt with in the volume is "the absence of theory that can be utilized in empirical [and perhaps applied?] research" (Cole 1994, p.129), the tone is generally one of distress over apparent disciplinary prestige. Lipset, for example, is convinced that "We are an endangered discipline" (p. 215). This appraisal is based on (1) the disapproval registered by 144 American deans several years ago (Lynch and McFerron 1993); (2) "Contested elections" such as those held in the ASA and Modern Language Association which accounts for the lack of respectability of such organizations as compared with the American Political Science Association whose elite nominating committee makes a wise presidential selection for the members; and (3) the fearful threats to sociology departments in certain elite institutions. (He mentions Yale and Washington University. In both cases there is some merit to the argument that the sociology department may be disposable.) He seems more concerned about departments in such "leading universities" than with some of the others he mentions in passing. In that same volume, Harvey Moltach's pessimism is at least rational. Taking as a point of departure the American tradition of individualism, Moltach (1994) concludes that "We are misfits. The most developed sociology in the world exists in a country inhospitable to it" (p.221).

Despite all that gloom and doom, the temper of the times is right and the outlook is rosy! But the kind of social movement we are talking about requires, above all, organizational coherence. There must be a unified voice lobbying for the interests of all sociological practitioners. It may be that the greatest cost of creating a movement is the ruin of the friendly little clubs--the end of the Society for Applied Sociology, and the Sociological Practice Association as we know them. On the other hand, such a coherent organization can provide a new home and revitalization for such groups as Sociologists in Business, Sociologists in Government, and even our fading ancestor, The Rural Sociological Society. It is of no little importance that the practice section provides a base of operation within the ASA.

Although organizationally fragmented, there is a growing collective identity among practitioners and funny terms like "sociological practice" and "clinical sociology" are more acceptable and better understood as part of the disciplinary vocabulary than they were a decade ago. Committed scholars have invented a legitimate (and legitimizing) history of the enterprise, along with heroic ancestors in whom we can take pride (e.g., Fritz 1987, 1988, 1990a, 1990b).[3] Some of the elementary ingredients of a social movement exist. What is most lacking besides organizational unity is the sort of charismatic leadership experienced by the women's movement and the teaching movement. It takes effort, time, persistence, and dedication to mobilize this motley crew of restless sociologists into enthusiastic and excited participants in a social movement. Who among you is willing and able to do that?

I chose the words "influence" and "respect" in describing what we might hope to achieve. Taking our cue from the women's movement and the teaching movement, it should be enough to know that we will no longer be perceived as second class citizens of the discipline and we will have a say in where our discipline is going. "Influence" and "respect" are more appropriate in this context than are terms like "power" and "control." Besides, as the little guy declares, who wants to be boss over nothing?

NOTES

1) Sam Strong published a paper on this topic in *The Midwest Sociologist* somewhere between 1954 and 1956. That journal, under the editorship of Paul Meadows at the time, has since been re-named *The Sociological Quarterly*.

2) In the last of a series of three articles in *The Washington Post*, Rensberger (1994) documents the likelihood of federal research resources shifting steadily in the near future from basic to applied research.

3) The origins and traditions of sociology both in Britain and the U.S. emerged as efforts to understand and resolve social problems. Until the invasion of the science creatures shortly after the second world war, sociologists were by and large do-gooders, reformers, preachers, and the like. It is not at all difficult for sociological practice to discover heroic ancestors among them.

REFERENCES

Cloward, Richard A. and Lloyd E. Ohlin. 1960. *Delinquency and Opportunity*. New York: The Free Press.

Cole, Stephen. 1994. "Introduction: What's Wrong with Sociology?" *Sociological* Forum 9(2):129-131.

Deutscher, Irwin. 1984. "The Moral Order of Sociological Work." *Journal of Applied Sociology* 1:1-11.

Fritz, Jan M., 1990a. "In Pursuit of Justice: W.E.B. DuBois." *Clinical Sociology Review* 8:15-25.

_____. 1990b. "Notes From the History of American Sociology: Frank Blackmer's Last Years at the University of Kansas." *Mid-America Review of Sociology* 14(1-2, Winter):13-26.

_____. 1988. "Charles Gomillion, Educator-Community Activist." *Clinical Sociology Review* 6:13-21.

_____. 1987. "The Whyte Line." *Clinical Sociology Review* 5:13-16.

Fritz, Jan M. and John Glass. 1982. "Clinical Sociology: Origins and Development." *Clinical Sociology Review* 1:3-6.

Larson, Calvin J. 1993. *Pure and Applied Sociological Theory*. Fort Worth: Harcourt Brace Jovanovich.

Lipset, Seymour Martin. 1994. "The State of American Sociology." *Sociological Forum* 9(2):199-220.

Lynch, David M. and J. Richard McFerron. 1993. "A Discipline in Trouble: Why More Sociology Departments May Be Closing Shortly." *Footnotes* 21(2):3,7.

Mills, C. Wright. 1959. *The Sociological Imagination.* New York: Oxford University Press.

Moltach, Harvey. 1994. "Going Out." *Sociological Forum* 9(2):221-239.

Myrdal, Gunnar. 1944. *An American Dilemma.* New York: Harper and Brothers.

Rensberger, Boyce. 1994. "Fundamental Research at Risk: Political Favor Shifting Toward Applied Science." *The Washington Post.* December 27, pp. A1, A12.

Stouffer, Samuel A. 1949. *The American Soldier, Vol. I, Studies in Social Psychology in World War II.* Princeton, NJ: Princeton University Press.

Irwin Deutscher

1923 -

Irwin Deutscher is a charter member of the SAS and a regular participant at annual meetings. The major thrust of his presidency of SAS was an effort to further propel a vibrant, young, and largely regional organization into a more cosmopolitan national and international one.

He began his career in 1953 at Community Studies, Inc. in Kansas City where he became Director of Research in Health and Welfare before moving to Syracuse University as Director of the Ford Foundation funded Youth Development Center. He later joined the faculty of Case Western Reserve University in Cleveland where he did extensive work in evaluation research and received an NSF Senior Postdoctoral Fellowship. Most recently Deutscher taught at the University of Akron where he also directed the evaluation of the ASA programs to improve undergraduate teaching. His teaching included graduate seminars on evaluation research and applied research, the latter sometimes team-taught with Alex Boros, the founder of SAS. In 1980 he was loaned to the U.S. Department of Health and Human Services for one year in order to do a pilot study for use in preparing an RFP synthesizing twenty years of evaluation research on Project Head Start. In 1995 he received an NSF travel grant to establish cooperative relations with applied sociologists and anthropologists in India.

Deutscher has published over 100 articles and monographs, including three books. His most recent book, co-authored with Fred and Fran Pestello, received a special recognition award from the Society for the Study of Symbolic Interaction in 1994. Two new books are nearing completion. His current work focuses on government policies toward ethnic, racial, and national minorities.

In addition to serving as president of the Society for Applied Sociology, Deutscher is Past President of the D.C. Sociological Society, the Society for the Study of Social Problems and the North Central Sociological Association. He has also served on the Council of the ASA. Deutscher received the distinguished alumni award from the departments of sociology and rural sociology at the University of Missouri, the Lester F. Ward award from the Society for Applied Sociology for distinguished contributions to applied sociology, the Aida K. Tomeh award for Distinguished Professional Service from the NCSA, and a certificate of recognition for leadership and support from the Sociological Practice Association. In addition to the post of Professor of Sociology at Syracuse University, Case Western Reserve University, and the University of Akron, he has been visiting professor at U.C-Berkeley, U.C.S.D-La Jolla, Ohio State University, and the University of Amsterdam.

He is Professor Emeritus, University of Akron, and currently resides in Washington, DC where his spouse is a lobbyist for the American Association of University Women, a volunteer worker at the White House, and an information specialist at both the National Gallery of Art and the Smithsonian Institution.

12 Sociology at a Crossroads: The Challenges of the New Millennium*

Joyce Miller Iutcovich
Keystone University Research Corporation
Gannon University

It was the best of times, it was the worst of times,
It was the age of wisdom, it was the age of foolishness,
It was the epoch of belief, it was the epoch of incredulity,
It was the season of Light, it was the season of Darkness,
It was the spring of hope, it was the winter of despair,
We had everything before us, we had nothing before us...

Charles Dickens, A Tale of Two Cities (1859)

Many of you, I'm sure, recall this memorable introduction to Charles Dickens' novel, *A Tale of Two Cities.* Dickens' novel provided a secular depiction of dual themes: one of burial and death, the other of rebirth and resurrection. The setting of his novel was the period prior to the French Revolution, an event that brought about a new era--a regeneration of society.

In my presentation today, I will examine the challenges that sociology faces as we enter the 21st century. I have borrowed from Dickens to provide a backdrop for my discussion of these challenges and the strategies we can take to bring about a "rebirth" of the discipline. Before I begin my discussion, however, I must preface it with some comments about my point of departure. Although I am here before you as President of the Society for Applied Sociology and I am a dedicated applied sociologist, I will be talking about sociology, as a discipline, as a whole. I do recognize both its basic and applied side, however, as I will articulate later, these two components of the discipline are inextricably linked. Therefore, to focus on one aspect at the

*Presidential Address, Thirteenth Annual Meeting of the Society for Applied Sociology, San Diego, October 12-15, 1995. Copyright, Society for Applied Sociology. Reprinted with permission from the **Journal of Applied Sociology**, Volume 13, 1996.*

expense of the other will do more harm than good to the "rebirth" of the discipline. Our efforts must be directed toward fostering the interdependence between basic and applied sociology instead of independence. If this interdependence came to fruition, perhaps then the general climate would be filled less with fear and uncertainty, and more with hope, encouragement, and a sense of renewal.

In what follows I will summarize, first, what has been identified as the crisis facing sociology. Next, I will elucidate on what I have identified as a number of fundamental dilemmas within the discipline--dilemmas that cannot be easily resolved. I then present a vision of sociology for the future--one that provides guidance as we face the challenges ahead. Finally, I discuss a number of specific challenges along with strategies to deal with these challenges as we enter the 21st century.

The Crisis Within Sociology

The recent sociology literature is filled with descriptions of the crisis within sociology. Departments have closed, faculty have been retrenched, fewer students are majoring in sociology, and so on. A recent issue of Sociological Forum (1994), entitled What's Wrong with Sociology? identified specific problems, as articulated by a number of well-known sociologists:

- Sociologists are self-destructive, denouncing one another and giving nonsociologists contradictory messages about what good sociological work is and ought to be.

- Sociology is incoherent, poorly written, arcane, and mystifying.

- Sociology has no core knowledge, it is not cumulative; there is no consensus and no scientific unity.

- Sociologists do not refute, nor confirm, nor expand ideas.

- Sociology has no distinctive subject matter, but shares topics with other social sciences; it tends to be all concepts and methods with very little substance.

- Sociology attracts the academically weakest graduate students in the university.

- Sociology is vulnerable to politicization.

- Sociology results are obvious.

- Sociologists are parochial and ignorant of solutions to problems that require a multidisciplinary approach.

All of these point to some significant warning signs that must be taken seriously if the discipline is to survive. They raise questions about the field's vitality and direction.

However, what's really wrong with sociology (and was overlooked by the sociologists writing in *Sociological Forum*) is its neglect of the practice side (Dotzler, 1995). Koppel argues that "the blindness to practice is self-destructive; academic sociology's best solution is in a closer relation with practice" (Koppel, 1995:4).

Indeed, as summarized in a 1992 article in the Chronicle of Higher Education, these "discussions about the current health of sociology call to mind the old conundrum about whether the glass is half empty or half full" (Coughlin, 1992:A6). There are those who point to rising enrollments, significant scientific contributions of the discipline, etc. In assessing the laundry list from What's Wrong with Sociology? Wendell Bell recently commented:

> Although there may be some truth to each of them, in nearly every case I can think of a contrary example, exemplars of sociological work that are soundly scientific, that focus on socially important topics, that are not obvious in results, that fairmindedly build on past work, and, that without being fanatically ideological, contribute to the policy debates of the day (Bell, 1995:6).

Regardless of the interpretation of the current state of the discipline--whether the glass is half full or half empty--there are some dilemmas that we face as a discipline that cannot be easily resolved; they are dilemmas that present us with a number of challenges as we enter the next millennium.

Dilemmas Within the Discipline

Three dilemmas facing sociology are: 1) The Knowledge Dilemma; 2) The People Dilemma; 3) The Marketplace Dilemma.

The Knowledge Dilemma. On one hand, the breadth of our disciplinary knowledge and skills is unparalleled in other fields of study and it provides us with vast opportunities for establishing our utility for society. On the other hand, this breadth of knowledge results in a fragmentation of our discipline and the lack of an intellectual core that defines our discipline and establishes our legitimacy in the larger social order. Let us examine this dilemma more closely.

There is a profusion of subjects and specialty areas within the discipline of sociology; it ranges from a focus on general questions about social structure and the social order, to very narrowly defined research that dissects peculiarities of behavior, by particular types of individuals, in particular types of settings. We operate at the macro, meso, and micro level of analysis. We collect and analyze data using both qualitative and quantitative techniques.

Given the variety of our knowledge and skills, some have argued that we are a victim of our own success (Newsweek, 1992; Porter, 1992; Coughlin, 1992). Sociology "has given rise to a number of new intellectual fields, such as criminal justice, social work, and survey research" (Coughlin, 1992:A6). Such specialties as market research, opinion polling, management studies, and urban studies also trace their heritage to sociology. Some point to this as solid evidence of the utility of our discipline. Enlightened others contend that we have "given away the store." As Billson has stated, "every time sociology gives birth to another one of these specialized areas, the number of majors shrinks" (Newsweek, 1992:55).

The other side to this dilemma is how this breadth of knowledge and variety of methodological approaches has led to fragmentation of the discipline and the lack of an identity and intellectual core. As argued by Glass (1992: 6),

"we have failed to position ourselves in the forefront of public consciousness like other social sciences--psychology, for example." We do not have
an identifiable external market. Political science has its niche--government;
economics has business; psychology has clinical practice (Coughlin, 1992).
Indeed, sociology's neglect of its practice side has resulted in the present
problems associated with sociology's "giving away the store." Areas that
have demonstrated practical usefulness have been siphoned off by others
who have recognized the importance of utility to society and its relationship
to the vitality of a discipline.

Not only do we lack an identifiable external market, but as well, many of the
core concepts of sociology have entered into the lexicon of public discourse
or have been incorporated into the writings of other social scientists, educators, journalists, etc. (Merton, 1991; D'Antonio, 1992). For example, we
often hear about the racial, gender, and class inequities, feminization of
poverty, organizational structures and functions, self-fulfilling prophecies,
the underclass, networking, and the use of such techniques as public opinion
polling. This shows the usefulness of our conceptualizations and methods;
unfortunately, these notions are seldom associated with the discipline of
sociology. If one were to pick up journals in related areas--for example,
education or public health--you would be hard pressed to differentiate the
contributions of sociologists from those who are trained in other disciplines.

The People Dilemma. By the very nature of our discipline, we tend to
attract individuals who are "rebels" and relish in the critical assessment of
the status quo (Turner and Turner, 1990). But, given this very nature of the
"beast," we are inhibited in our ability to come together as a discipline and
present a unified front. Our "presentation of self" is severely hampered
given our lack of consensus about which "theoretical, methodological and
empirical approaches are best, about which scholars are the most important
in the field" (Lipset, 1994:215). This quote from Lipset (1994:199) on the
state of American Sociology is very telling:

> Sociology appears to be one of the most internally divided
> disciplines, if not the most. Departmental struggles, which
> have led to sociologists complaining to administrators about
> each other, have put the field in bad repute among campus

officials and have endangered its survival in some schools.
The American Sociological Society and American Sociological Association have been among the most conflict-
ridden associations in academe for generations...It may be
suggested that they are related to the propensity of the
field to attract social reformers and political activists.

Although academicians, for the most part, tend to be more liberal than individuals from the larger population, across disciplines, sociology stands out
as one of the most radical and to the far left, as a number of studies have
substantiated (Lazarsfeld and Thielens, 1958; Ladd and Lipset, 1976; Lipset,
1982; Lipset and Ladd, 1972; Lynch and McFerron, 1993). Other social
sciences and those fields of study that are associated with establishment
activities and the free professions--e.g., economics, psychology, business--
tend to draw from a more conservative population. As a result, not only are
we considered pariahs on campus, (Lynch and McFerron, 1993) but we are
often labeled "socialists" by the larger society. This does little to enhance
our image in government and the business world where we might find considerable opportunities to apply our knowledge and skills.

The Marketplace Dilemma. In the effort to legitimize the discipline via
rigorous scientific research, we have undermined our viability in the marketplace. "Ironically in an effort to achieve institutional legitimacy like other
pure sciences, sociology's century-old emphasis on theory and statistical
testing, ...unwittingly undermined its ability to establish an incontrovertible
niche in the professional workplace and marketplace like its sister social
sciences" (Fleischer, 1994:6). And, it is not that sociologists during this time
period were opposed to the application of their knowledge, rather their emphasis was elsewhere. As Lipset (1994) asserts:

> Although the principal figures in sociology in the 1940s and
> 1950s strongly espoused what might be called a scientistic
> orientation, they, like their predecessors, believed that meth-
> odologically rigorous social science research was a pre-
> requisite for effective social reform, often radical change.
> This meant that basic research and theory had to come
> first, they should take priority over activism...To simply have

a worthy goal, to say that we have to get rid of what we do not like, will be ineffective, in lieu of scientific knowledge about the underlying factors that bring about the negative effects. The major departments concentrated, therefore, much more on basic theoretical and methodological issues than on substantive social problems (205).

However, since the passing of the Golden Era of sociology (Rhoades, 1981) the social, economic, and political climate in our society, as well as worldwide, has changed. There is greater emphasis on usefulness, practicality, and training students "to be able to do, as well as to know" (Clark and Fritz, 1986).

Marketplace issues are now at the forefront. Demonstrating our usefulness is the vehicle for establishing legitimacy. Thus, as sociologists in the academy have barely moved beyond their intellectual and political struggles over theory and method, a new source of contention has entered the picture--sociological practice and how this impacts the position of basic sociology in the academy. Those of us here today are well aware of this struggle and how it has further fractionalized our discipline. But, as we continue to debate these issues, as pointed out earlier, other fields have taken our knowledge and methods, put it to practical use, and prospered in the meantime--a few good examples of this are business management, marketing, and criminal justice.

Admittedly, these three dilemmas--the Knowledge Dilemma, the People Dilemma, and the Marketplace Dilemma--present us with some difficult choices for charting our future path. There are both advantages and disadvantages in being a field of study of such broad scope, in being a "critical" discipline, and in recognizing the importance of knowledge grounded in sound scientific research. The task at hand is to maximize the advantages and minimize the disadvantages. Given these dilemmas, there are a number of specific challenges we face as we enter the 21st century. However, before we can tackle these challenges, we must have a vision of our future.

Sociology 2000: A Vision of our Future

If we are to move ahead into the next millennium and prosper as a discipline, we must first have a vision of where we want to be. We will rise or fall, succeed or fail, by the image we hold in our minds. I ask you to close your eyes, think about sociology as a discipline, envision where we have been and what we can become. It is the year 2095. A hundred years from now. What do you see?

Others have advanced their visions of a future. In 1979 Costner wrote "A Vision and an Image." He argued that "many different research styles and specialties are compatible with a common goal, but that no such goal has been articulated to provide a common purpose to current diversity" (Costner. 1979: 74). His vision was one that focused on the importance of theory-- i.e., the need for sociology to have a set of "basic and general principles of social change such that the circumstances that sustain major social trends can be confidently identified and such that probable ramifications of specific social changes can be reliably anticipated under specified circumstances" (Costner, 1979:74). In addition, Costner recognized the utility of such knowledge for *policy relevant* or *action relevant* endeavors.

More recently Coleman (1994) advanced his vision of sociology. In his vision, quantitative methods/techniques typical of contemporary sociology are put to use in the analysis of the social system (whether large or small), rather than the individual, which is the unit of analysis in much of today's quantitative research. "The most formidable task of sociology is the development of a theory that will move from the micro level of action to the macro level of norms, social values, status distribution, and social conflict" (Coleman, 1994:33). In addition, Coleman's vision included an emphasis on the utility of social theory for the ongoing functioning of society. "It is extremely important for sociology to demonstrate its utility to society if it's going to be viable in the long run" (Newsweek, 1992:55).

Steele (1995) advanced a number of depictions of sociology as taught in the year 2005 (1995). He envisioned a sociology with a shift in focus from goals internal to the discipline to one in which the needs of clients and the community become a priority. The instructional techniques and content of the introductory course would also be much different. Students would engage in active, experiential learning; faculty and students, together, would become part of a total instructional environment in which learning takes place via multiple modalities. The new technologies associated with the electronic communications revolution would be at the forefront of the total instructional environment (e.g., computer-assisted learning modules, satellite downlinks with interactive capabilities, virtual reality learning, and e-mail and Internet connections to sources of knowledge worldwide). Sociology would be a vehicle for multiple career paths--that is, students are aware of the skills transferable to a variety of emerging career opportunities. Students would be life-long learners using their sociological analysis skills to make them better at identifying and planning social interventions to solve social problems.

Also, at the 1995 annual meeting of the American Sociological Association, the Section of Sociological Practice engaged in a process of defining a vision of sociology. The results of that session are enlightening. Two focus groups were established based on one's place of primary employment--either academia or in practice. Both the academics and practitioners, when asked to articulate their vision of sociology for the future, could not do so. Instead, the emphasis was on the "roadblocks" that sociology faces as it moves into the 21st century along with suggestions for improving the overall status of the discipline. They both emphasized the need to bring applied and basic sociology together; to market the discipline; to develop a common language; to bridge the gap between basic and applied; and to claim our identity (ASA Section of Sociological Practice, 1995).

How do these visions compare with your own? My vision includes one in which the distinctions between basic and applied sociology are no longer debated. Where the interface between social theory and social policy is accepted as commonplace. Where sociological practice provides opportunities to refine theory, generate new methodological techniques, and encourage multidisciplinary endeavors. Where techniques of analysis, both quantitative and qualitative, are used in conjunction with one another to provide a broader understanding of human behavior, whether on the micro, meso, or macro level. Where sociologists are called upon as experts in the analysis of social problems and the identification of solutions. Where they become part of interdisciplinary teams that attack the multifaceted aspects of societal problems. Where the majority of sociologists are "practicing" as physicians practice medicine. Where this practice is grounded in theory and in turn, it becomes a *reality test* for the theory from which the practice was derived.

We have a long way to go! And the path to this future will be challenging, to say the least.

The Challenges Ahead

Given this image, what are the challenges we face as we begin our journey into the next millennium? These challenges are not mutually exclusive, and they have a number of interlocking themes as well as potential solutions that are common to them. The first two challenges I will examine together since each relates to the *professional* status of sociology.

Challenge One: How do we become a "profession" and all it entails, yet still maintain our breadth of knowledge?

Challenge Two: How do we establish our legitimacy as a profession, yet maintain the flexibility of our discipline in the marketplace. And specifically, how do we avoid being "locked out" of jobs that are within the expertise of sociologists?

There are a number of essential features of a profession. Carr-Saunders and Wilson (1933) state that a *strong association* and a *monopoly of function* are key features.

Practitioners who desire to be a profession come together in associations and they work together with political authorities to establish a legal monopoly over the pursuit and practice of that occupation. Similarly, Wilensky (1964) describes the process through which occupations become professions: 1) making the occupation a full-time pursuit; 2) linking the training of workers to a special training institute 3) establishing an association; 4) obtaining a legalistic monopoly over their sphere of work; and 5) developing a code of ethics that regulates their professional behavior.

However, these features could apply to many of the trades (e.g., plumbing, electrical work, etc.), which are not considered professions. Thus, what are the core characteristics? According to Goode (1960), professions have a prolonged specialized training in a body of abstract knowledge, and a collectivity of service orientation. Freidson (1970) has further emphasized that professions have been extended autonomy or self-direction by a society that recognizes the value and reliability of an occupation. He further states that being a professional means engaging in behavior befitting the avowed promise of that profession.

Given these key features of a profession, I would have to argue that sociology is not a profession. Although most of us sitting here today would like to think of ourselves as professionals, the discipline of sociology comes up short in the area of "service orientation" and "monopoly of function." First, we do not have professional practice (or service) that is legally recognized by some form of licensure. Indeed, for those of us who do engage in practice, we are not alone in that there are others, trained in other disciplines, who practice right along side of us. Second, because of our breadth of knowledge, sociologists can be found fulfilling a wide variety of functions-- e.g., research, management and administration, counseling, system design and implementation, etc. And as other more astute fields of study seek closure of and the exclusive jurisdiction over the provision of their services through job reclassification and state-level licensure (i.e., a monopoly of function), sociology sits back, allowing these fields to take our knowledge and methods, claim them as their own, then restrict our use of them in practice settings. But our unwillingness to "stake our claim" comes not only from the purists who have labored to establish the institutional legitimacy of a scientific sociology. The problem comes from our inability to really know what is ours. Since we have been "giving away the store" for many decades and our own historical roots can be found in philosophy, theology, history, and the like, delineating the boundaries of sociological knowledge and methods is an extremely difficult task. But I contend that we either "stake our claim" or we lose it all.

The issue is to what do we "stake our claim" and how do we do it. There needs to be a common purpose to which all the diverse research styles and content specialties can contribute. This common purpose must be clearly articulated and the activities of sociologists, whether basic research or practical applications, must be tied back to this common purpose.

Costner (1979:75) talked about the development of basic and general principles "that will enhance our understanding of social change in ways that can be usefully applied to a broad range of specific situations other than those from which our knowledge was derived." Coleman (1994:33) also emphasized the need for sociology to develop a theory with the focus on the *social system*--one that moves "from the micro level of action to the macro level of norms, social values, status distribution, and social conflict."

Such a broad theoretical framework for understanding the social system-- what it looks like, how it changes, and how it can be used in the formation of social policy--becomes the common ground. That which we claim as our own. And, the practical applications of the knowledge become other means of *testing* the knowledge, in addition to the *testing* conducted by basic scientists. In fact, the practical applications become the most important means of testing since it moves from the *abstract intellectual level* to the *concrete real world level.*

Now, how do we do it? How do we stake our claim? Again, we note that the legitimacy of a profession is grounded not only in a body of abstract knowledge, but as well through a service orientation. This legitimacy is granted by a society that recognizes these areas of expertise and extends autonomy to a occupational group over its practice. This, of course, brings us back to the issue of licensure, which will require a delineation of our areas of expertise--which could also circumscribe our flexibility to provide services within our wide areas of expertise. Given this, at this point in time, rather than pursue specific legislation that licenses *sociological practitioners,* in general; the real concern is not to be *locked out* of certain fields of practice.

Thus, the tasks we must take up today are:

1) To monitor state occupational legislation to guarantee we are not excluded from practice.

2) To provide professional certification for areas of specialization as a first step in legitimizing our areas of expertise.

3) To establish a program of accreditation for our training programs so that we have clearly articulated standards that define the fundamentals of our knowledge and skills.

Whether we like it or not, we must move in this direction and we must be vigilant in our efforts. As sociologists we should understand political systems and how interest groups use their combined strengths to lobby on their behalf. As sociologists we should therefore use the same strategies and tactics that we advise others to use.

Challenge Three: How do we "become one" as a discipline--both applied and basic sociology?

As I stated previously, my vision focuses on an *interdependence* between basic and applied sociology, instead of the current state of *independence* in which we exist. If we examine other professional fields, this has not been a problem. Look at the professions of medicine, engineering, social work, psychology, geography, and anthropology.

The struggle between the basic and applied dimensions of sociology has been chronicled by others. At issue is whether we can move beyond the earlier phase in which our energies, as a discipline, were directed to the establishment of legitimacy. We must now move to the next phase where there is a new momentum that results from the interdependence between the basic and applied dimensions. But how will this come about?

Some of the changes in higher education today are facilitating the movement in this direction. There are significant outside forces impacting the landscape of higher education (Graff, 1995; Rice, 1995; Gamson, 1995). Demands for more relevance and accountability are echoing everywhere. There is a growing demand for the practical application of our academic disciplines, for practicums to prepare students for the job market, and for rewarding professional service within the community (not just basic research that results in publications in academic journals). As these winds of change affect higher education as a whole, there is a window of opportunity for sociology to couple its basic and applied side in a partnership that will not only enhance its marketability as a major, but as well, such a partnership will improve the overall status of sociology within the academy. This partnership and subsequent status enhancement will not result, however, if it is perceived by "basic" sociologists as a threat to their existence. Thus, the *basic* sociologists must be convinced that such a partnership provides them with a *reason for being*. How this relationship is articulated and strengthened should be the focus of an accreditation process for applied and clinical programs. Indeed, the Commission of Applied and Clinical Sociology has recognized this as an important component of the standards for accredited programs [1].

Challenge Four: How do we become recognized by the public as a "useful discipline"?

There are a number of examples of policy relevant sociological work-- Coleman's work in education, Wilson's study of the underclass, William Darrow's pioneering work in the understanding of AIDS, Matilda Riley's work related to the problems of aging and the life course, and Paul Starr's study of American medicine--just to name a few. And today, there are more sociologists who are quoted and recognized by the mass media. However, too often, sociologists and their work go unrecognized or sociological revelations are not attributed to the sociologists who have made significant contributions. On the other hand, some might question whether there is anything worth reporting. Think about it. When was the last time the nightly news, CNN, or Nightline featured the newest finding published in the *American Sociological Review*? In medicine we routinely hear about the latest scientific findings published in *The New England Journal of Medicine*.

Why don't we have good press coverage? There are multiple reasons. As stated previously, we lack a clear identity that the public can recognize, thus the media doesn't come to us; also, we cannot reach any agreement as to what is important enough to publicize. But, most significantly, we don't pursue press coverage--as a discipline. I do recognize that in recent years there have been more attempts to solicit press coverage for ourselves, but it is spotty and haphazard. We must deliberately and aggressively market ourselves. For many this is a dirty word, and it is anathema to a "scholarly discipline." In essence, that may be true, but we live in a different world today, and truth is seldom relevant. If we do not present a common front, and aggressively sell our wares, no one else will.

Challenge Five: How do we keep sociologists affiliated with the sociology profession?

This is an issue of professional socialization. The percentage of individuals trained in sociology (at all levels) who remain affiliated with the discipline is deplorable. We have not done this well, which is ironic since, as sociologists, we of all people should recognize the importance of socialization. As expressed previously, without significant numbers in our professional associations, the legitimacy of our profession becomes problematic. But what should this socialization process involve?

There are two aspects of the professional socialization process that are important. First, and particularly in graduate education, we can talk about an *orientation* that students acquire--that is, how are students socialized into a particular view of what it means to be a sociologist. Undoubtedly, the predominant view is one that emphasizes the role of the basic scientist. Thus, the *real* sociologist is one who has completed a Ph.D., taken a position in the academy, and engages in basic scientific research that is published in scholarly journals. The perpetuation of this view, of course, hinders the development of an *interdependence* between basic and applied sociology. Thus, it is critical that the socialization process begin to foster the view that there are multiple roles that sociologists play--both within and outside the academy. Just as the current socialization fosters the development of different specializations, it can also foster the dual roles of basic and applied.

In addition to acquiring a sociological *orientation*, a part of professional socialization means keeping our graduates connected with the discipline via professional associations. This is particularly important for those who may not pursue the Ph.D.--but this only happens with a select few. In part, this comes from a bias within the academy that only Ph.D.s pursuing the basic science degree are *real* sociologists. The thinking goes like this: although the training of *lesser* sociologists might pay our salaries in the academy, these students are not deserving of our attention and efforts toward social-ization for this group would be futile. I contend this cannot continue if we are to remain viable in the 21st century.

We must do follow-up on students, encourage their participation in the field, formalize the mentoring process for students, nurture their emerging abili-ties, and help them find jobs. Furthermore, we must provide what is needed to keep our graduates affiliated--graduation from accredited programs, useful continuing education for the work in which they are engaged, certification in specialty areas, and licensure. We may not keep all of our graduates affiliated, but we could do a far better job than we do currently. We tend to write them off.

Now, tying all of this together--the crisis we face, the dilemmas inherent in our discipline, and the proposed vision for our future--what do we have? Sociology is at a crossroads.

Sociology at a Crossroads

The metaphor of a journey and a crossroads implies that sociology now faces a fork in the road. Either sociologists raise their sights and take the difficult steps required, or we shall face the certain and unpleasant prospect of a demise of the field. Sociologists can continue to lament the current state of affairs of shrinking departments, budget cuts, identity problems, etc. We can maintain our small *social clubs* or we can move forward and take concrete action that will enhance our viability, as Deutscher eloquently described in his SAS Presidential address last year (Deutscher, 1995).

In essence, we must "get our act together." On an abstract and ideological level, we must establish a vision of sociology for the future--one that in-cludes a delineation of the basic and general principles of *how things work* within which the discipline's variety of methods and content specialties can fit. Furthermore, we must, as a group, support our rich diversity and facili-tate the *peaceful coexistence* among us.

On a concrete level, we must take the following actions, as identified in previous sections:

1) Move on accreditation of our educational programs, establish standards for learning, and eventually establish a credentialing system for our graduates (via certifications or state licensure).

2) Provide internships and job placement for our students.

3) Provide professional socialization within the academy--socialization that supports an identity with a discipline that has both a basic and applied side.

4) Work collaboratively with each other and other disciplines and tolerate each others' orientations rather than perpetuate theoretical/methodological divisions.

5) Tie our departmental and professional priorities to the priorities of higher education (e.g., cross-disciplinary work, accountability through outcomes based education, professional service both inside the academy and within the community, etc.).

6) Mount a significant public relations campaign that emphasizes the contributions of our discipline--both our methodological expertise as well as our understanding of social issues (such as diversity, immigration, family, crime, deviance).

In closing, I want to add that if the field of sociology is to preserve a distinct and separate identity and guarantee its future, we must accept *collective* responsibility for the current state that it is in as well as the direction it takes. The ideas presented herein are not revolutionary. But, undoubtedly, there are suggested strategies that will result in considerable resistance on the part of some sociologists--particularly marketing ourselves, accrediting our programs, and licensing our practitioners. For others, inaction is a matter of motivation. We may buy into the strategies that will preserve the discipline, but we believe it is someone else's responsibility to carry them out. It cannot be this way. It is the responsibility of each and every one of us. To mobilize the commitment within the discipline, is indeed, our biggest challenge. This humorous story captures my point:

> An elderly worker on a construction project opened his lunchbox, looked in, and growled, "Cheese sandwiches! Cheese sandwiches! Always cheese sandwiches for lunch."
>
> A fellow worker sitting close by overheard him and asked, "Why don't you ask your wife to make some other kind?"
>
> "Wife?" said the elderly man. "Who's married? I make these myself."

Thus, to the extent that we continue our internal bickering, blame outside forces, or continue with our ambivalence, we will be powerless to change anything. We need to be proactive rather than reactive in enhancing sociology's professional status. And, taking you back to Charles Dickens and *A Tale of Two Cities*, a *rebirth* of our discipline will not come easy; revolutionary periods are fraught with turbulence. However, as Dickens' character, Sydney Carton, sacrificed himself for the survival of his friends and the regeneration of society, so must we sacrifice (in terms of time, energy, and commitment to change) if we are to see our discipline as vital and robust in the year 2095.

NOTES

[1] The Commission on Applied and Clinical Sociology was formed in 1995 as a joint initiative of the Society for Applied Sociology and the Sociological Practice Association. This Commission seeks to enable sociologists to make significant contributions to society, through the development, promotion, and support of quality sociological education and practice in applied and clinical areas.

REFERENCES

ASA Section of Sociological Practice. 1995. "A Participatory Session in Creating our Future." Focus group discussion at the annual meeting of the American Sociological Association, Washington, DC.

Bell, Wendell. 1995. "The Sociology of the Future and the Future of Sociology." Paper presented at the annual meetings of the Pacific Sociological Association, San Francisco, California.

Carr-Saunders, A.M. and P.A. Wilson. 1933. *The Professions*. London: Oxford.

Clark, Elizabeth and Jan M. Fritz. 1986. "The Clinical Approach to Successful Program Development." *Clinical Sociology Review* 4:173-81.

Cole, Stephen (ed.). 1994. "What's Wrong with Sociology?" Special issue of *Sociological Forum* 9 (2).

Coleman, James S. 1994. "A Vision for Sociology." *Society* 32(1):29-34.

Commission on Applied and Clinical Sociology. 1995. Discussions of the Commission members at their charter meetings, February, June and August.

Costner, Herbert L. 1979. "A Vision and An Image." *The American Sociologist* 14:74-76.

Coughlin, Ellen K. 1992. "Sociologists Confront Questions About Field's Vitality and Direction." *The Chronicle of Higher Education* August 12:A6-A8.

D'Antonio, William V. 1992. "Sociology's Education Foundations: Facing the Challenge of Ambivalence." *Sociological Focus* 25:111-120.

Deutscher, Irwin. 1995. "The Politics of Identities and Futures." *Journal of Applied Sociology* 12(1):1-9.

Dickens, Charles. 1859. *A Tale of Two Cities.*

Dotzler, Robert J. 1995. "What's Wrong with Sociology? A Practitioner's Perspective." Paper presented at the annual meetings of the Eastern Sociological Association, Philadelphia, Pennsylvania.

Fleischer, Michael S. 1994. State Licensing Monitors Handbook. Washington, DC: The American Sociological Association.

Freidson, Eliot. 1970. *The Profession of Medicine.* New York: Dodd, Mead.

Footnotes. 1991. "An Interview with Robert K. Merton." American Sociological Association, October: 4.

Gaff, Jerry. 1995. "Preparing Future Faculty." Workshop presentation at the annual meetings of the American Sociological Association, Washington, DC.

Gamson, Zelda. 1995. "Professional Service." Workshop presentation at the annual meetings of the American Sociological Association, Washington, DC.

Glass, John E. 1992. "The State of Sociology." *Footnotes* 20(6):6-7.

Goode, William. 1960. "Encroachment, Charlatanism, and the Emerging Profession: Psychology, Sociology, and Medicine." *American Sociological Review* 25:902-914.

Kantrowitz, Barbara. 1992. "Sociology's Lonely Crowd." *Newsweek* February 3:55.

Koppel, Ross. 1995. "Why a Dichotomy between Teaching Sociology and Doing Sociology?" *Sociological Practice Letter* Spring/Summer: 4.

Ladd, Everett C. Jr. and Seymour M. Lipset. 1976. *The Divided Academy.* New York: W.W. Norton.

Lazarsfeld, Paul and Wagner Thielens, Jr. 1958. *The Academic Mind.* Glencoe, IL: The Free Press.

Lipset, Seymour M. 1982. "The Academic Mind at the Top." *Public Opinion Quarterly* 46:143-168.

Lipset, Seymour M. 1994. "The State of American Sociology." *Sociological Forum* 9:199-220.

Lynch, David M. and J. Richard McFerron. 1993. "A Discipline in Trouble: Why More Sociology Departments May be Closing Shortly." *Footnotes* 21(2):3,7.

Porter, Jack Nusan. 1992. "Sociology's Identity Crisis." *Footnotes* 20(6):7.

Rhoades, Lawrence. 1981. *A History of the American Sociological Association: 1905-1980.* Washington, DC: American Sociological Association.

Rice, Eugene. 1995. "Faculty Roles, Faculty Rewards Forum and Tenure Project." Workshop presentation at the annual meetings of the American Sociological Association, Washington, DC.

Steele, Stephen F. and Sherry Marshall. 1995. "On Raising Hopes of Raising Teaching: A Glimpse of Introduction to Sociology in 2005." Hans O. Mauksch Award Recipient Presentation at the annual meetings of the American Sociological Association, Washington, DC.

Turner, Stephen P. and Jonathan H. Turner. 1990. *An Institutional Analysis of American Sociology.* Newbury Park, CA: Sage Publications.

Wilensky, Harold. 1964. "The Professionalization of Everyone." *American Journal of Sociology* 70:137-158.

Joyce Miller Iutcovich

1950-

Joyce Miller Iutcovich, President of the Society for Applied Sociology 1994-1995 completed her undergraduate degree in sociology at Edinboro University of Pennsylvania (1971) and her Ph.D. in sociology at Kent State University (1981). As a student of Alex Boros, who served as her mentor over the years, Joyce was initiated into the ranks of the executive officers of SAS in 1980--shortly after its founding in 1979. Her first role included the publication and distribution of the *Bulletin,* the newsletter of SAS from 1980 through 1984, when its title changed to *The Useful Sociologist.* In addition to newsletter responsibilities, Joyce also administered membership campaigns and renewals, and served as part of the planning committees for the first and third annual meetings at Kent State University (1983) and Edinboro University of Pennsylvania (1985). In 1983 she and Harold Cox were appointed as the first editors of *The Journal of Applied Sociology*, both of whom served in this capacity until 1990. She also served as part of the planning group and one of the Associate Editors for *Social Insight: Knowledge at Work,* the first issue of which was published in 1995.

Upon leaving the editorial position of *The Journal of Applied Sociology* in 1990, Joyce served as the Chair of the Publications Committee until elected as Vice President for 1992-93. As Vice President, Joyce chaired the Program Committee that planned and organized the annual meeting held in St. Louis, Missouri, October 1993. In her continued movement through the ranks of SAS officers, Joyce was elected President and served her term of office in 1994-95. The theme she selected for the annual meeting in San Diego, California, 1995, was "Sociology 2000: A Vision of Our Future." During her tenure as President, the Commission on Applied and Clinical Sociology was formed. This is a joint initiative of the Society for Applied Sociology and Sociological Practice Association with the goal of developing accreditation standards and process for applied and clinical sociology programs. This Commission evolved from the initial efforts of Steve Steele, who formed a SAS Committee on Professional Standards and Accreditation during his term as President in 1992-93.

As an applied sociologist, Joyce has maintained a dual career path. One career has been in academia where she began as an instructor of sociology at Villa Maria College in Erie, Pennsylvania in 1978. Over the years she progressed through the academic ranks, moved from Villa to Gannon University when the two institutions merged in 1989, and achieved full professor status in 1991. In 1996 she was asked to served as Associate Provost at Gannon University, where she has taken over the responsibility for the assessment of student learning outcomes and the development of a center at the university that integrates faculty scholarship with the enhancement of the teaching-learning process.

Another career path involves an independent research and consulting practice that began in 1975 through the joint efforts of Joyce and Mark Iutcovich. Keystone University Research Corporation, of which Joyce serves as President, began modestly from their basement, but it is now housed in a former school building and has an annual revenue of approximately $5-6 million. The projects undertaken by KURC range from short term marketing, evaluation and needs assessment research to multi-year contracts to set-up and administer programs for state governmental agencies. In her capacity as an applied social researcher, Joyce has expertise in evaluation research, primarily in social service and educational fields.

Over the years she has published a number of articles related to her research in *Evaluation and Program Planning, Journal of Applied Gerontology, Journal of Applied Sociology, and Social Insight: Knowledge at Work*. She also has an number of chapters in edited volumes and in 1987, she and Mark Iutcovich published the book, *Consulting as a Sociologist* (Praeger Publishing).

APPENDIX A:

Society for Applied Sociology
Officers and Committee Chairs

Society for Applied Sociology Officers and Committee Chairs

Board Position	1984-1985	1985-1986	1986-1987
President	Alexander Boros	Alexander Boros	Mark Iutcovich
Vice President	James Hougland	James Hougland	Jeanne Ballantine
Secretary	Sonia Alemagno	Sonia Alemagno	Francine Jefferson
Treasurer	Nancy Dukes	Robert Kubiak	Robert Kubiak
SAS Board Members	Richard Ball	Richard Ball	Kathryn Grzelkowski
	Charles Norman	Charles Norman	Stephen King
	Mark Tausig	Mark Tausig	Grace Marvin
Archives			
Awards			
Bylaws	Mark Tausig	Mark Tausig	Darryl Poole
Development	Ruth Pickard	Ruth Pickard	
Ethics			
Finance			
Liaison	Terrence Russel		
Membership	Ruth Pickard	Ruth Pickard	Sonia Alemagno
Newsletter Editor	Sonia Alemagno	Sonia Alemagno	Francine Jefferson
		Julie Zieglar	
Nominating	Alexander Boros	Alexander Boros	Alexander Boros
Professional Standards		Nancy Dukes	Stephen King
Program		James Hougland	Jeanne Ballantine
Publications			
Student Coordinator			

Board Position	1987-1988	1988-1989	1989-1990
President	Marvin Olsen	James Hougland, Jr	Jeanne Ballantine
Vice President	Howard Garrison	Penelope Canan	William Brown
Secretary	Francine Jefferson	Dora Lodwick	Dora Lodwick
Treasurer	Dru Tiliakos	Dru Tiliakos	Patricia Ryan
SAS Board Members	Kathryn Grzelkowski Stephen King Grace Marvin	Sue Blanshan Gerry Gairola Harrold T. Curl	Sue Blanshan Gerry Gairola Harrold T. Curl
Archives	Alexander Boros	Alexander Boros	
Awards	Elizabeth Darrough	James Thompson	Marvin Olsen
Bylaws	William Brown	Max Burchard	Max Burchard
Development	GeAnne Pankey-Thompson	GeAnne Pankey-Thompson	Brian Pendleton
		Brian Pendleton	
Ethics	John Kennedy	John Kennedy	Eugene Royster
Finance	Dru Tiliakos	Dru Tiliakos	Patricia Ryan
Liaison			
Membership	Val Fonseca	Val Fonseca	Harrold T. Curl
Newsletter Editor	Harry Perlstadt	Harry Perlstadt	Dora Lodwick
Nominating	Mark Iutcovich	Marvin Olsen	James Hougland
Professional Standards and Accreditation			
Program	Howard Garrison	Penelope Canan	
Publications			William Brown
Student Coordinator			Joyce Iutcovich

Society for Applied Sociology Officers and Committee Chairs

Board Position	1990-1991	1991-1992	1992-1993
President	Howard Garrison	Harold Cox	Stephen Steele
Vice President	Stephen Steele	John Kennedy	Joyce Iutcovich
Secretary	Gerry Gairola	Gerry Gairola	Mark Peyrot
Treasurer	Patricia Ryan	Eleanor Lyon	Eleanor Lyon
SAS Board Members	Lynn Atkinson	Lynn Atkinson	Toni Pickard
	Eleanor Lyon	Eleanor Lyon	Harry Perlstadt
	James G. Thompson	James G. Thompson	Hayward Horton
Archives	Alexander Boros	Alexander Boros	Alexander Boros
Awards	Ruth Pickard	Ruth Pickard	Scott Lauder
Bylaws	Marvin Finkelstein	Marvin Finkelstein	John Kennedy
Development	Kathryn Gzrelkowski	Stephen Steele	Martin Jaeckel
Ethics			
Finance	Patricia Ryan	Eleanor Lyon	Eleanor Lyon
Liaison	Martin Jaeckel	Martin Jaeckel	Robert Dotzler
Membership	Brian Pendleton	Phil Obermiller	Donna Fletcher
Newsletter Editor	Dora Lodwick	Dora Lodwick	Susan Stein
Nominating	Jeanne Ballantine	Howard Garrison	Harold Cox
Professional Standards and Accreditation			
Program	Stephen Steele	John Kennedy	Joyce Iutcovich
Publications	Joyce Iutcovich	Joyce Iutcovich	Dora Lodwick
Student Coordinator	Sonad Sabash	Sonad Sabash	Ann Walawander

Society for Applied Sociology Officers and Committee Chairs

Board Position	1993-1994	1994-1995	1995-1996
President	Irwin Deutscher	Joyce Iutcovich	Dora Lodwick
Vice President	Patricia Ryan	Duane Dukes	William Hauser
Secretary	Mark Peyrot	Marvin Finkelstein	Marvin Finkelstein
Treasurer	Anne Hendershott	Anne Hendershott	Brian Pendleton
SAS Board Members	Harry Perlstadt	Hayward Horton	Phil Obermiller
	Hayward Horton	Phil Obermiller	James C. Peterson
	Phil Obermiller	James C. Petersen	Kathy Trier
Archives	Alexander Boros	Alexander Boros	Alexander Boros
Awards	Scott Lauder	Mark Iutcovich	Duane Dukes
Bylaws	John Kennedy	John Kennedy	John Kennedy
Development	Anne Hendershott	Rick Stephens	Rick Stephens
Ethics	James Wolf	James Wolf	James Wolf
Finance	Anne Hendershott	Anne Hendershott	Brian Pendleton
Liaison	Robert Dotzler	Robert Dotzler	Robert Dotzler
Membership	Dona Fletcher	Stephen Steele	Kathy Trier
		Kathy Trier	Augie Diana
Newsletter Editor	Susan Stein	Susan Stein	Sheila Anderson
			Sam Sloss
Nominating	Stephen Steele	Irwin Deutscher	Joyce Iutcovich
Professional Standards and Accreditation	Harry Perlstadt	Harry Perlstadt	Harry Perlstadt
Program	Patricia Ryan	Duane Dukes	William Hauser
Publications	Dora Lodwick	Dora Lodwick	Harold Cox
Student Coordinator	Ann Walawander	Sherry Marshall	Cathy Mobley

APPENDIX B:

BYLAWS OF THE SOCIETY
FOR APPLIED SOCIOLOGY

1995 and 1985

BYLAWS OF THE SOCIETY FOR APPLIED SOCIOLOGY*

PREAMBLE

The name of this organization shall be the Society for Applied Sociology. The rules and regulations listed in these Bylaws shall govern and direct the activities of the Society for Applied Sociology (SAS).

The major proposes of the SAS shall be:

1. to provide a forum for sociologists and others interested in applications of sociological knowledge;

2. to enhance the understanding of the interrelationship between sociological knowledge and sociological practice;

3. to increase the effectiveness of sociological research and training.

ARTICLE 1: MEMBERSHIP IN THE SAS

1. Persons and organizations sufficiently interested in applications of sociology to accept the responsibilities of membership shall be eligible for membership. A person or organization may become a member of the SAS by submitting a membership application, and by the payment of dues.

2. Individual SAS members are entitled to hold office, attend meetings, and receive all official SAS publications.

3. Non-payment of dues will terminate membership.

4. Questions concerning eligibility for membership shall be resolved by the membership committee.

*Approved in October 1995.

ARTICLE 2: BOARD OF DIRECTORS

1. The SAS shall constitute a Board of Directors from among its members. The governance of the SAS and the management of its affairs shall be vested in the Board of Directors, except insofar as the Bylaws delegate functions to other officers or committees.

2. The Board shall consist of the President, Vice-President, Immediate Past President, President-Elect, Vice-President Elect, the Secretary, the Treasurer, and four Members-at-Large. The Board will be directly elected by the members of the SAS.

3. The President and the Vice President shall serve for one year. The President-Elect and Vice President-Elect shall serve for one year and shall then become President and Vice President, respectively, for one-year terms. The Secretary and Treasurer shall be elected for two-year terms which are staggered so that their terms do not end in the same year. The four Members-at-Large shall be elected for two-year terms which are staggered. The Board members may not succeed themselves in office.

4. The Board shall be responsible for formulating the policy and the general direction of the affairs of the SAS.

5. The Board shall have the authority to fill vacancies in its elective membership, except for the President and the Vice President, due to death, resignation, or failure to elect. Such appointees may hold office until replacement by officers elected at the next election.

6. The Board has the authority to interpret these Bylaws.

7. The Board may establish membership categories and set annual membership dues, which may vary by membership categories.

8. The Board may terminate membership of any member.

9. The Board takes office at the termination of the annual conference. The Board shall meet twice each year. The first meeting shall be held as soon as

possible after the annual conference (post-conference meeting). A second meeting shall be held immediately prior to the annual conference (pre-conference meeting). The Board may meet at other times as called by the President. The actions of all Board meetings shall be printed in the subsequent issue of the official SAS newsletter. A majority of the Board constitutes a quorum. A quorum is required for official actions to be approved by the Board.

10. The Board meetings are open to all SAS members.

11. The Board shall hold any property belonging to the SAS and shall have such other authority as shall be vested in it by the SAS.

12. The Board will appoint the Editor(s) of the Journal of Applied Sociology, a Newsletter Editor, and an Administrative Officer.

13. The Board may create temporary committees not provided for in the Bylaws as may seem useful for promoting the work of the SAS.

14. The Secretary, Treasurer, and Members-at-Large may be replaced at any time by a majority vote of the Board.

15. The Board proceedings shall be in accordance with Robert's Rules of Order, unless otherwise determined by the provisions of these Bylaws.

ARTICLE 3: DUTIES OF THE OFFICERS AND EDITORS

1. The officers of the SAS shall include the members of the Board of Directors, the Editor(s) of the Journal of Applied Sociology, the Newsletter Editor, and the Administrative Officer.

2. Duties of the President:

A. The President has overall responsibility for coordinating the activities of the SAS.

B. The President will perform the following tasks:

i. preside over the Board meetings;

ii. preside over the annual business meeting;

iii. set the agenda for the annual business meeting and Board meetings;

iv. appoint the chairs and members of committees unless otherwise provided for in these Bylaws;

v. authorize and appoint special officers and/or committees;

vi. appoint a committee of at least three members, one of whom must be a Board member, to conduct an annual review of the Administrative Officer.

vii. provide overall supervision of the annual conference.

viii. act as the official SAS representative.

C. The President is authorized to sign checks for disbursements whenever the Treasurer is unable to do so.

3. Duties of the Vice President:

A. The Vice President shall serve as the chair of the program committee for the annual conference. The Vice President shall be responsible for planning and organizing the annual conference.

B. The Vice President shall be responsible for the preparation and printing of the program booklet for the annual conference and ensure that the booklet is distributed to the membership.

C. The Vice President shall be responsible for distributing registration materials to the membership prior to the annual conference.

D. If the President should not be able to hold office for any reason, the Vice President shall become President.

4. Duties of the Treasurer:

A. The Treasurer shall chair the finance committee.

B. The Treasurer is responsible for a permanent record of receipts and disbursement of the SAS.

C. The Treasurer shall be responsible for the dues collection.

D. The Treasurer shall be responsible for compiling financial reports as necessary.

i. Financial reports shall be prepared for the annual business meeting and at the end of the fiscal year. Other financial reports shall be prepared as requested by the President or the Board.

ii. In January, any not-for-profit tax forms shall be prepared, as well as any required Federal tax forms.

E. The Treasurer shall invest SAS funds with the President's approval.

F. The Treasurer shall be responsible for securing an independent review of SAS accounts at the expiration of the term of office of the Treasurer, and at any other time requested by the President or the Board. The results of all reviews will be published in the official SAS newsletter.

5. Duties of the Secretary:

A. The Secretary shall record and distribute minutes of the Board meetings and the business meeting(s) .

B. The Secretary is responsible for placing the summary of the minutes of all Board meetings and the business meeting(s) in the official SAS newsletter.

C. If the Board has not appointed a Parliamentarian, the Secretary shall serve as the Parliamentarian.

D. If the Vice President should not be able to hold office for any reason, the Secretary shall assume the duties of the Vice President.

6. Duties of the Members-at-Large:

A. The Members-at-Large will be assigned duties deemed suitable and necessary by the President.

7. Duties of the President-Elect:

A. The President-Elect shall perform those duties assigned to him/her by the President.

8. Duties of the Vice President-Elect:

A. The Vice President-Elect shall serve on the program committee.

9. Duties of the Immediate Past President:

A. The Immediate Past President shall chair the nominations committee and serve on the awards committee.

10. Duties of the Editor(s) of the Journal of Applied Sociology:

A. The Journal of Applied Sociology (JAS) is the official journal of the SAS. The Editor(s) shall collect manuscripts of papers submitted to the JAS so that they can be considered for publication in the JAS according to the peer review process.

B . The Editor (s) shall be responsible for the editing of the manuscripts accepted for publication and complete the JAS.

C. The Editor (s) shall be responsible for printing and distributing the JAS.

D. The Editor (s) shall periodically evaluate the distribution of the JAS to ascertain if the SAS would benefit by a wider distribution and make appropriate recommendations to the Board.

E. The Editor(s) may make recommendations to the Board for change and improvements in the JAS.

11. Duties of the Newsletter editor:

A. The Newsletter Editor shall serve as the Editor of the official SAS newsletter.

B. The Newsletter Editor shall be responsible for compiling the newsletter.

C. The Newsletter Editor shall be responsible for printing and distributing the newsletter.

12. Duties of the Administrative Officer:

A. The Administrative Officer shall be the general manager and fiscal agent responsible for the administration of the SAS within the framework of the policies, principles, and practices established by the Board. The Administrative Officer may disburse funds from SAS accounts.

B. The Administrative Officer shall be responsible for the administrative management of the affairs of the SAS business office subject to the approval and direction of the President and shall be responsible for working within an approved budget established by the Board.

C. The Administrative Officer shall count the ballots for all SAS elections and Bylaws revisions.

D. The Administrative Officer shall serve at the pleasure of the Board.

ARTICLE: 4: NOMINATIONS AND ELECTIONS

1. The President-Elect, Vice President-Elect, Secretary, Treasurer and the Members-at-Large shall be elected by mail ballot of the members. Their terms of office shall begin at the termination of the annual meeting in the year in which they are elected.

2. For the positions of President-Elect, Vice President-Elect, Secretary, and Treasurer, a majority vote is required before a candidate is declared elected. For the Members-at-Large, the candidate(s) receiving the largest number of votes shall be declared elected. In case of a tie vote, the President shall decide by lot between them.

3. The nominations committee shall send a mailing to all members by January 15 requesting nominations for the offices that will be elected during that year.

4. The nominations committee will provide a list of at least two (2) candidates for each position to be elected. The nominations will be announced, either in a mailing to all members or in the official SAS newsletter, by March 15. Nominees shall be members of the SAS.

5. Members will have until 30 days after the announcement of the candidates by the nominations committee to nominate additional candidates. Nominations from members shall be accepted provided that a petition is signed by 25 members.

6. Elections shall take place by mail ballots which shall be sent to all individual members by no later than May 15. Ballots must be returned by no later than June 15.

7. The ballots will be counted by the Administrative Officer, and the election will be certified by the Secretary.

8. Election results will be available by July 1. The chair of the nominations committee will announce the results in a mailing to all members or in the official SAS newsletter.

ARTICLE 5: MEETINGS

1. The annual conference of the SAS shall be held in locations determined by the Board.

2. At each annual conference, there shall be at least one business meeting

at which the Board shall respond to questions from the members.

3. The agenda of the business meeting (s) shall be determined by the President.

ARTICLE 6: STANDING COMMITTEES

The standing committees of the SAS are: membership, program, publications, nominations, local arrangements, finance, ethics, awards, bylaws, development and planning, educational and professional standards, and student. All members are eligible to serve on committees. The President is an ex-officio member of all committees.

1. Membership Committee: The function of the membership committee is to foster the growth of the SAS and promote communication and liaison among members and persons eligible for membership.

2. Program Committee: The function of the program committee is to plan the program for the annual conference. The Vice President shall chair this committee.

3. Publications Committee: The function of the publications committee is to oversee the SAS's publications and to make recommendations to the Board concerning changes in the directions of the SAS's publications. The chair cannot be a current Editor of any of the SAS's publications. Other members of this committee shall include, but are not limited to, the current Editors of the SAS's publications.

4. Nominations Committee: The function of the nominations committee is to nominate candidates for the Board and other duties as described in Article 4. The Immediate Past President shall chair this committee.

5. Local Arrangements Committee: The local arrangements committee is responsible for identifying a suitable facility to host the annual meeting, to include hotel arrangements, meeting rooms, and other amenities as provided for in the budget. The committee shall consult with the President on coordination of events and local arrangements. The committee shall coordi-

nate with the Vice President on meeting rooms and facilities.

6. Finance Committee: The function of the finance committee is to advise the Treasurer and the President on financial matters, including investment practices, budget planning, and financial policies. The Treasurer shall chair this committee.

7. Ethics Committee: The ethics committee shall investigate and make recommendations to the Board concerning any dues of professional ethics that are referred to it by SAS members or that the committee considers relevant to sociology. This committee is responsible for interpreting the SAS Code of Ethics.

8. Awards Committee: The function of the awards committee is to administer the SAS awards as described in Article 8. The Immediate Past President shall be a member of this committee.

9. Bylaws Committee: The function of the bylaws committee is to draft and propose to the Board appropriate amendments to these Bylaws, as specified in Article 9.

10. Development and Planning Committee: The function of the development and planning committee is to raise all funds other than dues and annual meeting fees.

11. Educational and Professional Standards Committee: The function of the educational and professional standards committee is to improve the quality of education, training, and practice of applied sociologists, and to work with other associations and commissions to achieve these ends.

12. Student Committee: The student committee shall support and coordinate student activities and serve as a liaison between students and the Board.

ARTICLE 7: BUDGET

1. The fiscal year of the SAS shall basin on the first business day of each calendar year.

2. At the post-conference Board meeting, a budget covering all anticipated income and expenditures of the SAS for the coming year shall be submitted by the President and the Treasurer for approval by the Board. The President and Treasurer shall review the budget at least quarterly and adjust the budget if needed.

3. At the end of each fiscal year, the accounts of the SAS shall be reviewed by the Board.

ARTICLE 8: AWARDS

1. The SAS may present four awards each year. These awards are:

A. The Lester F. Ward Distinguished Contributions to Applied Sociology Award is presented to a person who has made a significant contribution to applied sociology over a period of time.

B. The Alex Boros Award for Contributions to the Society for Applied Sociology is presented to a member of SAS who has served SAS with distinction.

C. The Award for Sociological Practice is presented to an outstanding sociologist who has demonstrated how sociological practice can advance and improve society.

D. The Community Service Award is presented to a person or organization in the community where the annual conference is held. The recipient of this award will have made significant and noteworthy applied sociological contributions in the community.

2. The awards committee shall issue a call for nominee for the Lester F. Ward Distinguished Contributions to Applied Sociology Award, the Alex Boros Award for Contributions to the Society for Applied Sociology, and the Award for Sociological Practice in the first newsletter after the annual conference. The awards committee will nominate candidates for these three awards. It will review, evaluate, and rank candidates in written recommendations to the Board. The Board shall select the recipients at the pre-con-

ference meeting, and these recipients will be announced at the annual business meeting. The chair of the awards committee shall inform the recipients that they will receive the awards at the annual conference the following year.

3. The local arrangements committee, in consultation with the chair of the awards committee, shall select the recipient of the Community Service Award. The chair of the local arrangements committee shall prepare a Citation and plaque, and present it at the annual meeting.

4. The Board may establish additional awards and prizes and set specific criteria for all awards and prizes.

ARTICLE 9: AMENDMENTS

1. Amendments to these Bylaws may be proposed by a majority of the Board at any Board meeting or by a petition of at least twenty-five (25) members.

2. The Bylaws may be amended only by approval by a majority of individual members voting in a mail ballot. Proposed amendments will be included in the mail ballot for the election of the Board.

ARTICLE 10: TERMINATION

1. Proposals to terminate the SAS may be approved by the Board at any Board meeting. The SAS may be terminated by a majority vote of all members in a mail ballot.

2. Upon such termination, all funds shall be transferred to a not-for-profit organization chosen by the Board.

Society for Applied Sociology
Bylaws of the Society*

PREAMBLE

The name of this organization shall be the SOCIETY FOR APPLIED SOCIOLOGY. The rules and regulations shall govern and direct the activities of the SOCIETY FOR APPLIED SOCIOLOGY (SAS).

The major objectives of the SAS shall be:

1. to provide a forum for Sociologists and others interested in applications of sociological knowledge;

2. to enhance the understanding of the interrelationship between sociological knowledge and sociological practice; and

3. to increase the usefulness and effectiveness of sociological research and training.

BYLAWS

Article 1
Membership In The SAS

1. The Board of the SAS shall have the power to establish different classes of membership. There will be both regular membership and student membership. All persons who are sufficiently interested in applications of Sociology to accept the responsibilities of membership shall be eligible for membership. A person may become a member of the society by submitting membership application and payment of due. Non-payment of dues by the final deadline for such payment will automatically terminate an individual's membership. Membership may also be terminated through extraordinary

*Approved October 1985

action of the Board of Director. Decisions concerning eligibility for membership in any class shall be mate by the membership chairperson.

2. Those whose membership lapses because of non-payment of dues may submit a membership application and current year dues and be reinstated as members.

3. The Board of the SAS shall have the power to fix the amount of annual dues, which may vary with the membership class. The treasurer shall have the power to designate sub-treasurers to collect dues.

4. Regular and student members are entitled to vote on all SAS business, hold office, attend all meetings, and receive all SAS publications. Privileges of other classes of membership shall be determined by the Board of Directors at the time they are created.

Article 2
Officers

1. The officers of the Society directly elected by the voting membership shall be a President, a President-Elect, an Immediate past President, a Vice President, a Vice President-Elect, a Secretary, a Treasurer and three (3) Members-at-Large. The President and the Vice President shall serve for one year. The President shall then automatically become the Immediate Past President. The President-Elect and Vice President-Elect shall serve for one year and shall then automatically become President and Vice President respectively for one year terms. The Secretary and Treasurer shall be elected by the voting membership for two year terms staggered so that the terms do not end in the same year. The three Members-at-Large shall serve simultaneous two year terms. Elected officers may not succeed themselves in office.

2. The duties of the President shall be:

A. The President has the responsibility of supervising and coordinating the activities of other officers and committees of the SAS.

B. As Chairman of the Board in meeting and as general executive officer, the President shall:

a. preside over Board meetings and secure facilities for this purpose;

b. preside over the annual meeting;

c. by consultation with the other directors, set the agenda for the annual business meeting and Board meetings, and send out agendas for the latter;

d. appoint the members and chairpersons of committees unless otherwise provided;

e. authorize and appoint special committees;

f. appoint the local arrangements committee for the annual meeting; and

g. propose an annual operating budget at the designated board meeting.

C. The President is authorized to sign checks for disbursements whenever the Treasurer is unable to do so. The President shall be bonded.

3. The duties of the Vice President shall be:

A. The Vice President has the responsibility of serving as the Chairperson of the Program Committee of the Annual Meeting. The Vice President shall see that the committee has finalized the program by April 1 and that other officers are informed of the participants and titles of paper to be presented.

B. The Vice President shall organize the plenary session of the Annual Meeting and preside over it. This officer should encourage early planning of program themes and securing of speakers. Speakers should be finalized by April 1.

The Vice President shall report the names of all speakers to the Editors as soon as possible, and if necessary secure a commitment from these speakers for manuscripts usable by the Editors.

C. With cooperation from others involved in preparing the Annual Meeting, the Vice President and Program Committee shall compile the program, have it printed and distribute it, along with related materials, to the membership.

4. The duties of the Immediate Past President shall be:

A. The Immediate Past President has the responsibility of serving as Chairperson of the Nominating Committee, and shall report to the Board and President thereon.

B. The Immediate Past President shall supervise programs designed to honor all members who have made significant contributions to the promotion of the SAS.

5. The duties of the Treasurer shall be:

A. The Treasurer shall maintain a permanent record of receipts and disbursements of the SAS, and collect dues. After the Secretary has mailed due notices, the Treasurer shall collect dues from members of the society. Periodically, the Treasurer shall inform the officers of dues collected, distribute membership cards, and create a list of individuals who have paid dues.

B. The treasurer shall compile reports as necessary:

a. A financial statement shall be prepared for each Board and Annual Meeting and at the end of the calendar year.

b. When necessary, reports shall be prepared for any foundation providing financial assistance for the SAS.

c. In January, a state Not-for-profit tax form shall be prepared, as well as any required Federal tax form.

C. The Treasurer shall invest the society's funds with the Board's approval.

D. A certified audit of the Treasurer's books shall be conducted at the expiration of the term of office or at any other time requested by the Board.

E. The Treasurer shall be bonded.

6. The duties of the Secretary shall be:

A. The Secretary shall record and distribute appropriately minute of Board meetings and annual meetings.

B. The Secretary shall maintain the society's mailing list which shall include the SAS membership, but not be limited to it.

C. The Secretary shall prepare address labels for mailing of the SAS Journal.

D. The Secretary shall be responsible for the Newsletter sent to all those on the SAS mailing list.

E. The Secretary shall serve as the editor of the quarterly publication 'The Applied Sociologist Bulletin.'

7. The duties of the Members-at-Large shall be:

A. Three Members-at-Large will be elected for two years each. They will be given duties deemed suitable and necessary by the SAS Board of Director. They will have voting privileges on all Board matters.

Article 3
Board of Directors

1. The Society shall constitute a Board of Directors from among its members. The Board shall be the governing body of the Society, except insofar as eke Bylaws delegate governmental functions to other officers or to committees.

2. The Board of Directors shall consist of thirteen voting members. The ex officio members shall be, the President, Immediate Past President, President-Elect, Vice President Vice President-Elect, Secretary, Treasurer and Members-at-Large. In addition, the ex officio members of the Board will appoint to the Board two (2) editors of the *Journal of Applied Sociology* and a Membership Chairperson. The editors and membership chairperson shall be appointed for two year terms. The terms of the editors shall be staggered so that the terms do not end in the same year. The President-Elect and Vice President-Elect shall serve on the board for one year before succeeding to office. Appointed Board members may be reappointed if the ex officio members of the Board so decide.

3. As the governing- body of the Society, the Board shall be responsible for the formulation of policy and the general direction of the affairs of the Society. It shall have the power to fill vacancies in its elective membership occasioned by death, resignation, or failure to elect, such as appointees to hold office until replaced by officers elected at the next election. The authority to interpret the By-Laws resides in the Board. The Board shall appoint and may remove by majority vote the Membership Chairperson and the Editors of the various publications sponsored by the Society.

4. The Board shall meet at least once annually in conjunction with, the annual meeting of the Society. The Board may meet on additional occasions but may make no decisions binding on the membership without a majority of Board members in attendance. All actions taken by the Board must be communicated to the membership promptly in an appropriate publication of the Society. The Board may create such temporary committees not provided in the By-Laws as may seem useful for promoting the work of the Society.

5. Board members may be replaced for non-feasance, with particular reference to the job descriptions at the discretion of a majority of the full membership of the Board.

6. The Board shall hold any property belonging to the Society and shall have such other authority as shall be vested in it by the Society.

7. The Board proceedings shall be in accordance with Robert's Rules of Order, unless otherwise determined by the provisions of the By-Laws of the Society.

8. All Board members shall have the power to vote on Board decisions.

9. The duties of the Membership Chairperson are:

> A. The Membership Chairperson has the responsibility of serving a the Chairperson of the Membership and Development Committee. This officer shall maintain a permanent record of the individual members by discipline and school as well a institutional members. A list of individual members, by discipline and school, and a lit of institutional members shall be prepared for Board meetings and the Annual Meeting.

> B. The Membership Chairperson shall be responsible for publicizing the SAS with the intent of fostering its growth; and for maintaining communication with, and serving as liason to, other groups. The Membership Chairperson shall use the mailing list to prepare and send out notice of dues in March, and past due notices at the designated time.

10. The duties of the Co-Editor are:

a. The two Editors shall make recommendations to the Board for changes and improvements of the SAS Journal.

b. By April 1, the Co-Editors should receive the titles of papers and the names and addresses of those presenting them at the Annual-Meeting from the committee in charge of sectional meetings. This information will allow the Editors to send guidelines for the preparation of papers to all those presenting papers at the Annual Meeting.

c. The Editors shall collect eke manuscripts of all papers submitted so that they can be considered for publication in the SAS Journal according to the peer review process. The Editors shall then edit the manuscripts, compile the journal, and have it printed and distributed.

d. The Editors shall periodically evaluate distribution of the SAS Journal to ascertain if the society would benefit by a wider distribution than currently in practice, and make appropriate recommendations to the Board.

Article 4
Elections and Voting

1. The President-Elect, Vice President-Elect, Secretary, Treasurer and the Member-at-Large shall be elected by mail ballot of the members qualified to vote. The term of office shall begin at the close of the Annual Meeting of the Society to be held during the year in which they are elected.

2. For the positions of President-Elect, Vice President-Elect, Secretary and Treasurer, a majority vote is required before a candidate is declared elected. For the Member-at-Large, the candidates receiving the largest number of votes shall be declared elected. In case of a tie vote the President of the Society, in the presence of witnesses chosen by the candidates concerned, shall decide by lot between them.

3. The Nominating Committee shall prepare a preliminary list of nominations for publication in the Spring edition of the SAS bulletin. At that time, additional nominations shall be accepted, provided that a petition is signed by at least 15 members of the Society. Nominees must be members of the Society.

4. Elections shall take place by mail ballots which shall be sent to the full membership by no later than May 30. Ballots must be returned by no later than June 15.

5. Election results shall b published in the Summer edition of the SAS Newsletter.

Article 5
Meetings

1. The Annual Meeting of the Society shall be held in such places as the Board decides proper.

2. The agenda of the annual business meeting shall be determined by the President of the Society, in consultation with the Board. The President shall exercise discretionary powers in accepting additional agenda items from the floor during the meeting.

3. At each Annual Meeting there shall be at least one business meeting at which the Officers and Board shall respond to questions from the membership.

Article 6
Committees

1. Committees shall be chaired by Board Members as provided in the By-Laws. Any member shall be eligible to serve on the committees and may express this desire by submitting a written request to the Board. The Board shall then determine the membership of each committee. The President shall be an ex-officio member of the committees of the SAS.

2. Membership and Development Committee: The Membership Chairperson shall serve a the chairperson of this committee. Its function shall be to foster the growth of the SAS and communication and liaison among members and persons eligible for membership, and shall be responsible for publicity of the Annual Meeting and other notable activities of the SAS.

3. Program Committee: The Vice President shall be the chairperson of this committee. Its function shall be to plan the program for the Annual Meeting. Solicitation of papers should begin immediately after the theme of the Annual Meeting is determined and should be as widespread as possible.

a. In the absence of completed papers, substantial proposals submitted in outline form can be considered. Committee should try to use at least one referee in evaluating proposals.

b. The titles of selected papers and names and addresses of writers shall be forwarded to the appropriate officers, as well as any changes in the sectional programs.

c . This committee shall insist that authors provide a finished manuscript by September 1 so that the committee may assist the Editor in an editorial capacity. Paper writers should be encouraged to provide copies of their papers for distribution at sectional meetings.

d. Members of this committee shall preside at their sectional programs of the Annual Meeting.

4. Nominating Committee: The Immediate Past President shall be chairperson of this committee. Its function shall be to nominate candidates or officers. The committee shall accept recommendations for candidacy from members for review.

5. Local Arrangements Committee: For the purpose of the Annual Meeting, a local arrangements committee and chairperson shall be appointed by the President of the SAS.

a. The committee shall work with the President on overall coordination of events and local arrangements.

b. The committee shall work with the Vice President and the Program Committee on rooms and facilities for the plenary session and sectional meetings.

c. This committee shall work with the Membership and Development Committee on local publicity for the Annual Meeting.

6. Editorial Board: The Editors of the Journal of Applied Sociology shall serve as co-chairs of the Editorial Board. The function of the Board is to

work with the Co-Editors to see that the journal publishes materials pertinent to the field and the SAS membership and to see that the journal is published in a timely and professional manner. The Co-Editors shall submit names to the Board of Directors for their review and acceptance.

Article 7
Budget

1. At the Board of Director meeting held in conjunction with the Annual Meeting, a budget covering all anticipated expenditures and income of the Society for the coming year shall be submitted by the Treasurer for approval by the entire Board. The President, Vice President and Treasurer shall review the budget at least every six months and make appropriate adjustments.

2. At the end of each fiscal year (Annual Meeting to Annual Meeting), the accounts of the Society shall be reviewed by the Board. If they desire, the Board or any Board member may request an independent audit by a certified public accountant. The cost of this audit will be borne by the Society. The report of any such audit will be published in an appropriate Society publication.

Article 8
Amendments

1. All proposals for amendment of thee By-Laws shall be made available to the entire membership three months prior to voting on the proposal. Amendments may be proposed by majority vote of the Board or by petition of at least ten (10) voting members of the Society.

2. The By-Law may be amended by majority vote of the members present and voting at the annual business meeting of the SAS.

Article 9
Termination

1. The SAS may be terminated by two-thirds vote at the Annual Meeting,

provided this proposal has been published three months prior to voting on the proposal.

2. Upon such termination, all funds shall be transferred to a nonprofit organization chosen by the SAS Board of Directors.

Approved at SAS Business Meeting
October, 1985
Edinboro, PA

APPENDIX C:

Annual Meetings, 1983-1996

Annual Meetings of the
Society for Applied Sociology

Meeting	Dates	Theme	Location	Keynote Speaker
First Annual Conference	October 14-16, 1983	Sociologists in Applied Settings	Kent State University, Kent, Ohio	Irwin Deutscher
Second Annual Conference	October 12-14, 1984	Applied Sociology: Premises, Products and Prospects	Northern Kentucky University, Covington, KY	Arthur Harkins
Third Annual Conference	October 4-6, 1985	Sociologists Serving the Community	Edinboro University of PA, Edinboro, PA	John Ball
Fourth Annual Conference	September 26-28, 1986	Applied Sociology in Sociopolitical Context	Indiana State University, Terre Haute, IN	Peter Rossi
Fifth Annual Conference	November 6-8, 1987	How Applied Sociology Could Change the Profession	Radisson Plaza Hotel, Lexington, KY	Art Shostak
Sixth Annual Conference	October 21-22, 1988	Creating Social Change	Hilton Inn of Oak Lawn, Chicago, IL	Andrew Greeley
Seventh Annual Conference	October 20-22, 1989	The Policy Relevance of Applied Sociology	Sheraton Denver Tech Center, Denver, CO	Richard Lamm
Eighth Annual Conference	October 12-14, 1990	Strategies for Problem Solving: The Role of Applied Sociologists	Terrace Hilton, Cincinnati, OH	Peter Rossi
Ninth Annual Conference	October 31-November 4, 1991	Generating Knowledge from Application	Annapolis, MD	Michael Cernea
Tenth Annual Conference	October 15-18, 1992	Applied Sociology in a Changing Environment	Cleveland Marriott East, Cleveland, OH	Paul Connet
Eleventh Annual Conference	October 14-17, 1993	The Craft of Applying Sociology	Hampton Inn, St. Louis, MO	Earl Babbie
Twelfth Annual Conference	October 20-23, 1994	Using Sociology Around the World	West in Hotel, Renaissance Center, Detroit, MI	Russell Dynes
Thirteenth Annual Conference	October 12-15, 1995	Sociology 2000: A Vision of our Future	Holiday Inn on the Bay, San Diego, CA	Bertice Berry
Fourteenth Annual Conference	October 17-20, 1996	United Through Diversity: The Blending of Many Voices	Best Western--American Hotel, Atlanta, GA	Robert Bullard

APPENDIX D:

Award Recipients, 1987-1996

AWARD RECIPIENTS

Society for Applied Sociology

Year	Lester F. Ward	Sociological Practice	Community Service
1987	Amitai Etzioni		
1988	Eugene Royster		Marijean Sueizle
1989	Alexander Boros	Elizabeth Peele	Bernie Jones
1990	Luther Otto	Diana Pearce	Tender Mercies
1991	Arthur Shostak		Annapolis Community Partnership
1992	Robert M. Hunter	Robert R. Brischetto	Cleveland Neighborhood Police Unit
1993	Marvin Olsen	William Darrow	Ray Hartman
1994	Irwin Deutscher	Howard Ehrlich	Mel Jerome Ravitz
1995	Peter Rossi	Ron Manderschied	Juliet Saltzman
1996	William F. Whyte	Omar K. Moore	Aaron Parker

APPENDIX E:

Mentoring Program, 1996

MENTORING PROGRAM OF
THE SOCIETY FOR APPLIED SOCIOLOGY

Introduction

Welcome to the first year of the Mentoring Program of the Society for Applied Sociology! In the past, SAS has attempted to recognize student contributions to the profession of applied sociology through such efforts as its Student Paper Competition and the Student Paper Sessions at the annual meetings. The Mentoring Program is a more recent effort to provide support and guidance to students as they begin to plan their sociology careers. By encouraging a dialogue and relationship between those applied sociologists who are firmly established in the profession and those sociologists who are starting out, we hope to assist students in countering the impersonality of the job market.

Since this is the first year of our program, we are starting with a limited number of student-mentor connections on a pilot basis. Twelve active members of SAS have volunteered to mentor students for the upcoming year. To ensure that we could get the program off the ground at this year's annual meeting, a number of students were paired up with mentors before the conference. We will expand the program next year to include more students and more mentors, based on feedback from this year's participants.

This guide sets out to provide general information about mentoring and some guidelines for the SAS Mentoring Program. A list and description of this year's mentors is also provided.

Objectives

The SAS Mentoring Program aims to:

* Foster within students a greater understanding of the work world in general and the field of applied sociology in particular.

* Develop within students a greater awareness of their strengths and skills as applied sociologists.

* Provide students with specific advice regarding their career goals and

* This program was designed and implemented by Cathy Mobley, Student Coordinator for 1995-96.

314

development strategies.

- Enhance students' connections to the Society for Applied Sociology and other professional organizations that could assist them in their career development.

- Increase the quality and quantity of communication and networking among members of SAS as mentors seek out information for their proteges.

- Provide mentors, and the organization, with a better understanding of the career needs of applied sociology students.

What is mentoring?

The word mentor comes from the Greek language and means "steadfast and enduring." As related in <u>The Odyssey,</u> legend has it that Homer gave the name Mentor to the friend whom Odysseus trusted to guide his own son. The term mentor has since become synonymous with a wise teacher, guide and friend. Other sources have defined a mentor as a friend, coach, counselor, tutor and sponsor. These definitions encompass the many roles that an individual takes on when they make a commitment to mentor a student. We hope that our mentors assist students in taking risks and in forming their identity as an applied sociologist. In other words, SAS recognizes that, first and foremost, mentoring is an important resource for students in overcoming the isolation that they may feel and in increasing their self-confidence.

At the same time, we realize that mentors themselves can benefit from participating in a mentoring relationship. That is, mentoring not only aims to open up doors for students, but also aims to "open the eyes" of mentors to the "student perspective." Some of the benefits that mentors stand to gain include increased feelings of collegiality and involvement with SAS and positive feedback from students who may have successfully applied the mentor's advice.

General guidelines

Two important qualities of a mentoring program are structure and flexibility. While these two qualities seem inherently contradictory, there is a need for both in any mentoring program. The pointers below aim to provide some structure to your efforts and to help you get started on your mentoring journey. But, also keep in mind the need for flexibility when establishing and maintaining your mentoring relationship.

Initial meeting: We suggest that you take time at the annual meeting to get together and set the parameters of your relationship and develop a strategy for communicating with one another. Some issues that you may want to consider during your initial meeting include: initial contact; frequency of contact, types of contact, and relationship goals.

1. Frequency of contact: A successful mentoring relationship relies on frequent communication between the mentor and the student. A number of sources suggest weekly to bi-weekly contact, even it's just to touch base and see how students are doing, to pass on a job announcement or conference announcements to let them know you are thinking about them, etc. We suggest that mentors and students communicate on at least a bi-weekly basis. If you have any problems communicating with each other, be sure to resolve them as quickly as possible. In terms of maintaining the relationship, we envision the annual meeting as a place to renew ties with one another and to set new goals for the relationship.

2. Types of contact: Ideally, the initial meeting between the mentor and student should be face-to-face. This will be possible for a handful of mentor-student pairs who will meet at this year's meeting. However, we expect that a number of students will express a desire to become involved with the program between now and next year's conference. Fortunately, with modern technology, we are able to extend and enrich the mentoring relationship. In these cases, a phone call would be the best way to initiate the mentoring relationship.

As the relationship progresses, count on e-mail as an important source of contact! But, please do not rely solely on e-mail. Be creative in the way that you communicate with one another! For those students and mentors who do not have access to the Internet, please rely on the telephone as a source of contact, in addition to letter writing.

3. <u>Relationship goals</u> While we expect that mentors and students will be communicating with one another on a frequent basis, we expect the content of their discussions to have some direct relevance to student needs. Both parties stand to benefit more if the relationship is more than just a pen-pal (or e-mail pal!) correspondence. Therefore, your first meeting should be devoted to not only introducing yourselves to one another, but also to setting some long-term goals and short-term objectives for the relationship. In thinking about the goals of the mentoring relationship, you may want to consider devising a longer term plan, which consists of a series of short-term goals and objectives. For example, a goal could be for the student to develop an applied sociology portfolio; a short term objective, then, would be to devise a resume or a cover letter. Be sure to set (and adhere to) deadlines for each of your objectives and your long-term plan.

Some additional pointers:

<u>For both the mentor and student:</u>

- Mutual respect and communication between the mentor and the student are essential.

- Reinforce for one another the importance of the relationship.

- Be attentive listeners.

- While you will set some initial rules and objectives for your mentoring relationship, recognize the need to be flexible. Deadlines and meetings may need to be rescheduled.

- Be consistent in maintaining contact.

- At certain points in your relationship, you may want to consider switching roles. This is in recognition that mentoring is a two-way relationship where both parties stand to benefit!

<u>For the student:</u>
- Take advantage of your mentor's knowledge and the field of applied

sociology. If you need assistance, just ask! Possible areas in which the mentor could advise you include: resumes, job hunting skills, interviewing tips, ideas for internships, and information about graduate programs.

- In order to reap the maximum benefit from your mentoring relationship, clarify what you need early on.

- Be sure to ALWAYS inform your mentor of any successes that you experience as a result of their advice. For example, if their advice resulted in a job lead, let them know! A thank-you is always a nice gesture.

- Share your successes and experiences with the mentoring process with fellow students.

- In addition to sharing your specific career concerns, let your mentor know your perception of student needs in general.

- Inform your mentor of any address changes.

For the mentor:

- Take the initiative in establishing the relationship.

- Become familiar with the student's career goals and their goals for the mentoring relationship.

- Make it easy for the student to get in touch with you. Inform them of any address changes. You may also want to let them know if and when you expect to be out of town for extended periods of time.

- Point out the various milestones that students may need to pay attention to (calls for papers, student paper competitions, graduate school application deadlines, internship application deadlines, etc.).

- Be aware that your mentee has much to contribute as well. Their enthusiasm can be inspirational as you face your own career challenges and decisions.

For all members of SAS
Any mentoring effort requires a commitment from all levels of the organization. We appreciate any suggestions that you may have regarding this program. And, of course, we look forward to your future involvement with this important effort!

Interested? If you are interested in having a mentor or in volunteering to be a mentor, please contact the Student Coordinator. Also, please send your comments and suggestions regarding the SAS Mentoring Program to the SAS Student Coordinator:

Teri Kepner
SAS Student Coordinator, 96-97
227 Tenth Street
Pasadena, MD 21122
e-mail: terik@annap.infi.net

Catherine Mobley
SAS Student Coordinator, 95-96
Dept. of Sociology Clemson Univ.
Clemson, SC 29634-1513
e-mail: camoble@clemson.edu

SAS Mentors
October 1996

Below is a list and a short biography on the individuals who have volunteered to be a mentor for the Society for Applied Sociology Mentoring Program. If you are an active member of SAS and are interested in having a mentor or in being a mentor, please contact the Student Coordinator.

Stanley Capela
Heart Share Human Services of New York,
191 Joralemon St. Brooklyn, NY 11281
Phone: 718-330-0385 Fax: 718-237-2040;
E-mail: 104437.3526@compuserve.com

Stan is currently Senior Director of Management Information Services for Heart Share Human Services of New York. His responsibilities include program evaluation and quality assurance; coordinating foster care training; overseeing information systems for foster care and prevention; conducting research activities - currently developing the planning component; and participating on various committees representing the agency. Stan has over 19 years experience in evaluation research, mostly in the non-profit area. His major focus at the present time is helping small community based agencies develop evaluation systems, designing evaluation and quality assurance systems for monitoring developmental disabilities programs; helping foster care and prevention workers develop an understanding of how to use computer technology to do their job and refining information systems to help directors develop more effective and efficient programs.

Bill Hauser
2534 Congo Street, Akron, OH 44305
Phone: 216-264-6464 Fax: 216-287-2248 E-mail: hauser@optimum.net

Bill is the manager of business development and research at Rubbermaid Incorporated. In this position, he is responsible for strategic planning, trend analysis, consumer and competitor research (domestic and global), acquisitions, and consumer/customer satisfaction. Bill has over 25 years experience in applied research in academic, military, and business environments. He is an adjunct professor at the University of Akron and teach courses in applied sociology, death and dying, and the environment. He is currently the Vice President and Program Chairperson for SAS.

Hayward Derrick Horton
Department of Sociology
SUNY Albany 1400 Washington Ave.
Albany, NY 12222
Phone: 518-442-4907 Fax: 518-442-4936 E-mail: H.H.@csc.albany.edu

Hayward is an Associate Professor of Sociology at the State University of New York at Albany. He holds a Ph.D. in Sociology from the Pennsylvania State University. His areas of specialty are Demography, Race and Ethnicity, and Rural Sociology. He has authored over 25 publications in the last six years. He is very much an advocate of Applied Sociology and its importance to sociology as a discipline and society itself.

Joyce M. Iutcovich

Associate Provost, Gannon University, University Square, Erie, PA 16541
Phone: 814-871-5334 E-mail: iutcovich@cluster.gannon.edu
President, Keystone University Research Corporation, 652 West 17th
Street, Erie, PA 16502 Phone: 814-453-4713

Joyce's areas of interest are evaluation research, needs assessments, and
social policy; sociology of education, gender studies, medical sociology, gerontology, substance abuse and prevention. Joyce is the Past-president (1994-
95) of the Society for Applied Sociology.

Mark Iutcovich

Professor of Sociology, Edinboro University of Pennsylvania Director of
Research, Keystone University Research Corporation, 652 West 17th Street,
Erie, PA 16502 Phone: 814-453-4713 Fax: 814-453-4714

Mark Iutcovich is a past-President of SAS. He is currently the editor of
Social Insight: Knowledge at Work. His areas of interest are theory, methods, substance abuse, and minority groups relations.

John Kennedy

Center for Survey Research Indiana University 10222 East 3rd Street
Bloomington, IN 47405 Phone: 812-855-2573 Fax: 812-855-2818
E-mail: kennedyj@indiana.edu

John Kennedy is president-elect of SAS. He was first involved with SAS as
chair of the Ethics Committee in 1987. As chair, he started the development
of the current code. As SAS Vice-President in 1992, he was responsible for
the annual meeting in Cleveland. In 1994, he re-wrote the SAS Bylaws to
bring them up-to-date with current organizational procedures and realities.

John received a sociology Ph.D. from Penn State. He has worked in a
small academic setting as a faculty member at the University of Hartford,
and as an applied sociologist in a large organization - the Census Bureau.
His current position, since 1987, as director of the Indiana University Center for Survey Research, is a mixture of academic and applied work. This
year, John is co-authoring a book with a colleague at NASA that will con-

tribute to NASA's redesign of its system for diffusing the results of federally funded R&D. He is also chair of the ASA's Committee on Professional Ethics that is rewriting the ASA's ethics code.

Phil Obermiller
5137 Salem Hills Lane, Cincinnati, OH 45230
Phone: 513-232-2669 Fax: 513-232-3770 E-mail:solotso@aol.com

Phil is self-employed as a researcher, writer, and editor. His current interests are in the history of migration, the development of social organizations by migrant groups, survey research methods among incarcerated populations, the effects of pollution on residents of low-income communities, and strategies for the economic development of neighborhoods.

Brian Pendleton
University of Akron, Department of Sociology, Akron, OH 44325 Phone: 216-686-1318 Fax: 216-972-5377
E-mail: bpendleton@uakron.edu

Brian received his Ph.D. from Iowa State. His research interests include qualitative methods, sociology of children, well-being, and international development. He has been very successful in obtaining funding for a variety of efforts, including the Decker Family Development Center, the Community Partnership for Drug and Alcohol Prevention, and for Children's Hospital. Brian has been the recipient of several awards, including the University Outstanding Teacher, Who's Who in the Midwest, and Citizens Awards from the State Senate and House.

Anne Marie Scarisbrick-Hauser
Associate Director, Institute for Policy Studies, Polsky #285, University of Akron, Akron, OH 44325- 1911 Phone: 330-972-5419 Fax: 513-232-3770
E-mail:rlash@vml.cc.uakron.edu

Annie is Associate Director of the new Institute for Policy Studies at the University of Akron and an Adjunct Associate Professor in the Dept. of Political Science at UA and Fellow of the Bliss Institute for Applied Politics. She has her Ph.D. in Sociology with major areas of interest being social science research methodology, collective behavior and socio/political movements, sociology of sport, environment and applied sociology. She has coordinated over 140 projects for a grant income total of $2 million in the past eight years. Annie also has supervised and trained junior survey researchers and has supervised interns. Having led a very active 'hands on' applied life, she is looking forward to serious work in writing and publishing in the next few years.

Gene Shackman
NYS DOH - Nutrition, 1215 Western Aye, Albany NY 12203
Phone: 518-458-6210 E-mail: gxsO3@health.state.ny

Gene currently works at New York State Department of Health, and Nutrition. He mainly does evaluation research on how well the WIC program works for infants and children, and some main areas of interest are data quality, evaluation and organizations. He also has some experience in the government public health organizations. He also does surveys and focus groups of WIC participants and eligible people, He is interested in methods as well. Gene completed his Ph.D. in sociology at SUNY-Albany three years ago.

Stephen Steele
Anne Arundel Community College, Applied Data Associates, Inc.
101 College Parkway   901 Randell Road
Arnold, Maryland 21012   Severna Park, Maryland 21146
Phone: 410-541-2369   Phone/Fax: 410-544-6814
Fax: 410-541-2239   E-mail: ssteele@clark.net

Steve Steele has applied sociology's concepts and tools for over two decades. As a teacher, practitioner and leader, he has been an advocate for understanding the practical value of the application of social science. He obtained his undergraduate and masters degree from Eastern Michigan University. Steve established the Center for the Study of Local Issues (CSLI) in 1978. CSLI has proven to be an important source of training for his sociology students at Anne Arundel Community College. Steve has been active in promoting the interests of applied sociology through his service to the American Sociological Association and the Society for Applied Sociology.

Steve was President of SAS in 1992-93. In the early 1990s, Steve formed Applied Data Associates, Inc., a small research and consulting partnership to assist organizations in the public and private sectors to gather information to address their concerns and solve their problems.

Susan L. Stein
President, OMNI Research and Training, Inc.,2329 West Main St. #330, Littleton, CO 80120-1951
Phone: 303-797-2633, ext. 18 E-mail: susan@omni.org

Susan received a doctorate from the University of Denver Sociology Department in 1974. She incorporated OMNI Research and Training, Inc. (OMNI) in 1975. OMNI's mission is to offer learning opportunities, for knowledge is the key to power that enables the improvement of social conditions. Susan has over two decades of experience in research, training, and client service. Susan's book *Breaking the Chain: The Bonds of Delinquency,* published in 1994, reports on her research with juvenile delinquents.

APPENDIX F:

Commission on Applied and Clinical Sociology
1995

Professional Workshop:
The Development of Education Standards for Applied and Clinical Programs*

A Brief History of the Formation of the Commission on Applied and Clinical Sociology

Harry Perlstadt, Michigan State University
Chair, Commission on Applied and Clinical Sociology

1. ASA Certification Program
In the early 1980s the ASA identified about a half dozen areas in which sociologists might seek certification from a professional association. These included, among others, demography, social policy and evaluation; organizational development, and social psychology. A core group of distinguished ASA members with experience and publications were appointed to an appropriate area certification committee. These committees set up criteria and began reviewing applications for certification.

After the first year or so, the few applicants who did apply were almost all individuals with master's degrees or uncompleted dissertations who had been working in an applied or clinical area for several years. They were seeking the certification based on experience and practice. ASA realized that most of its members, who possessed doctoral degrees, did not want certification— there was little demand for it. So by the late 1980s the several committees were combined into a single certification committee and shortly thereafter were combined with the state licensure committee.

2. State Licensure
In the succeeding years, the *ad hoc* State Licensing Monitors Advisory Committee submitted reports to the ASA Committee on Certification and Licensure substantiating that several disciplines in the social and behavioral sciences have successfully passed state licensing legislation. The net effect of these laws is to interfere with unregulated sociological practice, particu-

Prepared for presentation at the 1996 American Sociological Association annual meeting, New York, "The Educational Standard for Applied and Clinical Programs."

327

larly in matters of title, definition of practice, educational qualifications and state examination requirements.

A study by Michael Fleischer revealed that sociologists, in their efforts to find suitable work as qualified clinical interventionists and applied social scientists, most often join the ranks of social workers followed by psychologists and marriage and family counselors both in title and practice. That is, their identity as sociologists is lost. Further, in order to qualify for either professional certification or state licensure examinations, sociologists often must take courses available only through an accredited social work or psychology program. There is a link between disciplinary program accreditation and the acquisition of professional certification and state licensure.

3. Sociological Practice Association certification process.
SPA became interested in the accreditation of programs as a result of its own activities in the area of Certification. At one point they considered the possibility of certification at the BA level. Certification on the basis of degree was popping up in other areas, particularly among Social Workers as a criteria for state jobs. This was particularly true in Wisconsin, where the social workers tried to corner certain types of jobs for BA social workers. SPA decided that if clinical sociologists were to compete on a BA level, it would need to attest to the competence of undergraduate sociology majors in the same way that having a BA from an accredited social work program credentialed BA level social workers. Through the efforts of Jan Marie Fritz, SPA and the ISA work group on clinical sociology had produced a resource book including descriptions of specialized courses and internships. SPA quickly realized, however, that this was a tremendous job, particularly since it did not have a clear idea of what criteria should be used, or how to measure individual competence.

4. Society for Applied Sociology Needs Assessment
In 1992/93 under the guidance of Stephen F. Steele, SAS conducted a systematic needs assessment survey of its members in an attempt to identify goals and objectives for the organization. The survey revealed an interest in strengthening training programs, including the undergraduate level. People wanted ways to improve and assure the quality of their programs. As SAS President, Steele challenged the SAS Board and its committee on Profes-

sional Standards and Practice to look into this. In the year that followed, the committee learned that sociology departments in four year colleges and community colleges were especially interested in documenting the quality of their programs. Many were joint departments with social work and were well aware of the advantages and costs of accreditation at the undergraduate level. Accreditation was used to justify new courses and positions in Social Work, often at the expense of sociology. One or two departments, however, reported that establishing an applied or clinical program in sociology enabled them to add courses and faculty to cover both the applied/ clinical area as well as previously uncovered substantive courses. The committee name was changed to Professional Standards and Accreditation and given the charge to look into the possibility of creating a registry of applied and practice programs as a first step toward possible accreditation.

5. Resources and Directories
In 1990, Marv Olsen led a SAS workshop on Designing an Undergraduate Applied Program which resulted in a teaching note that proposed a rigorous model for such programs. The rationale was that such a program would demonstrate to academic administrators that sociological knowledge and skills can be relevant in the real world and would enable sociology majors to find employment related to their studies. In an effort to identify existing programs, Jeanne Ballantine, Carla Howery and Brian Pendleton assembled the first Directory of Graduate Programs in Applied Sociology and Sociological Practice which was a joint effort of ASA and SAS. Also in 1991, the ASA put out the Directory of Sociological Practitioners which updated and enlarged the 1986-87 ASA Sociological Practice Section Directory to include those not members of the section and a list of sociological practice organizations. In 1993 ASA began distributing *Embarking Upon a Career with an Undergraduate Degree in Sociology* by Janet Mancini Billson and Bettina Huber, and *Teaching Sociological Practice*, edited by Carla Howery, Novella Perrin, John Seem and Robert Bendikson.

6. Hearings and Formation of the Commission
In early 1994 the SAS Committee on Professional Standards and Accreditation developed a list of topics and courses based on the 1990 Marv Olsen teaching note. The committee chair, Harry Perlstadt, organized hearings at the Eastern and North Central meetings where the list was distributed and

feedback received. This was followed by a hearing at the ASA meeting in Los Angeles in August, 1994 which was well attended by people from the Sociological Practice Section, the Sociological Practice Association and the Society for Applied Sociology.

The results of the hearings were that skills and competencies should be stressed over a specific list of courses. This would put forward a set of standards but permit flexibility in terms of how the skills and competencies were gained. Programs would vary by degree level. A BA program would require a set of broad skills and competencies which would permit them to apply for entry level jobs in government and business while a masters level program would require specialization in a set of related skills in a particular area such as counseling, applied research (marketing, evaluation) or policy. Finally, a commission would be formed to improve undergraduate and graduate level education programs in applied sociology and sociological practice, to conduct research and other monitoring procedures, and to publish and distribute program information, monitoring reports, and related research. It was agreed that the Society for Applied Sociology and the Sociological Practice Association would pass resolutions to form a commission and contribute to its start up costs. The Sociological Practice Section, however, could not make any formal or legal commitments without the approval of the ASA Council. A letter was sent to ASA President Amatai Etzioni for distribution and discussion at the January, 1995 meeting. The decision was made not to formally join the Commission, but to wait to see what would emerge from the effort.

The Presidents of SAS (Joyce lutcovich) and SPA (David Kallen) proceeded to have enabling motions passed by their respective groups and appointed members to the first Commission meeting which was held in Phoenix, in February, 1995.

7. Activities to Date (August, 1996)
During the past year and a half the Commission has held its meetings in conjunction with meetings of SPA, SAS and ASA. At its first meetings the Commission approved bylaws, incorporated, and developed an agenda for action. The purpose of the Commission is to enable sociologists to make significant contributions to society, through the development, promotion, and

support of quality sociological education and practice in applied and clinical areas. The six action agenda items are to establish a Commission-sponsored accreditation of clinical and applied sociological practice programs; maintain a Commission sponsored registry of baccalaureate graduates who have successfully completed accredited general, clinical and applied sociology programs; create links between program accreditation and state sponsored professional registries, certification, and licensure; arrange a clearing house for dissemination of program models and resources to departments interested in developing clinical and applied programs; educate the public about applied and clinical sociology by representing to government, non-profit agencies, employers and other institutions and interested parties the objectives of clinical and applied sociological education and practice; and develop channels of communication between the Commission and other professional associations.

The Commission began working on its first action agenda item by creating two Task Forces: one on Accreditation Standards and the other on Accreditation Process. The Task Forces assembled materials and points for discussion between Commission meetings which were then reviewed and revised at the Commission meetings. A deadline was set to present findings at this ASA meeting, and this session is the result.

APPENDIX G:

Code of Ethics, 1994

Society for Applied Sociology

Code of Ethics*

PREAMBLE

We, the members of the Society for Applied Sociology (SAS), as social scientists engaged in the practice of our profession and its application to address issues of societal importance, are committed to the following principles of professional ethics and standards:

- the right of all individuals to be treated with culturally sensitive respect and dignity, regardless of their relationship to the professional activities being conducted,

- the right of members to engage in free inquiry and to publicly clarify their research and findings if either are misrepresented,

- the responsibility of members to be sensitive to their personal beliefs and advocacy regarding an issue as it relates to their ability to objectively perform professional activities related to that same issue,

- the responsibility of members to evaluate the potential positive and negative outcomes of their professional activities and act in a manner consistent with the principles of this code.

THE RESPONSIBILITY OF MEMBERS TO THEIR SUBJECTS

We believe that, in the practice of sociology, it is the responsibility of members, above all else, to knowingly do no harm to those they serve or their research subjects. This responsibility includes all individuals and social groups regardless of the member's assessment of the legitimacy or role in society of that person or group. Human subjects will not be coerced to participate in research. Study designs should assume voluntary cooperation on the part of

*Approved for Presentation to Members by SAS Board 10/23/94.

the research subjects if their participation is required; informed consent of subjects is encouraged whenever possible. All identifying information associated with participants in a study is to remain confidential, unless prior permission to release the information has been granted by the subjects or their legally designated representatives.

THE RESPONSIBILITY OF MEMBERS TO THOSE THEY SERVE

In addition to their subjects, we believe members have equally important responsibilities to those they serve; students, employers and clients. Members will provide those they serve with a realistic representation of their qualifications and limitations as they relate to the professional activity in question.

Members conducting research for clients should also clarify specific details of a project with their clients, either verbally or (preferably) in writing, prior to the beginning of a study. These details include the deadlines for key phases of the project, final deliverables (including reports, data and related electronic media), proprietary nature of study results and related publication rights of the client and member.

THE RESPONSIBILITY OF MEMBERS TO THE PROFESSION

It is the responsibility of all members to maintain a high level of integrity when dealing with research subjects, clients and the general public. No member will knowingly misrepresent data or study results to those they serve or to the public, either directly or through the media. No member will attempt to sell information for a personal profit that is confidential or proprietary unless they are authorized to do so.

THE RESPONSIBILITY OF SAS TO THE MEMBERSHIP

If a member feels they have been sanctioned by an employer or client because that person or group expected them to perform in a manner that would violate this code, that member can request support from SAS. In this situation, the member requesting assistance should contact the chair of the

Ethics Committee who will be responsible for notifying the appropriate individuals in SAS in order to resolve the matter in a timely manner.

PROCEDURES AND SANCTIONS

It is the responsibility of all members to report suspected violations of this code to SAS. Suspected violations of this code can be reported by anyone; members of SAS or not. The complaints should be sent to the SAS Administrative officer who will forward them to the Ethics Committee Chair. Complaints must be received within 12 months of the alleged violation. The Ethics Committee chair will notify the SAS President and members of the Ethics Committee of the details of the allegation. The Ethics Committee Chair is responsible for working with the members of the Ethics Committee and the member in question toward resolving the matter in a timely manner. The Ethics committee will make a recommendation to the SAS President. The recommendations can include suspension from SAS.

AMENDMENTS TO THE SAS CODE OF ETHICS

Amendments to this document can be made following the same procedures used to amend the SAS Bylaws.